Edward Pennell Elmhirst, Richard Mounteney Jephson

Our Life in Japanese Drawings

Edward Pennell Elmhirst, Richard Mounteney Jephson

Our Life in Japanese Drawings

ISBN/EAN: 9783337166687

Printed in Europe, USA, Canada, Australia, Japan

Cover: Foto ©ninafisch / pixelio.de

More available books at **www.hansebooks.com**

BY

R. MOUNTENEY JEPHSON,

AND

EDWARD PENNELL ELMHIRST,

9TH REGIMENT.

WITH ILLUSTRATIONS FROM PHOTOGRAPHS

BY LORD WALTER KERR, SIGNOR BEATO, AND NATIVE JAPANESE DRAWINGS.

LONDON:
CHAPMAN AND HALL, 193, PICCADILLY.
1869.

LONDON:
PRINTED BY VIRTUE AND CO.,
CITY ROAD.

TO

COLONEL T. E. KNOX, C.B.,

9TH REGIMENT,

TO WHOM WE OWE IN A GREAT MEASURE THE HAPPY

DAYS WE HAVE ATTEMPTED TO DESCRIBE,

THIS BOOK

IS DEDICATED, WITH EVERY FEELING OF RESPECT

AND AFFECTION.

CONTENTS.

	PAGE
INTRODUCTION	xiii

CHAPTER I.

Arrival in Japan—Harbour of Yokohama—Lovely Scenery—The Mountain of Fusi-yama—Slight Introductory Sketch of Manners, Customs, and Dress of the Japanese 1

CHAPTER II.

The Luxurious Dwellings of the East as experienced by our Heroes—*Ex uno disce omnes*—Their Interior Arrangement and General Advantages—A Terrible Mistake, or the Just Punishment of a Wicked Husband—Furniture and Decorations of the Huts—The Kennels—Master and Men—Mr. Aaron at Work—History of the Pack—Japan as a Hunting Country—Its Drops and Crops 9

CHAPTER III.

Reflections at Sea—Invitation to witness an Execution—The Procession—Prison at Kanagawa—Its Inmates—Japanese Punishments and Tortures—The Doomed Man's Breakfast—His Farewell—Official Politeness—The Death-stroke—After-treatment of Head and Body—The Gallows—Execution of Chinese at Canton—Horrible Fate of Mowung, the Rebel Chieftain 22

CHAPTER IV.

Different Views of the Early Rising Movement—Introduction of many Principal Characters—Tony's Escape—Our Morning Work—The usual Company—Belleville and the Aide—The latter's first Purchase—Aaron as a Musician—B. and the Murderer—The Biter Bit—Abdul: his Private Character and Political Opinions—Mulvey and old Ugly—Jolly enjoying a Joke—Japanese Bettoes 34

CHAPTER V.

Release of the Pack—Blanche's Misdemeanours and consequent Fate—A first Draw—Hitting off the Trail—A View—Settling to it—In or over—Paddy-fields—The Griffins—Forming the Stud—Mr. Micawber as a Purchaser—The Chief's Charger . 48

CHAPTER VI.

A Weekly Holiday—An Early Breakfast—A Picture of Youthful Depravity almost too horrible to contemplate—Our Cheery and Efficient Guide—A Refractory Steed—Coming Events cast their Shadow over one of the Party—Curiosity of the Japanese—Something *like* a Camellia Tree—A truly Rural Scene—Arrival at Kanasawa — Appalling Intelligence — Terrific Combat — Frightful Catastrophe—Al Fresco Juggling Entertainment—Temples of Kamakura — Sacred Ponies — Extraordinary Shrine—Scene of the Murder of Major Baldwin and Lieutenant Bird, 20th Regiment—DAIBOOTS—The Corpulent Priest: his Doubts, his Distrust, his Delight!—A Merry Afternoon in a Tea-house—The Return Home—The Evening Tub—A Conscientious Subaltern 60

CHAPTER VII.

The Hot Weather—Variety of Landscape—The "School"—A Specimen Performance—Mr. Aaron's Catastrophe—Tony's Consolation—Mr. Micawber as a *Maître de Cheval*—Loss of the Tackle—Mr. Micawber again takes the Lead 96

CHAPTER VIII.

Drawing up the Sweep—The Conditions—The Entries—The Preliminary Spin—Dr. De Pifet—The Start and the Result—Dr. De Pifet and Mr. Micawber preparing for the Race—The Post Entries—The RACE.—Do Pifet's Finish—The Liver Cutter and his Steed—The Slough of Despond—Awful Fate of Flying Isaac — A Second Struggle — Downfall of Do Pifet — Mr. Micawber's Domestic 103

CHAPTER IX.

A Leap in the Dark—The Mikado and the Tycoon—A short Description of a Visit to the Tycoon—His Castle at Osaka: its outward

Appearance and inward Arrangement—The Court Dress—The Tycoon himself: Deference paid to his Presence—Destruction of the great Palace of Osaka 121

CHAPTER X.

Aaron's Sanctum—Announcement of the Drag—The Lydias of Japan—Ladies, Horses, and Horsey Ladies—Japanese Aristocracy—Visit to the Stud—Start for the Meet—Messrs. Rudolph and Lothario—Aaron and his Horn . . . 129

CHAPTER XI.

The Meet, and who is there—Bobby has some Difficulty in Mounting—Laying them on—Smooth Going—Pericles, and Solon's Success—Going the Pace—The Fenian in the Paddy-field—Dr. Quock on Foot—The Selling Drop—Jorrocks and Bobby come to Grief—The Brook and its Catastrophes—The Final Drops—The Worry 141

CHAPTER XII.

The Banquet—Colonel Summers—The Yokohama Market—Mr. Micawber becomes the Subject of Conversation—Dr. Quock as a Satirist—The Captain: his Speech—The Chief's Maxim—Captain Puffles's Departure—Colonel Summers's Song—Ferozeshah—Aaron's Objection—The Fox—Captain Puffles's Return—His Adventure with the Ghost—A Dead Man as a Bedfellow 157

CHAPTER XIII.

A Visit to Curio Street—Games and Amusements—Kite-flying—Battledore and Shuttlecock—Curious Ceremony to commemorate the Birth of a Son—Abdul makes the Acquaintance of a wicked Spirit called Tenjo, and suffers therefrom—A Victim to the Belief in the Transmigration of Souls—Cleanliness—Pseudo-patriotism of the Japanese—Theatricals—Scene in a Theatre—A Cure for Sea-sickness (never before published) . . . 178

CHAPTER XIV.

Doubts and Difficulties—Who is *not* at the Meet, and who *is*—Late Introduction of some of our Chief Characters—The Aide—A Whiskered Darling—Hunting the Pig—The Dark Cavern—

Misplaced Confidence—The Fenian's Descent—The Finish—
Mr. Jorrocks's Opinion—Another Drag Hunt by Moonlight . 200

CHAPTER XV.

A Cocktail—The Arena—Japanese Wrestlers—The Struggle—
Ovation to the Victor—Kangoes—Public Bath houses—The
Wrestlers at the Camp—The Child and the Nippon—Bobby's
Success, or the Two Bantams—Wrestling a National Institution—Abdul on the "Revels"—Abdul's Pupils—Their Inquiries into the Conformation of our Army 223

CHAPTER XVI.

The Reader becomes acquainted with Captain Puffles; his numerous
Sobriquets; his Little Weakness; his Marvellous Stories;
their Effect on us in the Days of our verdant Youth; his Great
Valour; his Mighty Prowess; his Rival, Mr. Pop—The Challenge!—Death preferable to Dishonour!—Preparations for
Ensuing Struggle—Exciting Finish—Disgraceful Proceedings
on the Turf 238

CHAPTER XVII.

The Winner declared—The Liver Cutter allows himself to be carried
away by his Feelings—The Road Home—Tony renders himself
amenable to the Laws for the Prevention of Cruelty to Dumb
Animals—Captain Puffles becomes the Football of Fortune—
Fresh Difficulties—Dangerous Dilemma—Succour at Hand—
Safety—Sweet Repose 265

CHAPTER XVIII.

A Day's Sport in Prince Satsuma's Covers—Prince Tchikysan's
Deer Island—Hakodate—The Einos: their Appearance and
alleged Origin—Trout Fishing at Hakodate—A Burst with a
Buck—Varieties of Shooting near Yokohama—Pheasants—
The Copper Cock—Snipe and Wild-fowl Shooting—A Day at
the Pheasants—Fluffy and his Fair Charges—A Feminine
Squabble—An Early Start—Fluffy's Kennel—Riding to the
Ground—C——'s Leap in the Dark—The Half-way House—
Commencing Business—The Child counts his Chickens before
they are hatched—Beating the Ravine—Death of a Copper
Cock—Return to the Tea-house—A Lamentable Scene . . 279

CONTENTS. ix

CHAPTER XIX.

PAGE

Publishing of the Programme—Jolly and Aaron at Home—You visit the Training-ground—A Daybreak Trial—Selling Lotteries; their Effect on Racing in the East—The Yokohama Race-course—Rudolph again—B. and Bones at work—The Child and his String—Taking off Weight—A Universal Genius—" My horth Pluck," or how a Steeple-chaser *ought* to be trained —Saepius Tight and his Trainer—The two Greys, or Hayn's Pot —The Top of the Stand—A late Arrival—Tony's Valet—The Aide's Disaster—Public-spirited Smith—Bobby's Reward . 304

CHAPTER XX.

Japan makes a Start as a Naval Power—One of the Old Sort—Force of Habit—A Sunday Pleasure Trip and its Consequences— Carelessness of Japanese with regard to Precautions against Fire—The Reader is supposed to be present at a Fire in Yokohama—First Alarm—The Japanese Fire Brigade—The Fire-Standard Bearer—Arrival on the Scene of several Celebrities, amongst whom are Captain Puffles and Tony: the former shows much Cool Determination, proves himself Equal to the Occasion, and severely reprimands Tony, who harbours Revengeful Feelings—He (Captain P.) comes out in a new Light as a Linguist; carrying on a Conversation in French, that might lead you to believe he was a Native (of any Country but France, though)—He makes an Appointment, and keeps it—Tony fully revenged 324

CHAPTER XXI.

How will you go to the Races?—Fashions and the Fair Sex—The Night before the Races—Rudolph's Breakfast—A Melancholy Incident in the life of the Child—The Road to the Course—The Paddock—The Griffins' Plate—English Beauty at Yokohama— The Steeple-chase—Preliminary Canters—A Fair Field and no Favour—Mulvey in the Mire—Down the Road—More Haste less Speed, as exemplified by Ugly and the Aide—Jorrocks in Prosperity and Misfortune—The Last Jump—Bobby's Victory —All else that took place 350

CHAPTER XXII.

A late Reform—Who is in Fault?—Something at last about the Japanese — Dress, Courtesy, and Cleanliness — Language,

Lodging, and Living—Our first Japanese Dinner—Prince Satsuma's Banquet—The Bill of Fare—Subsequent Entertainment and Attentions—The Summer Palace and its Gardens—Kagosima—The Prince among his People—Yakonins' Swords—Harakiri; its various Phases and Causes 373

CHAPTER XXIII.

Is simply descriptive of some of the Difficulties connected with the Production of this Great Work 394

CHAPTER XXIV.

Old Times—Unpleasant Comparisons—24th May, 1867—Tunics and Red Tape—The Three "Gallopers"—Captain Puffles in his Full Dress—The Feu de Joie—Mr. Pop's Flight—Pericles Running a Muck—Extraordinary and Appalling Combat—Return of the Wearied—A Word about Shop—The Tiffin—The Aide holds an Imposing Position till found an Impostor—Colloquial French—How to prevent Ill-effects from a Heavy Luncheon—LAND IN SIGHT—Mr. Pop again in Trouble—Horticultural Pursuits—The Ball—A Word of Farewell . . 404

LIST OF ILLUSTRATIONS.

FUSI-YAMA, AS SEEN ACROSS LAKE HAYONI. From a Drawing by A. F. B.
WRIGHT, ESQ., 9th Regiment . . . . *Frontispiece.*

To face Page

CRIMINAL LED TO EXECUTION. Fac-simile of a Japanese Painting on Silk   25

EXECUTIONER AND CRIMINAL. From a Photograph by SIGNOR BEATO .   30

HEAD OF MATSUDAIRA, ONE OF THE KAMAKURA ASSASSINS. From a Photograph by SIGNOR BEATO 32

BETTOES, OR NATIVE GROOMS. From a Photograph by SIGNOR BEATO .   46

TEMPLE AT KAMAKURA. From a Photograph by LORD WALTER KERR .   85

BRONZE IMAGE OF DAIBOOTS. From a Photograph by LORD WALTER KERR 89

THE TYCOON IN HIS COURT ROBES. From a Photograph by FREDERICK SUTTON, ESQ., R.N. 126

A PICNIC GROUP. From a Photograph by SIGNOR BEATO   .   .   132

JAPANESE LADY IN HER BOUDOIR. From a Photograph by SIGNOR BEATO   133

KITE-FLYING FESTIVAL AT ISIHARA. From a Drawing by A. F. B. WRIGHT, ESQ., 9th Regiment 185

PROFESSIONAL WRESTLER. From a Photograph by SIGNOR BEATO . .   225

KANGO, OR NATIVE PALANQUIN. From a Photograph by SIGNOR BEATO .   230

ADMIRAL KING, WITH PRINCE SATSUMA AND HIS PRIME MINISTER. From a Photograph by LORD WALTER KERR 280

xii   LIST OF ILLUSTRATIONS.

To face Page

GROUP OF EINOS. From a Photograph by FREDERICK SUTTON, ESQ., R.N. 282

A RUSTIC MAID. From a Photograph by SIGNOR BEATO . . 302

JAPANESE FIRE BRIGADE. Fac-simile of a Native Painting on Silk . 334

JAPANESE LADY AND ATTENDANT, WITH PIPE AND TINDER-BOX. From a
   Photograph by SIGNOR BEATO 378

PRINCE SATSUMA'S SUMMER PALACE AT KAGOSIMA. From a Photograph
   by LORD WALTER KERR 388

GARDENS OF THE SUMMER PALACE. From a Photograph by LORD WALTER
   KERR 389

A TOUCH OF PAINT. From a Photograph by SIGNOR BEATO . . 403

INTRODUCTION.

A BOUNDLESS, dreary waste of waters; a good ship ploughing her way wearily; two "chums" having their afternoon smoke and confidential chat together—and there, reader, you are present at the scene of the nativity—so to speak—of this book.

Leaning over the bulwarks, and looking down into the deep blue sea, these two friends are languidly bewailing the tedious monotony of a sea voyage.

"Three months more of this," remarks the younger, adding an expletive implying intense disgust at the future prospect. "What a blank is one's life!"

"So much of existence thrown away!" says the other. "I've read until I hate the sight of a book."

"So have I; and I know what every fellow is going to say when he comes up to me."

"Backgammon is utter——"

"Rope quoits are worse."

And so on, until all the amusements resorted to on board ship are one after the other condemned.

"I say," remarks a corpulent old warrior, approaching, "did I tell you——"

"Oh, yes," reply the two discontented beings, with

one voice. "We know all about it! It happened at Bangalore. We've heard it often."

The communicative warrior retires abashed, and the two return to their occupation of looking down into the depths of the ocean.

"This will never do, you know! We shall be drivelling idiots by the time we get home!"

"I don't feel very far from it now," says his friend, shaking his head mournfully, "and we've only had a couple of weeks of it. Oh, confound him! here's old Dizzy!"

"Look here!" begins the last-named gentleman: "did you fellows ever hear how——"

"Now, which one is it going to be?" asks the younger, interrupting him snappishly. "Is it about when you played the Yankee skipper at *écarté?* for I'm hanged if I can listen to that any more!"

"No, it wasn't!" replies Dizzy indignantly. "I was going to tell you about——"

"Well, never mind! Whatever it was, you've told it us before."

Dizzy retires crest-fallen, and the friends continue their grumble uninterrupted.

What has the younger seen, that makes his face brighten up so?

Has his abstracted gaze into the deep been met by a glimpse of a lovely mermaid, or is he indulging in a happy day-dream?

No; it is the flash of a bright thought which is lighting up his features.

"I say, old fellow!" he exclaims, "I'll tell you

what we'll do ! Let's jot down our life in Japan, by way of amusing ourselves for the rest of the voyage!"

The elder one, although in reality snatching at the idea as eagerly as the speaker, thinks it becoming his two or three years' seniority to show a certain amount of caution ; so he shakes his head doubtfully, and responds: " Well, I don't know. You can, perhaps, describe a run, or anything of that kind, and I'm—I'm not bad at —at——"

Here the other comes to the relief of his friend, faltering in his modesty, and encourages him with a figurative pat on the back: " No, you're not half bad ; and between the two of us, I think we might, by giving a sketch of our two years in Japan, make an amusing book of it ; for, you know, old boy, we had some great fun there."

" Ah, yes," returns the elder, still riding the high horse, which he thinks he is duly entitled to mount, from the fact of his having made his *début* on life's stage a little in advance of his friend: " it might be all very amusing to *our* fellows ; but I doubt if the general public——"

" Oh, bother the general public !"—Here the authors apologise to the general public.—" At all events, it will be something to do ; and when we get home, some foolish individual might undertake to publish it."— Here the authors apologise to Mr. Chapman.

" All right !" says the elder one, suddenly becoming a convert to the other's views. " I vote we begin at once."

And begin at once they did with the utmost enthusiasm, though their labours were perforce carried on at times in rather a desultory manner.

Of these labours this book is the result.

P.S.—The authors feel that it is due to themselves to state that the arrangement and compilation of this book have been made under great difficulties.

Torn asunder by the cruel exigencies of the service, they have been unable to compare or arrange their work properly; and to this circumstance they beg the generous reader to attribute any tiresome repetition he or she may detect.

It is their virgin attempt; and, in fear and trembling, they offer it to the world.

"Be to their faults a little blind!" They are painfully conscious of their own shortcomings; and can only pray that the glaring deficiencies, to which they themselves are fully alive, may be lightly passed over, nor visited with the displeasure they deserve.

DRAMATIS PERSONÆ.

AARON.—Huntsman to the celebrated Yokohama Hunt.

B., MULVEY, THE CHILD.—His satellites, radiating round and reflecting the light of the above great planet.

BELLEVILLE—The beautiful, the beau.

THE FENIAN.—Not so beautiful, but still a *beau garçon*. Of these twain it may appropriately be said, "Look on *this* picture and on *this;*" but closely allied on one point—both keen promoters of sport: BELLEVILLE loving it even as the fragrant fat of the bear, or the savoury essence of almond; the FENIAN pursuing it with the fire of red pepper.

THE AIDE—Belonging to the Staff and lean kine.

CAPTAIN PUFFLES—To the (Fal)staff, or fat kine; stout of heart and figure.

MR. POP.—A great gun in his way, who appears on the scene as a leading character on several occasions—the most prominent being in his ever-memorable Race with the last-named welter weight.

ABDUL.—He to whom *we* owe our knowledge of drill (*acquaintance with* is perhaps a better term), and to whom *you* are indebted for more than one of the accompanying illustrations.

THE CAPTAIN.—A veteran warrior, bearded and bronzed, but also much bearded and cheeked by those to whom he often acts the part of bear-leader.

C——— now misses his old friends more oft than ever did he snipe or pheasant, catch or cannon, ere he left us.

JOLLY requires no description.

DR. PIERRE DE PIFET.—A martial medico, who on one occasion attains a high standard of equestrian celebrity—only to vanish again into obscurity, with the passing brilliancy of a meteor.

DRAMATIS PERSONÆ.

Dr. Quock Wock.—A young and promising member of the same profession, the clearness of whose delivery is scarcely commensurate with his fluency of diction and readiness of idea.

The Liver Cutter.—A most able theorist on the probable age of a horse, the proper weight of a cutting whip, or the fittest length for a spur; under whose able tuition any and every description of horse speedily becomes a thoroughly *finished* animal.

Tony figures during the occasional brief intervals he allows himself between his periods of somnolency.

Spiro.—A young gentleman of the Grecian style of beauty, the length of whose limb is only equalled by that of his narratory bow.

Tweeker.—A modern version of the Artful Dodger, known chiefly as the fortunate owner of the celebrated Pig.

Bobby may be described as the soul of wit—brevity.

Micawber.—So called from the many points he possesses in common with the immortal character of that name.

Bones.—A Sapper of renown. One of ye chief sporting characters of ye Great Work that men call "Our Life in Japan."

R——, a Minden Boy—wearing, like his first love, the badge of the double X - is here seen as the Guide to Daiboots.

Fluffy—Of the same corps; a mighty hunter.

Podgy.—One of Scotland's warlike sons.

T——, last, but very far from least, of the martial heroes. Rival of the fat priest at the Temple of Daiboots—conquered, but not disgraced.

Rudolph.—The Sir Joseph Hawley of Japan.

Lothario.—A gentle knight, combining in the modern sportsman all the romantic virtues peculiar to the days of chivalry.

Jorrocks has been drawn by an abler pen than ours.

Alexander.—Another daisy of the Yokohama Turf.

&c., &c., &c., &c., &c.

OUR LIFE IN JAPAN.

CHAPTER I.

OUR ARRIVAL.

ON the 9th May, 1866, we arrived in Japan, the Land of the Rising Sun, as its inhabitants proudly call it, a country of which so much has been written and so much has been talked for the last ten years, that to obtain a reader of one single more work on it is expecting a great deal from a generous and enlightened public.

This volume is not, however, entirely devoted to a description of the country and its inhabitants. Our object is more amusement than instruction; so the general reader may rest quite assured that he will not have to digest such dry facts as, "The population of Japan is estimated at about," &c., or, "Japan is a country rich in objects of interest to the naturalist, the historian," &c., &c.

If any one wants information on such points, are there not countless books, we repeat, wherewith he can satisfy his craving for knowledge? Let him consult one of these, and throw aside our volume; for in it he will find little more than a description of how a body of Englishmen, exiled for a time, at a distance of seventeen thousand miles from home, strove to while away the days, weeks, and years, until it should please Providence and the Horse Guards to recall them once more to their native land.

In it he will find scarcely anything but a chronicle of the doings of these Englishmen for the space of two years: how they rode, shot, ate, drank, and generally made merry; what they thought of the country and its inhabitants; and how they managed to amuse themselves.

To make a new start, as the first seems to have been a false one:—we landed on the 9th of May, 1866, after having been a year in Hong-Kong, where we had had the bad fortune to drop in for a particularly sickly season, the bitters of which only served to heighten our appreciation of the lovely, sunny land in which we found ourselves, on this bright spring morning.

We could not have seen it under more favourable circumstances; our eyes, accustomed to rest on the barren-looking hills of Kowloon and Hong-Kong, now feasted on every new feature of the beautiful landscape, which was spread before us like a panorama as we passed close along the coast on our way into the harbour.

Every one who was able was of course upon deck, and the expressions of delight that burst from many, as some new beauty in the scene opened before us, showed how keenly our poor fellows were enjoying once more the sight of green fields and wooded hills, which to many, no doubt, brought recollections of happy country homes far away in old England.

As the officers of the regiment were standing on the poop enjoying the scenery, full many a regret was expressed for the absence of one whom we had left sleeping peacefully in the Happy Valley at Hong-Kong, the last home of so many of our regiment. Probably similar regrets stirred the hearts of many forward on the forecastle, where the men were all crowding, eager to obtain a glimpse of their new quarters; and possibly the lovely landscape became blurred and indistinct before the eyes of more than one honest fellow as he thought of "poor ould Bill,"—how they "listed together," and how they had always been true and fast comrades, until Bill, what between that "Chiney fayver" and "them Guards," was carried down to the Happy Valley, one of the many victims of a certain scheme of false economy, of which the less we speak the better.

It was about seven o'clock in the morning when we anchored in the harbour of Yokohama, and the appearance of our future home for two years was all that could be desired.

That venerable, white-headed old mountain, Fusi-yama, monopolised most of the attention, as it would always be sure to do, no matter under what circumstances.

It is not its height so much (about 12,000 feet) that makes it remarkable, as its peculiar shape and isolated position.

After living some time amongst the Japanese, one begins to share their veneration for the grand old mountain.

There is also another, part of the range from which Fusi-yama springs, which is called O-yama, and has even a more sacred reputation than its bigger and more majestic neighbour.

At noon we landed, and marched up to the English camp, situated on a hill overlooking the town, at a distance from it of about half a mile.

In a few days the regiment we relieved embarked for Hong-Kong, and left us in undivided possession.

They, poor fellows, were very much down on their luck at the prospect of a summer at Hong-Kong; and as the last few boats' full were leaving the landing-place, and our band was playing "Auld Lang Syne," far above the strain of the dear old air, a voice from the ranks was heard to exclaim, "Begorra, ye'd better to change it to the Dead March in Saul, for we're off to Hong-Kong!" a remark which seemed to have anything but an enlivening effect on the comrades of this military "dismal Jimmy."

However, the passing cloud, we hope, was dispersed by the few hearty farewell cheers we gave them; and we are happy to say that the gloomy forebodings of this lugubrious warrior were never realised; for the ensuing summer at Hong-Kong turned out to be a healthy one, and few of the "Minden Boys" fell victims to the dire climate.

Before ushering you, kind reader, into strange scenes and strange society, we will give you a slight sketch of both, just as we would say to a friend who was going on a visit to a place we were acquainted with, "You'll find Jones a good fellow, gives capital dinners."—"Brown has some good shooting."—"Very good hunting country."—"People about inclined to be civil," &c.

The remainder of this chapter, then, will be devoted to initiating you, in a slight degree, into the peculiarities of the country, the story of our life in which we offer to you.

Novelty is ever charming as a rule, though it wears off in a very short time after arriving in a new place; but with us, Japan and its inhabitants never ceased to be a novelty. There was always something new to observe and wonder at. They are a people so totally different from any other in the world, that in a year's residence amongst them you get a less insight into their manners and customs than could be gained in six weeks into the habits of any other nation. Their manners are polished in the extreme; and, as a rule, they are exceedingly good-natured, and have a keen sense of the ridiculous—rather too much so—for we believe that if the most dutiful son, possessed of the greatest filial piety, were to see his father dying before his eyes, he could not repress a laugh if the old gentleman were to do it at all in a comical way.

Their laws are stringent, and we must presume well framed, as the government seem to have the "masses" pretty well in hand. We very much doubt whether there would be any "park railing" scenes amongst them. Their rules of etiquette are complicated and strict, and extend in a measure most absurdly down to the lowest classes. Two coolies meeting each other in the street, if they are personally acquainted and off duty—that is to say, not engaged in carrying any load—will, before they commence a conversation, bow, simper, and smirk in the most grotesque manner for several moments, and on leaving each other will repeat the same performance. This does look rather ridiculous when we consider that the probable tailor's bill of each of these gentlemen for the half year is the following:—"To one rag (summer suit complete) 3 cash." What a difference from the "Ulloa, old cockywax! what's yer little game?" accompanied by a tap on the chest or a dig in the ribs—the kind of salutation in vogue among this class of life with us. We confess that of the two we rather prefer the "old cockywax" style. We have seen two old women meeting in a street in a village, approaching each other for several yards, bowing, scraping, and cackling pleasantly the while, and with each bow shuffling a pace nearer to each other until they meet, when they probably observe that it is a fine evening, and then part in the same polite manner. This may have been the third or fourth time they have met during the day, and on each occasion the same thing has been gone through, with the only exception, probably, of changing the remark according to the time of day.

A meeting of two Japanese "swells" is something wonderful to behold: the bows, smiles, and scrapes are multiplied almost to infinity, and the foreign looker-on is apt to be repeatedly sold; for after they have approached each other in the correct style, and have got so near that they cannot bow without knocking their heads together, he naturally concludes that the conversation is going to begin, when all of a sudden it seems to strike them both simultaneously that they have not been quite polite enough, and they retire shuffling and facing each other for a few paces, then approach as before; when, after they have met, they may or may not, according as they think they have or have not been sufficiently formal, address each other. We cannot help contrasting this with the vacant and mutual "Il' are you?" of two of the same class with us. We have seen Europeans going through these antics with Japanese of high degree, and we have been strangely moved to mirth thereat—until it has come to our own turn. The Frenchman is far away the best at it, and almost comes up to the Japanese themselves; but the Englishman shirks his work disgracefully, and the little he does is done in an awkward, not to say sheepish way. He looks piteously out of the corners of his eyes, as he bows and rubs his knees—one of the minutiæ—to see if any of his countrymen are observing him, and if he finds out that he is watched, he becomes more heavy than ever.

Their politics are—well, we had better not go into that much, as it is a thing that no man can understand, and we should think that the person who knew about as little of it as any one was the supreme head of affairs in Japan himself. A little farther on we may possibly take a timid dip into this ticklish subject.

Their dress, though striking us as peculiar at first, we soon got accustomed to, and at last ended by admiring. We can vouch for the comfort of it, as we have sometimes for days, when out in the country, appeared entirely *en Japonais*. We recollect on one of these occasions one of our party went so far as to have his entire head shaved. This was not so much of a sacrifice on his part as might at first appear, for his locks were of a certain bright tinge, which had often induced little boys in the streets to cry out after him the name of a well-known vegetable.

We shall never forget the delight with which we took our first rides and rambles in Japan, through green lanes, and over wooded hills with lovely, peaceful views on every side.

How we did revel in all this after the heat and fever of that barren rock, Hong-Kong, which would be an unbearable place were it not for the kind and almost princely hospitality of the merchants there.

Many a pleasant reminiscence have we of their tiffins, dinner-parties, and balls.

Yes, Hong-Kong was not such a bad place after all in the winter-time. We often sigh as we think of *some* of its comforts. Where in the world is there such perfection in a servant as in a China boy? Scrupulously clean and attentive, he watches every movement with a view of anticipating your wants. Almost his only drawback is, that he has a mother who dies once a month at Canton. This is the form in which the request for leave is invariably put.

This looks uncommonly like a bolt off the course.

We must confine ourselves to Japan.

CHAPTER II.

HUTS AND KENNELS.

An Englishman's first care is always said to be to make himself comfortable; and, naturally, our earliest thought was to make our dwellings in some degree habitable.

Alas! in our case, how difficult, nay, impossible, was this of attainment! and, after many futile efforts and waste of money and patience—both notoriously scarce articles among the members of our honoured corps— even the most persevering were fain to retire from the conflict, and seek what consolation they could find either in groaning in silence or loudly anathematising the authorities.

For, gentle reader, may we ask you—reared, as you no doubt have been, in the lap of luxury—to imagine yourself condemned to take up your quarters in a frail erection, something between the old-fashioned dog-kennel and an overgrown bandbox, into which at one time the wind and rain would burst almost unrestrainedly, at another the hot sun would strike down on the head of the unoffending inhabitant, as if anxious to show how little such a so-called shelter availed against its might? Certainly, however, its advantages were patent to the most casual observer; and how much more so to him who could say, with a proud sense of proprietorship, "This is my home, and "—with a slight effort of imagination— " my castle!" for it combined the greatest economy of space and material with the freest possible ventilation. Many an able writer has moralised over and analysed every phase in that inherent failing of human nature— perversity; and this natural weakness of ours was here strongly exemplified. No doubt you turn back with anything but feelings of delight from the prospect we have put before you, and which, we assure you, appeared but little more pleasing in its reality to our eyes; but how many a one who would feel himself somewhat ill-used if honoured with a peremptory invitation to consider himself at home for a year or two under such a roof, would, following the bent of his own taste and inclination, willingly live for weeks, or even months, in the hot and swampy jungles of India or the trackless wilds of the American forests! And you, again, to whom we more particularly and in all humility address ourselves—the leaders and upholders of the grand old sports of England, where, indeed, true sport in all its perfection is alone to be found—who, by your example and keen participation, keep the patrician element to the fore in these degenerate (?) days, e'en as it ever was when the flower of old Rome turned out to compete for the laurel and the myrtle;—how many a one of you whose equanimity might be considerably upset by finding a cold wet stream dripping down unmercifully on his devoted head, when comfortably consigned to the capacious arms of Morpheus, from the one hole in the roof he had overlooked, would cheerfully mount his hack on the chilliest of damp days to canter off to Ashby Pastures; and, when there, stick manfully to the hounds through a blank morning—his personal discomfort increasing every moment—on the chance of a gallop in the afternoon, and the certainty of a cold on the morrow!

So much for the difference between necessity and inclination; but as our aim is to chronicle, not our causes for grumbling, but our endeavours to make time pass lightly, we touch but timidly on subjects the bare mention of which actuates a thousand good people to let forth oft-read homilies with regard to "the lot of a soldier," "the fortune of war," &c., &c. One more moment, though, you must give us, and we take it as Englishmen to whom the right to grumble is a time-honoured privilege. We ask you to judge for yourselves whether the picture we have drawn comes up to your preconceived ideas of what so many stay-at-home people, whose only notions of the far-off countries toward the rising sun are gathered from the "Arabian Nights," would induce you to believe with them is a land of Eastern luxury!

Suppose us to have taken possession of our new residences; and before proceeding any further, you may not find it out of your way, *en passant*, to look into one of them, which will answer much for the description of all, or, at any rate, of most of those occupied by the individuals whom we crave the honour of introducing to you.

The spacious apartment of ten feet square is bounded by boarded walls, whose weather-beaten and mouldy sides the sanguine owner (*pro tem.*) has fondly attempted, on more than one occasion, to conceal with Japanese screen-paper; the first wet night, however, showing how uselessly he had pitted himself against the elements. Through various well-designed chinks the gentle zephyrs come unbidden, and with the same ease and freedom sundry holes afford facility for the entrance of rats to this Liberty Hall. The centre of the room is taken up with a low stove, most conveniently placed for tumbling over, and of a pattern peculiarly adapted and ingeniously contrived for a cold climate and a frosty night, insomuch that it never fails to emit the smoke, which it generates in an extraordinary degree, from *below* into the room, thus almost obviating the necessity for the addition of a stove-pipe, but rendering it advisable to save life by opening wide all the doors and windows. Unlit, too, it has other uses, for the flue carries off the greater portion of the rain that falls on the roof, conducting it into its own recesses, and thence in safety on to the floor of the hut. Both from its position and natural beauty this piece of furniture would attract your notice prominently; and, illustrative of this point, we are reminded of a sad case of mistaken identity which occurred to one of "ours" who shall be nameless.

Comparatively a newly-married man, he had been compelled to join his corps in Japan, after having experienced the sweets of married life just sufficiently long to render not altogether unbearable the idea of the temporary separation, which his orders from the Horse Guards, and the delicate state of his wife's health "precluding, my dear, the possibility of your accompanying me," had enforced upon him.

As is usual with these faithless swains, a short time spent apart from his mate sufficed to effect a complete change in his treasonable mind; and that return of bachelorhood which had seemed so pleasant in the distance became more and more irksome. Absent and constrained at one moment, noisy and artificially high-spirited at the next, not even the firmest application to his studies for the Staff College—consisting, to the eyes of ordinary mortals, of caricatures without the faintest resemblance to anything or anybody, and a constant perusal of the first page of Victor Hugo's "Le Roi s'amuse"—not even the hourly repetition of his two favourite pieces, "Sally, come up" and "Van Amburgh is the Man," to the accompaniment of a most asthmatic harmonium—not even the innocent recreation of shaving a portion of his own face or his poodle's body till he had obtained every possible variation in the appearance of both, could distract his thoughts from her he loved so well. At length a climax came to what had already become almost insupportable. An intimate friend of his, and also of his better half, arrived on business per mail steamer. Bringing news of her as he did, how could he but be received with open arms? and it was agreed he should dine that evening at Camp. As the new arrival splashed, ankle deep in mud, in his patent leathers (poor soul, 'twas his first visit to Japan) up the hill for his dinner, no doubt his feelings of friendship cooled down somewhat from that boiler heat to which they had risen at meeting an old acquaintance on first arriving in a foreign land; but once seated with his legs under what—hidden as it was by a snowy cloth—might have been mahogany, but wasn't, his heart expanded gradually as it felt the influence of the good liquor with which his military friend plied him.

The latter, meanwhile, was anything but shirking his collar, and raised to the seventh heaven by the glowing accounts of Madame's ever-thoughtful anxiety for him, the enthusiastic way in which she was wont to speak of, and her many loving messages to the absent one, bumper followed bumper in alarming succession. He insisted on taking wine with his guest no less than six different times; toasted his spouse, himself, and the world in general; and, finally, ended a convivial evening by spontaneously bursting into song, and in the fulness of his heart treating the company to the "Bailiff's Daughter," which he evidently considered more or less appropriate to the occasion. By the time he had arrived at the third verse, however, his feelings proved too much for him; and, after several ineffectual attempts to walk through the wall of the dining-room, a lucky tack took him through the door, and with more than one providential escape he reached his own hut in safety.

With his earthly shell full of claret, and his mind of the one subject that throughout the evening had usurped his every thought, no wonder that the apparition that he now saw by the dim light of the night-lamp should appear doubly impressive to his dubious and uncertain vision. Before him, in the centre of the room, stood the longed-for object of his affections awaiting him. With a hiccup and a cry of delight, he rushed to fold her in his arms, screaming, "Shweetisht! Shweetisht!! Shertain you'd come!!!"

From these words all is oblivion, till a friend arriving on the scene at seven the next morning, bringing with characteristic kindness a bottle of soda-water, found the unfortunate husband stretched on the floor, his face scratched, his mess clothes and shirt-front red with rust and blackened with soot, and his stove-pipe, which he had torn down, clasped firmly to his bosom.

Continuing our examination of the interior economy of the hut in question, in which we were interrupted by the stove-pipe reminiscence, we observe that the floor can boast of nothing in the shape of carpet, though the hearth is protected by a piece of matting whose real worth had better not be estimated by its intrinsic value; and anything that might be wanting in the shape of ornament is amply made up by the presence of a picture gallery, which takes up three of the walls, and comprises half-a-dozen of Ackermann's Sporting Prints, a couple of German chromolithographs of a third-rate order, and some groups (photographs) of officers of the regiment, the whole collection more or less undistinguishable from the effects of smoke and damp. The fourth wall is hung with spurs—light and heavy, sporting and military; whips—crops and cutting—the greater number worn and curtailed to an unserviceable size; canes and sticks of all sorts, forage caps, bridles and bits, and a cracked looking-glass. The remaining furniture in this well-ordered establishment consists of a venerable camp-bed, standing very much over and extremely shaky on its legs, a portable chest of drawers, a ditto washhand-stand, and a saddle rack carefully covered up from the wet—for even in Yokohama we can appreciate Peat. A pair of gymnastic rings depend from a beam, and dumb-bells and clubs are lying handy in a corner; and the ingenuity has to be as thoroughly exercised as the muscle, in order to work these without danger to the articles of ornament and *vertu* already referred to.

Being released from your temporary confinement, you may be the less unwilling to accompany us at once to the kennel, where, this being the second day of our being left in possession, we shall be certain to find Aaron hard at work. *En route*, you will not object to a tankard of our last consignment of Allsopp from England, and then, armed with a Manilla and a switch, across the newly-made lawn in front of the ante-room to the wooden dwellings—apparently somewhat superior to those we have just left—that you may see at about a hundred yards' distance, and from which a Babel of sounds, consisting of rating, whip-cracking, and baying of hounds, is even now proceeding.

Arrived on the spot, our expectations are verified by finding Aaron in all the glory of dirt and heat, with his coat off, sleeves turned up, just rising from the act of rubbing sulphur ointment into the skin of an unhealthy-looking animal that it is a compliment to call a *dog*, much less should it be dignified with the name of *hound*— a word that some of one's holiest recollections are bound up with. His two assistants, the Child and B., are similarly employed; and, to judge by the bald appearance of many members of the pack, their task is likely to be a somewhat lengthy one. The two latter individuals have been described on a previous occasion,[*] when the first Moonlight Drag of the Holy Boys was honoured by a place in that green-backed volume that finds its way to the farthest corners of the world, and monthly serves to lighten and cheer the exiled sportsman, keeping alive his innate love for the glorious pursuits he has left behind him, and instilling a joyous anticipation of what he pictures and prays for on his return home.

"Our noble Patrons, Mr. Aaron; Mr. Aaron, our kind

[*] The chapter referred to is reproduced from *Baily's Magazine* as Chapter XIV. in this volume.

and sympathetic Readers;" and we turn round to apologise for introducing you thus. Mr. Aaron, as is but befitting a true sportsman and one of a good stock—hailing from the same county as Jack Mytton and others, keen and hard as he—belonging to a house that has ever done its utmost towards supporting Church and State, the County Pack and the Breed of Foxes—bows politely, expresses the extreme felicity he derives from the honour of making your acquaintance, and in the excitement of the moment gives you his greasy hand to shake.

The ceremony of introduction over, you will doubtless pardon him for continuing his labours. For this kind of work he is from his early habits much more fitted than any other of his brother officers, and hence he was unanimously elected to hunt the beagles we are now inspecting: brought up in the neighbourhood of a well-known pack of foxhounds, to the kennels of which he had ever the *entrée*, he had considerable opportunities of fostering his natural tastes, and of acquiring a better knowledge of the points of a hound, and his management at home and in the field, than is possessed by the ordinary run of amateurs.

He now appears thoroughly at home, and his whole mind is wrapped up in the thought of how to get the little pack something like fit; but, first of all, how to eradicate the mange, a disease which, in the hot climates of the East, rages like a plague, and is terribly speedy and virulent. Nearly half the entire number are now suffering from it; and the first steps to take are, of course, to separate the sufferers from the rest of the body, and after administering a dose of castor-oil to each, trust to clean and dry kennels, the sulphur ointment daily applied, and plenty of gentle exercise to effect a cure. This treatment we found to answer admirably—indeed, with the exception of three thorough incurables, who were at once consigned to a watery grave, all our patients appeared in a few weeks with new and glossy coats.

Another difficulty, that gave our friend Aaron considerable trouble, was that of providing them with new names, as well as new coats; for, on receiving them over, many were either wanting altogether in this last, or were possessed of such drawing-room titles as were more appropriate for a lady's lap-dog.

Nothing daunted, however, by the difficulties before him, Aaron went steadily to work to re-christen the beauties with the help of Stonehenge's list of names and his own early recollections; and, by dint of spending a considerable portion of each day in drawing them one by one to his voice, he at last succeeded in imbuing them with some faint idea that when one of the number was called, the whole pack was not necessarily wanted.

In very truth, it was an imposing sight to view the lord of the kennel standing in the yard, before a long trough filled with the morning meal, the baying pack vociferous for their food, and understanding no such distinction of persons, while their noble master in vain endeavoured to individualise by name his unruly children. Perhaps two or three were persuaded—or, more probably, accidentally happened—to come forward when called upon; but as, on the appearance of a hungry hound out of his turn, B. and the Child were ready at hand to fall upon him, these also would take the alarm and precipitately join their comrades; till at last, in sheer desperation, Aaron would rush at them, make one cut at a venture with his whip, and shouting, "By Gosht" (his favourite and universal interjection), "you beasts! you may feed yourselves!" retire to his own breakfast, only to repeat the same scene in the evening.

That he is not easily to be turned from a determination once taken is well known to his intimates, and the following incident will bear out the truth of the general opinion. On a certain occasion, when with two brother officers he was passing through Venice, it was decided to give up one day to enjoying the beauties of the Queen of the Adriatic. At breakfast, one of the party, who had been there before, said, "We shall leave again to-morrow morning, Aaron, and you ought certainly to see the lions of the place while you are here." The individual addressed said nothing, but it was evident that the advice sank none the less deeply into his mind. During the day he got separated from his companions, who, thinking nothing much of this, continued their rambles without him; but, as Aaron did not put in an appearance at dinner, they began to feel rather anxious about their friend. At last he returned, tired, dusty, and evidently out of humour; for, in reply to their inquiries as to where he had been, he answered: "By Gosht, you fellows have been humbugging me. You said there were lions here; I have been looking all over the place, but I can't find them."

Our pack* (or rather, the remains of it, for its numbers, from the effect of climate and disease, had dwindled fearfully), in the first instance imported to Shanghai by a Mr. Antrobus, were afterwards got over from that

* The remainder of this chapter is reprinted from *Baily's Magazine.*

place by the 20th Regiment, from whose hands they descended to us.

They were always a mixed lot, consisting of ten or twelve couple of harriers, half that number of long-eared beagles, and two or three couple of dwarf fox-hounds; and it is a question whether a judicious reduction by half, at the hangman's hands, would not have added materially to their efficiency.

Now let us try to give you some idea of the country, *i.e.*, in a riding point of view.

It is undulating in its general character; and the valleys being kept for the cultivation of paddy, and consequently always in a state of muddy swamp, we were compelled to confine our riding to the rising grounds.

The system of cultivation in Japan is much the same as that of China; viz., a succession of perfectly level plateaux, one above the other; the banks and drops separating these being, with the exception of an occasional stream and a few odd fences, the only obstacles you have to encounter. But these same drops appear, on first acquaintance, anything but tempting; varying, as they do, from about four to ten or even twelve feet in height (do not think we are romancing), sometimes with a slight incline, but more often perpendicular, frequently overhanging. It is only when you know by experience what a Japanese horse—or rather, pony, for they do not average much over fourteen hands—can do, that you feel a fair degree of confidence in riding at them.

As far as appearance goes, there is hardly an animal to be found in Japan for which you would care to advance much beyond twenty pounds at any fair at home; but, as regards their power of crossing this particular kind of country, their looks certainly belie them. As a rule, they are mis-shapen brutes, with few good points about them; but they will carry any amount of weight, and seldom make a mistake at their jumps. Indeed, with a heavy man on their back, and out of deep ground, they will reach the top of a bank that you would hardly care to put a weight-carrying hunter at.

Moreover—and this goes a long way to ease the mind of a poor man riding his only horse—they never hurt themselves at all seriously, a broken back or limb being a thing quite unheard of. It may truly be said of them, that "though rum 'uns to look at, they are devils to go."

They have a curious way of getting down their drops. Except when going at a great pace—as, for instance, in a steeple-chase, when they will fly off the top, and keep their feet in the most wonderful manner—they usually dwell a moment, then, putting all four feet together, and tucking their hind quarters well under them, slide half-way down, and jump the rest. In your first experience of this style of thing, you feel an almost irresistible inclination to leave your saddle and take a plunge over your horse's head, in which case you would stand a very good chance of being jumped upon. This kind of acrobatic feat we have seen performed with great success on more than one occasion.

With regard to our seasons for hunting, we were dependent not so much on the time of the year as on the gatherings of the crops, which really seemed to be always growing. No sooner was one cut than another was seen springing up in its place; and thus it was only for a few weeks immediately after the spring and autumn harvests that the country was really rideable.

CHAPTER III.

BEHEADING OF A CRIMINAL.

"Illi robur et æs triplex," etc., etc.

We have always noticed that the quotations best received are those most in use, and consequently most familiar to the general public. We do not suppose that many of our readers—if we may ever hope to have many—have kept up their classics to that standard to which they had attained when leaving college or school; but the brilliant ode in which Horace pays a pitying tribute to the courage of those who " plough the briny wave," when they might be comfortably housed on shore, must be familiar to all; and, indeed, so often has it been brought before us by novel writers and others, that we do not get the chance of forgetting it. What a debt of gratitude is owing from this class of writers to the poet from whose works a classical allusion appropriate to any subject and any occasion may always be culled! We have never yet attempted a novel—indeed, we are extremely doubtful of our ability; but should we ever venture on the field of fiction, we shall certainly prepare ourselves by a renewal of our acquaintanceship with Horace, and Lemprière's Classical Dictionary.

To return to where we started from. We were going to relate how, but yesterday, when suffering from the heat of 2° south latitude, and the showers of black smuts that the funnel unmercifully rained down upon us till we had serious thoughts of ending our wretched existence by plunging into the cool, blue water, whose peace it seemed profanity to disturb by our vulgar presence, we quoted this line lugubriously, but, as we thought, with infinite depth of feeling, to a non-classical friend. To our disgust, he answered with a miserable attempt at wit: "Don't talk rot; there will be neither *ease* (æs) nor comfort till we get on shore again and out of this blessed ship."

Though somewhat annoyed with the reception the neat extract from our favourite poet had met with, we could not help confessing that his sentiment—albeit not delicately expressed—coincided strongly with our own opinion; and the conversation, thus begun, ended in a united growl against the utter discomfort of the sea, and the amount of life wasted in long voyages—for life, when one is young and in possession of that happy power of appreciating the thousand enjoyments now open to one, is very jolly and pleasant, let soured men of the world and bilious cynics say what they will.

How the young ladies who warble so sweetly, "I'm afloat, I'm afloat," would shun the joyous melody, if under the influence of a tropical cyclone!

"Rocked in the cradle of the deep" sounds very differently when the deep is rocking the cradle too roughly. The very words suggest sea-sickness; and as for any beauty in a vast waste of restless water, we plead guilty to not having poetry enough to see it.

All these wanderings—no doubt feeble and vapid, and possibly scarcely even original, for the same feelings must have been experienced, and perhaps expressed, by numbers who have taken up pen to drive away *ennui* at sea—what have they to do with the subject of Japan? Nothing whatever; but having once been set going, we are too apt to take the bit between our teeth and rush off the track at random. They were suggested by the uncomfortable consciousness that we have undertaken a much more difficult task than we had imagined, in attempting here at sea, without notes or even our home-letters, to give you an account of our doings in the land of Niphon.

Leaving for the time our own immediate pursuits and amusements, we propose to give you a sketch of capital punishment by beheading, which we were privileged to witness.

One morning, as we were breakfasting after our early ride and subsequent toilet, a note was received in camp from the interpreter to H.M. Legation to the effect that an execution was about to take place at ten o'clock, and, thinking some of us might like to be present, he had obtained permission from the Governor of Kanagawa for any of the British officers to avail themselves of the opportunity.

Human nature is ever curious; and, as such a chance might not occur again, four or five of us at once ordered our ponies, and, having received leave from parade, buckled on revolvers, and cantered off towards the Japanese prison at Kanagawa—a distance of about three miles.

When within half a mile of our destination, we fell in with an immense crowd of people, and on inquiry, found that the criminal, who was even now being paraded on

horseback through the town, would pass here on his way back to the prison and the fate that awaited him.

Remaining where we were, we soon saw the *cortège* approaching, and even at a long distance could distinguish a solitary figure raised above the level of the accompanying crowd. As they neared, and then passed slowly, we had ample opportunity of looking closely at the procession.

First of all came two men bearing placards raised on poles—the one proclaiming the nature of the crime for which the offender was to suffer and the punishment he was condemned to undergo; the other inscribed with his name and native place. Immediately following rode the doomed man, tied to his horse, with his arms tightly pinioned behind him, and a rope fastened to his waist, held by a man who walked alongside.

Never had it been our luck before, and we trust it may never be again, to behold a creature in God's image reduced to such a state. With a skin blanched, parched, and shrivelled; features worn and distorted; eyeballs glazed and sunk; his cheek-bones appearing to be forcing themselves out, and his withered arms hanging nerveless at his side, the wretched being strove hard to bear himself bravely, and to behave at the last as became one of his race. As he passed, his eye lit on our party, and he called out, with a scornful laugh, for " the foreigners to come and see how a Nippon could die."

Assuredly, among the Japanese there still survives, in much of its native purity, that courage which moved the old Romans and the Spartans to bear up against the most trying sufferings and most killing hardships.

The spirit that filled the breast of the noble defenders of the pass of Marathon could not have been altogether wanting in those two-and-twenty yakonins of high blood who but the other day kept the bridge of Osaca against the entire armies of the Princes Chiosiu and Satsuma, and gave their beleaguered sovereign time to escape.

Before the bridge was captured, not even the one, as at Marathon, was left.

They all fell, and with their wounds in front.

A year in a Japanese prison—a year of torture and starvation—had brought what was said to have been once a fine, powerful man, to the repulsive and wasted form now before us; yet his heart had not died out, nor his pluck deserted him, and he could still hurl defiance at his hated persecutors.

The crime for which he was now to lose his life, and for which he had already undergone the year's preliminary imprisonment, was, having entered a house in the dead of night with, it was said, the combined objects of plunder and revenge.

Next in order in the procession came two spearmen; then some men on foot; and lastly, two officers on horseback, with their retainers.

Following them up, we soon reached and were admitted into the prison.

On being ushered into the court-yard, we found Mr. L.———, the interpreter, with one or two of his friends, and, after greeting him, were introduced to the authorities, who manifested the greatest possible civility, and invited us to take a tour of the premises.

A word or two will be sufficient to describe the prison itself.

Built entirely of wood, it consisted of a collection of low, black, one-storied edifices, whose dismal hue and sombre aspect alone must have been enough to crush out hope from the hearts of the unfortunates entering there.

In the centre of these, or rather, surrounded on three sides by them, was the court-yard or execution-ground, the whole being contained within a high wooden paling.

The different cells were all open on one side, and crossed and recrossed by stout wooden bars, through which you could look upon the occupants.

Some of these—probably suffering for lesser crimes—seemed tolerably well cared for; while others, huddled up together like sheep in a pen, appeared worn and emaciated—in some instances, to a degree horrible to contemplate. With no protection from the piercing night-air—which could penetrate through the open sides of their cages, and strike into frames almost as free from clothing as from flesh—we wondered how human life could survive the concentrated misery of agony, mental and physical, with existence barely supported on a meagre portion of rice and water.

Fearful tales are told of the tortures employed to extort confession or punish crimes. The coloured drawings of the Japanese (and we have been informed by various good authorities that they are no exaggeration) reveal scenes and phases of human suffering almost too dreadful to dwell upon. The fiendish ingenuity of the Roman Inquisition is outdone by the diabolical contrivances of the acknowledged jurisdiction of Japan.

Thieving, more particularly when accompanied by violence, stands almost highest in the list of crimes; and for this, in its worst forms, are reserved some of the most cruel tortures. Death—the shape to be determined by the amount stolen and the way the offence is perpetrated—is the punishment for robbery of anything over the value of forty ichiboos (about sixty shillings). Confessions, wrung out in sweating agony—too often, 'tis to be feared, from innocent men—by means of the bastinado, by the application of crushing weights piled gradually heavier and still heavier on the yielding chest; by severing member after member, and limb after limb, from the quivering trunk, by—— we forbear to sicken you by enumerating other tortures, if possible, more terrible and cruel still—may be followed by beheading, by crucifixion, by impalement on blunt spears, by tearing asunder by means of wild cattle, rendered mad by flaming torches, or by some other of the many awful forms of death at disposal.

While we had been making our tour of inspection, the doomed culprit had been unlashed, and dismounted from his horse at the gate; but when set on his feet, he was unable, from weakness and the constrained and painful position in which he had been kept so long, to stand; and they were obliged to carry him into the precincts of the prison. Here an ample breakfast had been provided, and any kind of refreshment that he chose to ask for was allowed him. This would appear to be a heartless mockery, as if it were intended to ridicule the poor wretch in his last moments; but, on the contrary, he applied himself vigorously to the meal, the completion of which was to be the signal for his own leap into eternity.

In all probability it was long since he had known

what it was to be properly fed; and the sufferings he had gone through had rendered his mind callous to the last punishment, or made death appear but a happy escape. At any rate, he ate heartily, and with evident enjoyment, of what was placed before him, talking the while to those around him. Suddenly he caught sight of two civilians, who had approached for a nearer view; and though he saluted them politely enough, he turned to his attendants with a curse on the "bocca tojins" (fools of foreigners).

When a full half-hour had elapsed, it was intimated to him that his presence was now expected; and accordingly, with the assistance of an attendant on each side, he walked slowly into the execution-ground, and was placed, kneeling and sitting on his heels (in the universal Japanese posture), behind a small hole dug out for the reception of his head. Some ten yards in front of him, and separated by a rope running across the square, sat the presiding yakonin and the prison authorities, calmly fanning themselves; and beyond these, again, were the six or eight foreigners who had been admitted.

The prisoner's arms were then pinioned behind his back; but, before the cloth was tied over his eyes, he requested that a minute's grace might be allowed him. This being granted, he raised a weak, quavering voice to its highest pitch, and screamed out, "My friends!"

Immediately an unearthly chorus of wails answered the poor wretch from his friends outside the walls, none of whom could be seen from the interior.

The effect of this was positively startling to the nerves of us strangers: Mr. L—— alone was at all prepared, and explained to us the meaning of what passed.

"Friends!!" again shouted the unfortunate man,— and after each sentence the same thrilling response was sent back to him,—"I am about to die, but think not that I care!" a horrible attempt at a laugh following the last words. "Do not mind me! It is quite indifferent to me! Rather look out for yourselves! Syonara (goodbye)!!" and with a deeper and more prolonged wail, the crowd outside answered, "Syonara!!"

He then signalled to his guards that he was ready, and submitted quietly to the operation of blindfolding.

The executioner, who had hitherto been standing by his side—with the greatest *sang-froid* pouring water on the keen blade of his long two-handed sword—now stepped up, and carefully adjusting his head a little on one side, and in such a position as to hang exactly over the hole prepared to receive it, signed to the officer that all was prepared; but before the latter would give the signal— and while the wretched being before us was momentarily expecting his death-stroke—he inquired of Mr. L——, with every mark of politeness, if the English officers were ready.

Of course he quickly answered "Yes," and the word was given—when, without raising his weapon more than a foot above the neck of the condemned, the executioner brought down his heavy blade with a plainly audible thud, and the head dropped instantly into the place prepared for it.

We had always fancied ourselves possessed of very fair nerves; but we must confess to a most sickening feeling as the dull splash of the sword meeting its victim —turning at the instant living flesh into senseless clay —struck on our ears, and the cleaving of the neck

showed for a moment a ghastly red circle, with the blood leaping out in streams from the headless trunk.

As we turned to look at the others of our little group, we could see by the whitened faces of the strong men around that they, too, were not altogether unaffected by the scene they had just witnessed.

Immediately the head fell, it was seized, carefully washed and cleaned before the features could get set, and put into a bag. At the same moment, two men jumped on the body, and by means of kneeling on, squeezing it, &c., strove to drive out all the blood while it was warm. This having been as much as possible effected, it was rolled up, tied into a bundle, and carried off.

Thinking all was now over, we proceeded to pay our respects to the Japanese officers, and were about to move homewards, but were requested to await the performance of the final ceremonial.

The procession having been re-formed much the same as before—with the exception that the horse previously ridden by the deceased now carried the executioner, in charge of the lifeless head—wended its way to a raised mound at the side of the high road, about a quarter of a mile away.

On this spot a kind of gallows had been erected, and on this was placed—after having been sponged and combed—the dead man's head, supported in its position by clay, there to remain for six days in sight of all passers-by, and a warning to all evil-doers.

The accompanying engraving is from a photograph, taken by Signor Beato, of the head of Matsudaira, one of the murderers of the ill-fated Major Baldwin and

Lieut. Bird, 20th Regt., which was exposed in the same manner and place.

The pleasant ride back to Camp was sufficient to drive away the blue feeling that had stolen more or less over the whole party.

Only a year or so before, we had been present at the beheading of three Chinese at Canton, where it is of such daily occurrence, and is thought so little of, that in one corner of the execution-ground some scores of heads —without any exaggeration—may always be seen piled in all stages of preservation or corruption. But there it was done in such a business-like, informal way, and the Chinamen seemed to be so little affected by their approaching fate—actually laughing and talking till the moment when, as they knelt down, their tails were pulled forward and the short, heavy sword took their heads off one by one—that we looked upon it in quite a different light from the scene we have just described, nor experienced any of the disagreeable sensations as on that occasion.

It was in the same great city that some of "ours" witnessed, in the year 1865, the cruel and barbarous fate awarded to the rebel chief Mowung, whom, after they had claimed and obtained him from the English Acting Governor of Hong-Kong as a pirate, the mandarins resolved to punish as a traitor, for the lead he had taken in the revolution of the north.

Accordingly, he was condemned to suffer the "execution of twenty-one cuts," by which, before the last stroke lets out together his quivering bowels and his life, each of the previous twenty severs a fresh portion of flesh and muscle from the wretched sufferer.

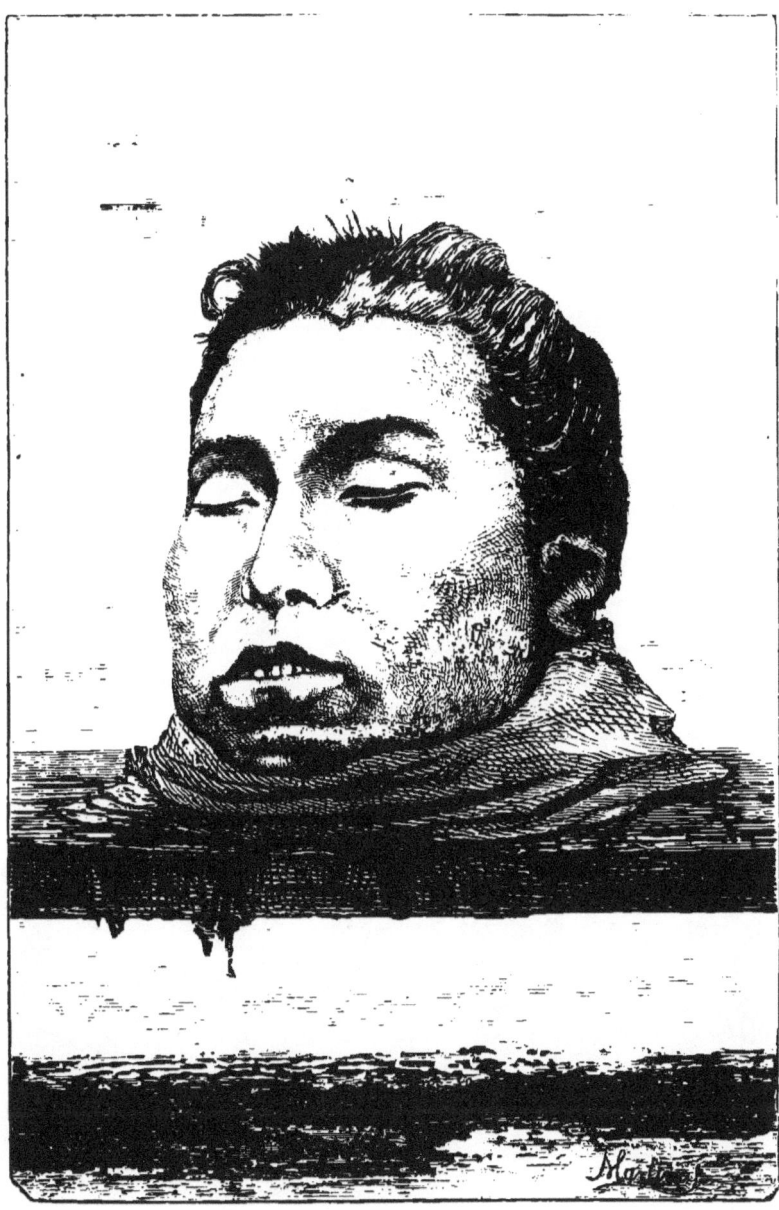

With superhuman command of self, the unhappy Mowung bore silently the slow and deliberate slicing off —first of his cheeks, then of his breasts, the muscles of upper and lower arms, the calves of his legs, &c., &c., care being taken throughout to avoid touching any immediately vital part. Once only he murmured an entreaty that he might be killed outright—a request of course unheeded by men who took a savage pleasure in skilfully torturing their victim.

With superhuman command of self, the unhappy Mowung bore silently the slow and deliberate slicing off —first of his cheeks, then of his breasts, the muscles of upper and lower arms, the calves of his legs, &c., &c., care being taken throughout to avoid touching any immediately vital part. Once only he murmured an entreaty that he might be killed outright—a request of course unheeded by men who took a savage pleasure in skilfully torturing their victim.

CHAPTER IV.

THE EARLY MORNINGS.

How much has been said, read, and written, both in favour of and against the practice of early rising! And, after all, how little has it affected the habit of those whose inclinations lead them to adopt one side or the other!

Since our early infancy it has appeared to be the aim of our nearest relatives—the while they feel themselves by no means bound to follow their own precepts—to impress us with the expediency of what they term "rising with the lark;" that being, at the same time, a most indefinite expression, for, to our certain knowledge, the larks themselves are as much divided about the hour for a morning flutter as we are.

Then, too, they would have us believe that "early to bed and early to rise" must necessarily lead to a man's becoming "healthy, wealthy, and wise."

Now, we can conscientiously state that for some years past we have religiously followed the latter part of the precept; though we must admit that, owing to sundry unfortunate combinations of circumstances, we have been at times unable to follow out the remainder in its strictest sense; and it is no doubt due to this, or our want of faith, that we have not yet succeeded in reaping in full the advantages held forth as the reward. For, though we may congratulate ourselves without any great self-flattery on being at present possessed of the "mens sana in corpore sano," which—at all events till hoary old age creeps in and holds up his withered finger as a warning—may so generally be induced by strong exercise and the society of good fellows, we still look upon the attainment of wealth as being as far out of our reach as ever, and we fear not even our most indulgent friends will do us the justice to come forward and bear testimony to our character for wisdom.

Again, there are an equal, or even greater number arrayed on the opposite side, who take Lord Dundreary's well-known view of the case. These men say, and with some reason, "If you people choose to turn out of your beds when we are just settling down to our second sleep, why in heaven's name don't you do it, and let us alone?"

A very clever article appeared some little time back in the *Saturday Review*, or, as its enemies dub it, the "Saturday Reviler," from the pen of a late riser, who, after setting forth what he called "the absurdity of turning night into day," charged the man who gets up early—and who, he said, is also almost invariably a ranting exponent of his own views—with being a perfect social nuisance—going about with the air of a superior being, and looking down with a most irritating pity on all who differ from him.

Why one should be bound by any rule on this point more than on any other mere question of taste, we cannot understand. The happy majority of the present day —and here we hope, respected patrons, we can exchange mutual congratulations—who, though it cost many a youthful struggle to attain a habit they then yearned after as the "correct thing," have long looked upon the pleasant luxury of pipe or cigar almost as an absolute necessary. *These* are not ever seeking to enrol the rest of the world on their side! Content to rest satisfied in the enjoyment of their quiet indulgence, they willingly adopt the charitable theory of "Live and let live."

As an instance of the *plausibility*—they cannot expect *us*, who are advocates for the early-rising movement, to say more—of the arguments of those who go in for what they term their "proper amount of rest," one of the Holy Boys will have reason as long as he lives to thank Providence for his love of sleep.

In the summer of 1865 his passage was engaged in the *Chanticleer*, about to proceed the next morning from Hong-Kong to Shanghai. The early hour fixed for her departure, however, viz., 9.30 A.M., was extremely distasteful to Tony's habits; thus, when nine o'clock arrived—by which time he should have been on his way to the pier—his anxious servant did all in his power to get him up, but he merely grunted out that "he shouldn't go," and rolled over for another snooze.

Naturally, when his usual hour for rising came on, and brought with it a return to consciousness, he had ample time to reflect on the step he had taken, and to mourn over the passage-money he had forfeited.

The next day ensued a typhoon, which will long be remembered in China. Houses were blown down; vessels at anchor were driven ashore, or dashed against each other; junks and boats were swamped or stranded in great numbers; some two thousand Chinese were drowned at Hong-Kong alone; and for days afterwards dismasted or water-logged vessels were towed into harbour, but no trace has ever yet been found of the ill-fated *Chanticleer*, or her luckless companion, the *Corea*.

So it happened that habitual laziness was the means of saving Tony from an early death, and of preserving to his friends a cheery companion, and—despite his indolence—a keen shot, a good welter-rider, and a useful cricketer.

Sad is it, though, to know that his natural fondness for sleep has been so increased and excused to his mind by this escape, that there now appears every chance of his relapsing into a chronic state of torpor, and becoming but a sleeping partner in the great joint-stock company—Society.

We have been allowing our pen to run terrible riot all this time; and unless we hark back at once to the true line ere the scent becomes cold, our patient field will be moving off home in disgust.

We were led into this long digression by our intention of noticing the way in which our early mornings were spent for some time after we were fairly settled in Yokohama.

At 5 A.M. Aaron would issue from his diggings, got up in a venerable patrol-jacket and the seediest of breeches and boots—an elaborate toilet being considered quite *de trop* at that hour—and, on being joined by B. and the Child, with, probably, two or three others of the corps, all similarly attired, would jump into the saddle, and trot down to the kennels. Among the additions to the party are usually numbered Belleville and the Aide, with both of whom you are perhaps already familiar, and whose portraits will be found transcribed in Chapter XIV.

The former of these does not appear to advantage at this time; and, with his whiskers uncombed, his ambrosial locks guiltless of macassar, and his delicate throat bare of collar, suggests strongly the parallel of a theatre as seen at a daylight rehearsal. Since his arrival in Japan, he has been tormented by an unpleasant dread of becoming corpulent—hence the unwonted amount of exercise he is in the habit of taking; and as he assures us—in using a pet Yankee expression of his—that "he doesn't care who is around" at this ungodly hour, we must excuse his present appearance.

The Aide is mounted on his new and maiden purchase in horse-flesh—or *pony-bones* would be a more appropriate term. We cannot say he made use of the consummate judgment in this instance that he usually displays; for his meagre little beast, in addition to being much under size for him, has brought from the native wilds, that he left so lately, a disagreeable trick of determining for himself the moment when he fancies he has travelled far enough, and from that point refusing, in spite of all moral and physical persuasion, to move another step in advance. Even if he has to resort to backward travelling like a crab, he always contrives to assert his opinion, and invariably returns in triumph to his stable.

Such conduct would try the temper of a Job; and sweetly serene as is that of the Aide, it finally broke down after some months of repeated trials—when many a prospectively pleasant ride had been cut short; many an expedition, carefully planned and arranged, had been —as regarded his share in it—brought to an abrupt termination by the vagaries of his wilful steed. Then, and not till then, did he heartlessly give him away to two midshipmen, who—disregarding all vulgarly-accepted ideas as to the necessity of food, in favour of the more economical plan of starvation—galloped him about the country till you could almost see through his attenuated carcass.

At length the unhappy brute contrived to break away from his tormentors; and, fleeing into the country, returned no more.

Aaron is riding a well-shaped bay, which, under his careful management, is rapidly becoming handy and clever; though at present he is chiefly distinguished by an extraordinary fancy for rushing, neighing and openmouthed, at every other quadruped that meets his view. He is also very averse to the cracking of the long hunting whip that his master is armed with. A horn is not yet possessed by the accomplished huntsman, though even now one is on its way out from England, to the dread of his nearest neighbours, who are but too well acquainted with the musical talents to which he daily gives frequent exercise, in performing with much feeling and expression the thrilling solo of "Woodman, spare that tree," accompanying the performance with many original variations and generous repetitions of certain chosen parts.

Many a hearty prayer has gone up that the woodman would be induced "to spare that tree," and be hanged to him; but, to the present moment, Aaron has continued to invoke him without effect.

B.'s animal is another raw specimen of the produce of the country; in colour something like mouldy oatmeal, but not badly shaped—as Japanese horses go—and already giving promise of jumping power. His eye affords a pretty good insight into his disposition, which is so thoroughly vicious as to have obtained for him the title of "the Murderer."

'Tis but a week ago that, as B. was passing through a crowded village, the Murderer took the opportuninty of setting on and worrying almost to death a harmless native.

Just arrived in the country, straight from England, and having vividly before his mind visions of yakonins, with their revengeful characters and two fearful swords, his owner adopted the only course that at the moment presented itself to his terrified mind, and betook himself to ignominious flight. The next day, however, accompanied by a body-guard of friends, he returned to the spot, when the relatives of the injured man demanded and received the sum of twenty ichiboos—about thirty shillings—as compensation for what they loudly protested to be his speedily-approaching dissolution.

After serving his master faithfully for some months, the Murderer supplied the means for the successful carrying out of what will always be looked upon as the cleverest and most praiseworthy action of B.'s young life, viz., "doing in the eye" one of that astute race of men who, though they may occasionally prove a little *out* in their expressed opinion when describing a horse to an expected customer, but seldom err in over-rating his merits when the respective positions are reversed.

One morning, when out with the beagles, the Murderer got deeply bogged in a paddy-field, and the next day was found to have sprung a most undeniable curb.

On being taken out of the stable, he was naturally as lame as a tree; but not a word of this was whispered beyond the circle of the distinguished and horsey trio, of which B. made one worthy unit.

After a diligent course of arnica and cold-water bandages, bran mashes, and a total rest from work, the " ginger-coloured 'un " was to all appearance sound and well again; none but those in the secret being at all likely to detect the much-reduced lumps on his hock. At a stable-consultation it was unanimously determined that the Murderer should, if possible, be sold forthwith. Accordingly, as buyers were very scarce at the time, an individual who combined the equally ingenuous professions of horse-dealer and livery-stable keeper—and who, in consequence of the arrival of the admiral's fleet in harbour, happened to be just now much pressed for mounts—was, as a kind of forlorn hope, appealed to.

After the Murderer's mane and tail had been carefully trimmed and attended to, his pasterns dressed, the long hairs just above the coronet—inseparable from coarse breeding—rounded off, his feet tarred and oiled, and his coat brought to as high a pitch of glossiness as the persevering use of hard strapping and damp clothes could bring it—or the low caste of the animal in question would allow—the coper was introduced to the screw, that " only the reduction of our rate of pay and the increased price of forage would induce me to part with."

" He is a rare good jumper,"—which was true.

" I don't know much about him,"—which was *not* true.

" His temper? Oh, you have only got to look at his eye to be satisfied about that!" This was again literally true; but B. was well aware, when he said it, that a tightly-tied headstall kept those tell-tale eyes shrouded in a dark corner.

Cleverly drawing the dealer on one side, to show him the points of the occupant of a neighbouring stall, he gave room for the Murderer to be led forth without the chance of venting his ill-humour on the bystanders.

During the usual inspection, walk and trot, he went as sound as B.'s most sanguine wishes could have hoped for; but when his spirits got the better of him—after a month's confinement in the stable—and he commenced a series of kicks and plunges, the feelings of anxiety and apprehension of his owner can be better imagined than described.

"I declare I can't give that horse work enough! He always wants to be at play. Bailey, walk him about for an hour or two!" and, with this last direction to his groom—who obeyed by moving the object of his care out of sight behind an out-building, and immediately on the withdrawal of the pair, brought him back to his stable and a cold bandage—he asked Mr. Whiteman what he would take to drink.

That worthy preferred "a little brandy—no water, sir, thank you;" during the discussion of which the bargain was concluded by his agreeing to give our friend one-half of what he asked—which, *par parenthèse*, was three times what he originally paid for the moke—with the additional agreement, that the ex-owner was to be provided on the Thursday of the following week with a hack for an already-settled excursion.

For four days the Murderer nobly performed his part of carrying sailors out for the day's ride—generally amply remunerating his master by getting rid of, and in two instances nearly killing, his rider after an hour's departure; when, returning to his stable, he would be let out to another Jack, who in all probability quickly shared the fate of his comrade. For this invigorating amusement the tar had the satisfaction of "stumping up" the sum of five dollars—rather more than a guinea.

At the end of these four days, however, the Murderer completely broke down, and became an incurable cripple, the other hock following the lead of its companion.

Revenge is sweet, and how truly enviable must have been the feelings of the injured horse-dealer when, on B. presenting himself for his mount on the appointed Thursday, he found his late steed ready saddled and bridled for his use! And how thoroughly did the latter reap the reward of his sin, when, after attempting a painful hobble for half the ten miles to the rendezvous where he was to join his party, he had to dismount and walk the remainder!

To return to the party who are preparing to accompany the hounds for their morning exercise—their chief inducement lying in Aaron's fondness for a little by-play on the way, such as throwing the pack into some outlying cover, which he may think likely to hold a fox. The Child is on his big-hocked, big-maned little chestnut, Iona, whom you have already met with in the chapter to which, in order to avoid repetition, we are obliged so frequently to refer you.

Besides those already mentioned, there are one or two others out who require a word or so of introduction.

Imprimis, there is he who instilled into us—and, indeed, all those present—their first knowledge of the rudiments of drill. For years the "father of the subalterns," he is ever ready to lend the guidance of his sterling common sense for assistance when appealed to,

or to aid with his quiet tact in settling any of those
trifling disagreements which, even among the closest
friends and most boon companions, will occasionally
present themselves—and which, when each side is ready
and willing to meet the other, and more particularly
when such a mutual pacificator as Abdul is at hand to
smooth over the preliminaries, will dissolve into a still
firmer cement of friendship than had hitherto existed ;
but if left to themselves, soon widen into a breach that
it is a work of time and difficulty to heal over.

He is just as keen as the youngest of us in matters of
sport ; and will watch the working of a pack of hounds
with as much interest as he does that of the Conservative
party—to whose policy, as becomes a "rank old Tory "
(to quote his opponents), he is enthusiastically devoted.

Though his once black hair has become much changed
in hue of late, and he has grown a little bit shaky about
the pins, we know few things we should enjoy more
than, after priming him with some of the leading Radical
speeches of the day, to let him into a room alone with
John Bright, or his worthy colleague, Mr. Beales.

Reduced in purse and credit though we are, we would
willingly lay £50 that he would effect a complete
change in the views of either of those oily politicians
within half an hour.

Then there is one whose flowing moustache and ex-
pansive smile are ever seen to the front when hard work
—or, as we say in China, "pigeon"—is to be done.
Universal in his occupations and pursuits, Mulvey—who
is a light weight, with a proportionately light hand—
takes to hunting as he does to everything else ; and
after poor Aaron succumbed to the effects of service in

China, and returned to the home of his fathers with little else but his bones and an enlarged liver, he took his place in the kennel, and was unremitting in his care of our then sadly-diminished pack. He is now riding Ugly, a rare tough old animal; who, in the hands of his late owner—a hard "thruster" and able jock in the 20th Regiment—won several steeple-chases, and now looks fit to win another.

Loud above the morning salutations, and whatever conversation may be going on, we hear Jolly's intensely vociferous laugh as he revels in the enjoyment of some joke, which was probably uttered a quarter of an hour previously, and every one else has by this time forgotten. The following is a tolerable instance of this enviable faculty. When the Holy Boys were quartered in that paradise of stations, that has since passed from our hands —to wit, Corfu—Jolly was one of a party returning in their yacht from the opposite coast of Albania, where they had been on a shooting trip. As they entered the harbour one of his companions observed, "Why, the *Beeswing* has left port."

Abdul, who was also on board, and who is, you must know, a "bit of a joker" in his way, seized the opportunity and replied, "Oh, impossible; *beeswing* is always in *port*."

The *jeu de mot*—like many others, weak, but appropriate—was received with great applause; but throughout the storm of merriment Jolly was observed to maintain a dignified silence.

A full half-hour elapsed, and they were in the act of dropping anchor, when Jolly suddenly burst out with "Haw! haw! haw!" in his own deep bass. Peal followed peal in unrestrained enjoyment, and he finally rolled on the deck as if he would choke. His friends thought he had been seized with a fit, and were preparing to throw buckets of water over him, when he found breath enough to gasp out, "Haw! haw! Capital! I see it! *Beeswing in port!* Haw! haw! haw!"

He is now mounted on a black Bellerophon—if possible more determinedly vicious than the Murderer, and consequently boasting of an equally engaging *sobriquet*. Having completely disabled one betto, and, but a few days ago, taken a piece out of the shoulder of another—he has been christened the Maneater, under which name we shall hear something more of him hereafter.

One word about the bettoes just mentioned: a separate caste of their own, they are looked upon by their countrymen almost as a distinct tribe. Capital grooms *if they choose*, they will face and handle the most dangerous horse—and Japanese horses are seldom to be trusted;—but you never know when they will take it into their heads to shift their quarters and leave you without the slightest warning. They are quick and intelligent, but the greatest thieves in the universe. It is wonderful what distances and at what a pace they will run alongside their masters, when riding into the country—being always at hand to take charge of the horse when a halt is called, and to throw over him the rug they have carried rolled up on their shoulders.

In the summer they dispense altogether with the clothing that a false state of society would insist upon; but this is not so much noticed, as they supply its place

by a tight-fitting flesh surtout of tattooing of the most wonderful pattern.

The accompanying photograph shows exactly what we have attempted to describe; and we leave it to our readers to determine whether this is not a cooler and more appropriate dress for hot weather than what we in our civilised barbarity are in the habit of adopting.

CHAPTER V.

THE EARLY MORNINGS (*Continued*).

THE whole party that are likely to turn out being now assembled, Aaron waxes impatient, and saying, "Come along, you fellows, or we shan't be back before the sun gets hot!" moves off in the direction of the kennels.

At the sound of approaching hoofs, the pack, in expectancy of their liberty, grow clamorous to be free; and immediately the door is opened, rush boisterously out—jumping up at the ponies at the imminent risk of being "savaged"—and testify their joy by baying, rolling on the grass, and other eccentricities indicative of canine delight.

Of a sudden, a little, rough, terrier-looking sort of beagle, rejoicing in the euphonious but unsporting-like name of Blanche, catching sight of a strange dog in the distance, goes off at score in full cry, followed by the whole mob, who, not to be behindhand, give tongue enough to awaken the bones of their forefathers in Great Britain. This is too much for Aaron's temper; and rating and whipcord are freely applied to bring back the delinquents to a sense of duty, while the ringleader is caught up and at once consigned back to the kennel.

The pack has now become so reduced in numbers that it is with the greatest reluctance that we can make up our minds to part with any one of its number; but in this instance there is no alternative, and Blanche is forthwith condemned. Loth, though, to shorten the poor animal's existence, Aaron looks round for some other means of getting rid of the mischievous one; and of a sudden, as a brilliant thought strikes him, he exclaims, with the usual preliminary, "By Gosht, I know what to do with her! A fellow to-day asked me if I knew of a good *terrier*, so we will send Blanche to him."

Accordingly, in the course of the day, Blanche journeyed down to the settlement in a basket, with Aaron's compliments, and a collar round her neck; and though hardly deemed an acceptable present, was credited with a good supper and a warm lodging. The very next morning, however, when the kennel doors were opened, out rushed Blanche and repeated the scene of the previous day. By some means she had escaped from her incarceration, and regained her old quarters. A fresh imprisonment was followed by a fresh escape; and finally, the hunting establishment was put to the expense of a charge of powder and an ounce ball, in order to rid itself of her presence.

Something like order being at length restored, we move off in rear of the hounds, who, though now comparatively quiet and orderly, require a watchful eye to guard against a repetition of the break-out just witnessed.

As we trot gently along a country path—the whole landscape presenting one mass of green luxuriance; the spring crops just rising above the ground, and the many woodland patches bursting into their new life; with the fresh breeze causing one's chest to heave and expand, and the first colouring of the sun throwing a varied tint over the peep of ocean that smuggles itself into view through a cleft in the hills—we acknowledge to a feeling of triumph—an obtrusive sense of superiority over those whom we left snoring among their blankets, or only awake enough to cast an anathema after "those mad fellows, who go cracking their whips in the middle of the night."

Arrived at a likely-looking bit of detached cover, Aaron sends his assistants on to commanding points at the far end of it; and, after allowing sufficient time for them to reach their posts, himself enters, and does his best to induce his somewhat slack-drawing lot to disperse and work for themselves. Much breath and energy does he waste in "Eleu, in there! Heigh, brush him out!" &c., &c.; for, till their game is found, the Yokohama pack appear to look upon hunting in cover as an unprofitable delusion, and treat it with contempt accordingly.

Nothing results from his efforts beyond a slight sense of irritation of throat and temper. The hounds are therefore quickly withdrawn, and we proceed in the direction of another piece of plantation, in which Aaron is morally certain of a find.

On our way there, however, Warrior and Countess—two dwarf foxhounds, who, as trusty, steady, old servants, are allowed to jog along a little ahead of the body of the pack, snuffling at every twig and blade of grass by the side of the path—stop suddenly, feather for a moment in joyous doubt, their sterns appearing to act as signal-staffs to their comrades, who rush up at once to join them, then throw one deep, thrilling note, and dash off at a tangent.

The dewy grass still proclaims Reynard's passage on his return from his last night's cruise in search of provender; and following this up a few hundred yards, brings us to a snug little hollow where he had hoped to pass the day undisturbed. Probably he was even now enjoying his morning nap; for not until the keen little pack are almost on the top of him does he attempt to leave his retreat. As the music bursts out into an ecstatic crash, Aaron catches sight of a grand old dog-fox stealing away beyond the cover, the white tag at the end of the brush showing plainly as he tops the hill. With a shrill scream, he gallops to the spot, and the little ones answering quickly to his cheer, we are soon cramming through the underwood for the open country beyond.

Regardless, in our excitement, of promising crops and agricultural interests, we send the raw griffins—*griffins* being the term for ponies newly reclaimed from the country—along at their best pace down several nice drops, as the country slopes gradually downwards from the high lands above, till we arrive on the top of a deep, precipitously-bounded valley, at the bottom of which runs the Rifle Range.

This brings us all to a stand; and, as the hounds dash merrily down the slope, we have the satisfaction of seeing skimming up the opposite hill that same worshipful little animal that has caused the heart of many a good man to rebound almost painfully, as he waves his brush and lays himself out over the grass, from Sulby or Waterloo. *Then*—as two hundred of the hardest goers, on the best horses in England, settle down to ride to hounds that can pull down a fresh fox in the open—may be experienced the true delirium of fox-hunting. We may be young yet; but at present we hold that he who, in such case as this, can keep his place without skirting or craning, should be content to let the gods themselves rest unenvied in their seats.

As the pack stream out across the grassy bottom, and their music is thrown back as they mount the hill, it becomes more than nature can bear to stand here inactive; so, sitting right back, and using the persuaders freely, we shove down into the thick cover on the chance of hitting off a part less precipitous than the rest. Once started, there is no stopping; and while one is nearly pulled out of the saddle by the bushes, the happy possibility of finding one's self taking a clear dive of thirty or forty feet is ever present to one's mind. Providence, however, befriends us, and, after much crashing and floundering, we emerge in safety, though each one bears marks of rough treatment; and Aaron's pet feature—the family nose—is sadly disfigured by a bloody scratch marking the whole length of its graceful contour.

The leaders having left a kind of lane in their track, like that caused by an elephant in his headlong course through the jungle, the whole party—with the exception of the Aide, whose pony had carried him home some time before—follow without accident, though at one moment Belleville had a narrow escape of being suspended — Absalom-like — by his "Piccadilly weepers." Alas that the ruthless War Office should have just issued a stern, but incontrovertible order that "whiskers, if worn"—for our part we look better without them—"are to be of the most moderate dimensions!" Ye who have any of the milk of human kindness left unsoured by the thunderstorms of this boisterous life, to you we appeal. Is it not hard that these, his friends in sickness and adversity, who have ever stuck close to him when other ties have been estranged, who have proved a source of employment in the morning and harmless display in the evening, should now be ruthlessly severed from him for ever by the whim of—— Beware! we are nearing holy ground; or—a better simile—about to tread on cracked ice, that bears the label DANGEROUS. Since this fell mandate has come forth, poor Belleville has scarcely raised his head. He has not even energy enough left to bestow the usual care on the immediate cause of his suffering; but amid his overwhelming grief, we must do him the justice to state, that we believe his sorrow is not so much for himself as for the feelings of the poor women, to whom (*D. V.*) another two months of "mare turgidum"—as hateful still to landsmen as it was in the easy-going days of Horace—will give back their treasured one, excepting the above-mentioned loss, more beautiful than ever.

Hark forward! we are losing time, while hounds are running; and the small jump into the Rifle Range has brought us opposite the very brook that caused so much disaster in the last Yokohama steeple-chases: so at it we cram, without the faintest hope of making a successful negotiation. Aaron, however, on Tom Brown, gets over with a scramble; but Iona, who faces it as if meaning business, bucks straight up into the air, and—after rolling the Child well into the mud at the bottom—concludes the performance by standing on his stomach, and, having thus obtained a firm footing, springing on to the bank.

B. slaps at it hard; and, hitting off a sound place, blunders in and out on the right side. Old Ugly, who knows the place of old, puts his head on one side, and, cocking his one eye, flies it like a bird. Abdul's stupid brute whips round, and, getting his hind legs in, falls backward, plunging his venerable rider into a stream as pure and clear as the Thames at London Bridge. Belleville's doubtful attempt ends in a steady refusal; and Jolly takes even longer than is his wont to find out the joke—of going at such a place.

Meanwhile, Aaron, with B. and Mulvey, is creeping up to the hounds, who soon get among a lot of small covers, where Reynard amuses himself by quietly dodging from one to another. These delays also give time to the Child—who, after shaking himself, has managed to roll again into his saddle and pound along the line—to get within hail.

Being at last forced into the open, the fox heads in the direction of Camp, and makes good his point, which is a strong fir and brushwood cover at a mile or two's distance. From this—owing to the smallness of the pack, both in number and individual size—it takes a full half-hour to dislodge him. When at length we succeed in pushing him out, he takes over a broad valley of paddy-field—the curse of the country as regards its hunting—across whose treacherous surface we are obliged to get off and lead, taking advantage of the narrow tracks left for the labourers.

This difficulty surmounted, we rattle happily along over some nice open country, past the site of the present British Legation buildings; the drops and up-jumps severely testing the almost unbroken animals. Still they go willingly and pluckily, though each jump at all bigger than the ordinary causes a struggle and a heartfelt "Come up!" At a deepish drop the Murderer falls head over heels; and immediately afterwards Aaron and the Child roll back together in an attempt to get up a five-foot bank out of boggy ground; but though for a moment heads and heels are all mixed up together, no harm is done.

The hounds are just approaching the wooded cliffs which border on the sea; and, as it is now not of the slightest use letting them continue the chase, Aaron contrives with some difficulty to get them off the line; and both horses and men, being pretty well satisfied, move slowly home.

Such is a pretty good specimen of many an early morning's fun during the continuance of the hot weather. The "griffins," of course, improved by degrees; and, after a time, we were in possession of animals which—if small and plain-looking—were handy and clever at this peculiar country.

The choosing, trying, and purchasing of the ponies produced of itself much fun and amusement. Some— and these were the majority—looked out for something that promised to be able to carry them across country; and, if possible, possessing pace enough to give their owners the chance of sporting silk—in person or by proxy—in the next races. Others sought for strong, steady-going hacks, such as might carry them a long day's journey into the country with safety; and this kind of animal—viz., one that will neither trip nor stumble, and whose straight legs, good feet, and safe action insure lasting properties—is most difficult to obtain in Japan, many that can go well and cleverly over soft ground being utterly useless, or even dangerous, on the road.

Then, too, there were a certain number—very limited, it is true—who, ambitious to emulate, or laudably anxious not to be behind, their brother officers, were now in quest of the kind of quadruped we see advertised in the *Times* as "a quiet cob, suitable for an elderly gentleman," on which to serve their novitiate.

Great numbers of every class that Japan could produce were brought in for purchase for some time after our arrival, and most of these were untamed and savage brutes, about as well acquainted with the feeling of a saddle on their backs as a Bengal tiger. The sharp and cruel bit used by the Japanese sufficed to keep them from breaking away; and the plan we usually adopted was to have them blindfolded on the parade ground, then —seizing an opportunity to get behind their shoulder in such a position as to escape a kick from behind, or a blow from the front—catch hold of their tangled, flowing mane, and vault on to their backs. A piece of stout cord, fastened round them like a surcingle, served to prevent one slipping too far forward, and the severe bit kept their heads up; so that, after a little practice, they very seldom managed to dislodge one. With another horse alongside, they would move along sufficiently willingly to give some idea of their paces—at all events, this was the only trial to be obtained, and one was therefore obliged perforce to be satisfied.

The operation of backing having been gone through, the animal, if approved, underwent a careful and would-be knowing examination of hocks, legs, &c., at the hands of a board composed generally of three or four members from the number already alluded to.

Occasionally, too, a few steady old pack-horses would be sent up to the Camp for sale, and from these the last-mentioned division of purchasers usually made their choice.

Of the men, in whose education that most important branch—*videlicet*, a practical knowledge of the points of a horse, and of the art of riding him—had been neglected, *most* acknowledged and wept over their shortcoming, avowing their firm determination to overcome the deficiency as quickly as lay in their power; but one or two, with excusable self-respect, did their best to gloss over, and prevent others from discovering the gap in their acquirements. A notable instance of this last plan of action was provided by one who, on account of many points of resemblance, had been christened Mr. Micawber; and though for some little time he contrived to carry on the delusion, he was soon bowled out as follows ("*et in omni veritate dico*"):—

A most suitable palfrey for our friend having passed his preliminary examination before a large party of "ours," he was brought up for closer scrutiny. Micawber stood by — his cap on one side; one hand in the pocket of the horsey breeches he had affected since his arrival in Japan, the other employed in tapping his boot with a bran new cutting whip—the while looking the knowing purchaser to perfection. Had he maintained his posture quietly, without venturing a remark, he would have gained rather than lost in his assumed character; but amid the numerous comments that were being passed by one or the other, Micawber stepped forward, and was seen to peer curiously into the docile animal's ear. After a careful survey, he again put his hand in his pocket with a calmly-satisfied expression, when one of the party called out—"What were you looking at?" "Why, what do you think?" he answered, while an air of conscious pride stole over his countenance. "To see if he has got *thrush!*"

Of course, roars of laughter greeted his answer; and though he tried hard to maintain his dignity, he was at last compelled to turn tail and make the best of his way, with a damaged reputation, to his hut. It appears that in his anxiety to impress us with his knowledge of things horsey, he had been in the habit of talking quietly to the adjutant's groom, from whom he had picked up the terms and expressions with which he had of late electrified us; but the man having a turn for chaff, Micawber had not always succeeded in learning the truth; and this piece of valuable information with regard to the locality of thrush was the last he had extracted from him.

After this, Mr. Micawber was most sensitive of ridicule—more particularly on this subject—and was ever most ready to resent any attempt at it; so much so, that on Aaron one day picking up the foot of the "Falling Star"—as his new purchase was most appropriately named—and observing, "Why, he's got no bars left in his feet!" he answered, with the most bitter sarcasm, "Well, so much the better; then he can't jump over them;" and added, *sotto voce*, to a friend, while winking knowingly, "Who *potted the thrush* that time, eh?"

Some few of the corps—chiefly among the seniors—provided themselves with horses by taking those of the officers of the regiment that preceded us off their hands, in preference to getting raw animals from the country, and the one most fortunate in this way was our gallant chief.

Right bravely had "Flying Isaac" borne himself and his different owners since his first entrance into a military stable, and more especially on that memorable occasion when he earned his name.

Departing for the nonce from his particular line, Isaac had in a weak moment essayed a hurdle-race. With courage becoming his profession, he rose gallantly at the first flight; but strength or pluck failing him half-way, he remained suspended on the top.

Vaulting ambition is ever subject to a fall; but here the difficulty lay, not in escaping one, but in managing a descent from his undignified position, for the bars were strong and the hurdles firmly rammed into the ground. At length a saw was produced and released him; but from that moment he was never seen in public but on the parade ground or the broad road. Here, however, with his grand big legs and portly form, he stood high—some sixteen hands—in the estimation of bystanders; his dignity never suffering him to betray any of the playful weakness common to horse-flesh, nor allowing him even to break out of a walk, without a threat of also breaking his knees.

In the end he was sold to a speculating black for the sum of twenty-five dollars; but the sense of degradation proved too much for him, and the very day after the sale he fell down in a fit, nor rose again alive—thereby probably saving a sable spouse from an early widowhood. But he had served his purpose—the dollars were *paid!*

CHAPTER VI.

TRIP TO DAIBOOTS.

Our chief, ever mindful of the welfare and happiness of his boys, as he delighted to look upon us, had established a rule in the garrison that every Thursday was to be set apart for purposes of enjoyment and recreation. The decree had gone forth, and on that day the hard-worked—and, we were going to add, miserably paid, but we restrain ourselves—sub felt himself a gentleman at large.

Whether the chief had pitched upon this particular day in a thoughtful and considerate spirit, inasmuch as it followed our guest night, or whether it was the result of accident, we know not; but, whichever way it was, we take this opportunity of recording the sense of gratitude which used to steal over us, on awakening on Thursday mornings, as we thought of the ride into the country before us, planned days before! How grateful would be the soft, balmy morning air! how invigorating would be the occasional larks across some favourite line of country! As we thought of all this, and then looked on the other side of the picture, with its courts-martial, orderly-room, military catechism—yes, military *catechism!* Oh, Mars, to think that your devoted sons should be thus treated!—and a host of such other abominations, too painful to dwell upon, our appreciation of the boon knew no bounds, until at last, with the same old familiar, delightful feelings we recollect so well experiencing when a little boy, we would jump out of bed, and dress in all the exhilarating consciousness of having a whole holiday before us. They were happy days those; and a slight shadow of regret, which even the idea that we are homeward bound is not able wholly to dissipate, casts itself over us as we reckon them amongst things of the past. Every moment, even while we are writing these words, as the old ship plunges onward on her course, increases the distance between us and that sunny land where those bright scenes were laid.

On these days we have seen aged captains, one or two, with their locks tinged with grey, and bearded subalterns trooping forth at six o'clock in the fresh morning, rollicking and skylarking in as mad spirits as schoolboys tumbling out of morning school.

Every one of these Thursdays was at first devoted to exploring different parts of the country within a day's reach, and the particular excursion we are about to hand down to posterity was on the occasion of our first visit to Daiboots, the great bronze Buddhist idol of Japan, situated at about seventeen miles from Yokohama. R——, of the 20th Regiment, who with a brother officer had stayed behind on the departure of their regiment for Hong-Kong, acted as our guide. The party, most of whom you have been introduced to, consisted of Tony, Aaron, the Aide, Spiro—this gentleman's name is peculiar, and requires some explanation: he obtained it at first in the Ionian Islands, from his likeness to several young Greeks, who were all known to us under the generic term "Spiro," that being the abbreviation for St. Spiridione, their patron saint—De Tabley, a medico belonging to the Royal Artillery, on leave from Hong-Kong, Belleville, and one or two other choice spirits, including T——, a very popular A.D.C., slightly inclined to *embonpoint*.

At six o'clock in the morning we assembled at the mess, where an early breakfast had been laid out for us. One by one we came dropping in, all breeched and booted, and with revolvers in our belts, in obedience to a strict order that this weapon was to be invariably carried on all long trips into the country. First of all appeared R——, looking rubicund and pleasant, and his cheery shouts soon brought in Aaron, who lived in a hut adjoining the mess; then followed in rapid succession the Aide, Belleville — the odour of Rimmel quite throwing the morning air into the shade— T——, the fat aide-de-camp, Tony, and Spiro. The majority of the party betrayed unmistakable symptoms of having kept it up rather late the night before. "I say, what do you fellows think of the tea one gets in Japan?" inquires that sly old fox, R——. Every one at table begins by saying it is insipid, and at last ends by agreeing that it is undrinkable. "Well," continues R——, gradually leading up to his point, "I'm of your opinion; it is insipid; but what's one to drink, you know? I say, Harvey!" suddenly changing his tone to one of reckless indifference, "bring me a glass of soda and B., and tell the cook to make some more of that grill, with no end of Cayenne pepper and Worcestershire sauce in it!"

R——'s soda and B. is brought, and every one else— led away by the expression of pleasure on his face while drinking it—follows his example; and by the time the new grill makes its appearance, we are all in a fit state to do justice to it. Now the reader is not to run away with the idea that this was a usual occurrence: it simply happened that we had had, the evening before, what is called a big night at mess; and when a man goes to bed at three o'clock and gets up at five, with a hard day's riding before him, there is nothing that smacks particularly strong of dissipation in doing as most of the party did. Is the following a picture of debauchery? Rice, a friend of ours, had been dining with us the previous evening. After leaving the dinner-table we say to him, "Rice, old fellow, take one of the big 'uns, you'll find them the best,"—alluding to the fact of the mess waiter standing with a cigar-box open,—"and come and sit outside, and listen to the band." Well, we go outside, each with a No. 1 manilla in his mouth, sit down in a delightful little arbour overlooking the bay, and listen to the strains of some selection. After it is over, Rice, who is lately from home, narrates some wonderful run or extraordinary day's shooting; he gets so enthusiastic over these subjects, and talks so much, that we begin to think he must be getting a little dry; so, actuated solely by the laws of hospitality, and of course without any ulterior views for our own benefit, we thus address him: "Rice, old fellow, what do you say to a liquor?" He responds with alacrity, "Come on!" Upon which we adjourn forthwith to the mess-room, where the wants of both are attended to. After this we resume our old seats in the arbour, each with a fresh cigar. The band is now playing a waltz. Rice begins to look sentimental, and taking the cigar out of his mouth, regards the light at the end of it in a dreamy sort of way. At last, when the first cornet plays that deliciously soft solo part, his feelings break forth in words: "Ah!" he says, with a long-drawn sigh, "the last time I danced to this was with such a stunning little girl. I say, old fellow, you promise you won't tell any one?" Thus enjoined, we pledge ourselves to secrecy; whereupon follows a most detailed and strict account of how little Rice has fallen in love at home, the colour of the young lady's eyes and hair, her height, her voice; on a certain occasion what he said to her, and what she then said to him, and all the rest of it. He even gives us an imitation of her smile; but what between the music, the brandy and soda, and these fond recollections, little Rice is getting quite unmanned, and his imitation impresses us with anything but admiration. We are now beginning to get on our mettle; for we, too, have a reputation for gallantry; and determining not to be outdone, we launch out into descriptions of several fascinating young creatures, who, we believe, have at different times succumbed to our fascinations. The band stops playing; but the evening is so deliciously cool outside in the open air, and so oppressively hot in-doors, that we continue sitting in the arbour and spinning out our yarns to a most surprising length.

It really is astonishing the amount of small talk—so small that there's nothing at all in it—that two friends can get through after dinner over a smoke. At last Rice looks at his watch by the light of his cigar, and discovers that it is past eleven o'clock. This time he takes the initiative, and says: "I say, old fellow, I think this child could do another B. and S. without sustaining any material injury!" We, of course, guided as before by the laws of hospitality, and admiring the delicate way in which he has put it, take his arm and conduct him to the mess, where the wants of both are administered to by the ever-attentive Harvey. After this, we go into the billiard-room; for, as Rice says, "it's no use going to bed, for those infernal mosquitoes will keep one awake until daybreak;" so we go in for pool, at which game Aaron is, of course, in his element, very red in the face, and keenly alive to the business in hand, which he finds most remunerative. We amuse ourselves at this work until our ichiboos have all more or less found a long home in Aaron's pocket. We say a long home advisedly, for Aaron loveth not to part with his shekels. Rice then finds out that it is past two o'clock, and announces his intention of departing. When he gets to the door, he finds that he is very much heated, and that the morning air is getting chilly; whereupon we become concerned for his health, and recommend a glass of brandy and water before starting, to keep the cold out. He falls in with our views with charming readiness, and says: "Yes; he thinks with another cigar and a glass of brandy and water he'll do." We add, that we don't think this treatment would do us any harm either; and, as we drink, we propose seeing each other home. However, we only accompany Rice to the Camp gate, where we wish him an affectionate good night. By the time we are in bed it is nearly three o'clock; so that when we get up the next morning for our trip at half-past five, we have had barely three hours' sleep. Now, do you think, under the circumstances, there was anything very depraved either in having a soda and B. in the morning, or in the events which led to our requiring one? The former picture from life has been drawn to convince you on the subject; and if it has not, we are sorry for you.

After we had done ample justice to our grill, R—— reminded us, in rather energetic terms, that we were wasting the sunny hours; and, taking advantage of his position as guide, declared his intention of waiting for no man. Lighting his cheroot, and mounting his chestnut pony, "Minden Boy," he started off at a steady jogtrot, followed by the remainder of the party, amidst much bustle and confusion, and many inquiries as to "why the devil he couldn't wait until a fellow lit his cheroot?" or, "Where the deuce is my revolver?" However, R—— trots on quite unconcernedly, puffing away at his cigar, in the proud consciousness of being the only one of the party who knows the way. At last we all catch him up, and emerge into the beautiful green country in a long string; the Aide bringing up the rear at a respectful distance, for he is mounted on an animal called Solon, who combines in himself all the vices which horse-flesh is heir to. This unfortunate young officer's finances were always at the lowest ebb; the consequence was, that his stud generally consisted of one or two animals who had gained for themselves reputations for having eaten a betto or brained a man. Solon, having attained considerable distinction in this particular line, had done both, in addition to many other little pleasantries of a like nature. He had some redeeming qualities, however, inasmuch as he was a capital pony across country, up to any amount of hard work, and throve well on chopped straw : all of which attributes were much appreciated by the Aide;

the last in particular. Solon, on this particular morning, was in a bad temper even for him, and had evinced several unmistakable symptoms of animosity towards all the ponies of the party in general, "Queen's Regulations," Spiro's pony, in particular: the consequence was, that the Aide was condemned to ride in rear of the whole party, any attempt on his part to close up and be sociable being met with an adjuration, in language more strong than polite, to "keep that d——d Maneater out of the way!"—a request which the Aide occasionally experienced some difficulty in complying with, as Solon seemed to burn with a desire to make a repast off Queen's Regulations' tail, perhaps under the impression that it would form an agreeable change to his usual diet of chopped straw. To turn to others of the party: Aaron was in great force, mounted on a China pony, surnamed "Tornado," who accomplished almost as much of the distance on his knees as on his feet. However, Aaron was proof against such trifles, and only grinned cheerily at his misfortunes: but who could have lost his temper on *such* a morning, with *such* scenery, and *such* boon companions? We own to not having the best temper in the world; but on that morning, if any one had administered to us a good sound kick, we should have looked upon it rather in the light of a joke than of an insult.

Our path lay, like the paths of all younger sons in fairy tales, up hill and down dale, through woods and valleys, villages and hamlets, and past peaceful farmhouses, from which chubby little children came trooping out, with shrill cries of "Tojin! Tojin!" and would then look at us, for the most part, in wonder and awe;

whilst others, more daring than the rest, would salute us with " Ohio! dókò maro, maro?" ("Good day; where are you going?") the invariable question addressed by every Nippon to any tojin—foreigner—he may meet in the country. Then, after we had passed, and they felt themselves secure, they would shake their little sides with laughter, to think what funny-looking people these foreigners were, and then rush into the house to tell all about us to the old people, who had watched us go by with looks which said plainly: "Ah, when we were young, such goings on as a lot of ugly tojins galloping about the country would not have been allowed." However, these old folks, generally speaking, were cheery and good-natured whenever we stopped to talk with them; and if they were addicted to a little grumbling, and to recurring to the days when they were young, why it is a privilege of old age in every country, Japan as well as anywhere else. As to the children, the fact of their being dressed exactly like the grown-up people, gave them, in our eyes, at first, an intensely comical appearance. The child of two years of age and the old person of seventy wear precisely the same description of clothes; the former looking very much like the latter seen through an opera-glass reversed.

As we trot on, contemplating the scenery, and as it varies, feeling joyous or sentimental by turns, our reveries are disturbed by a rattle, followed by the exclamation, "By Gosht!" The rattle proceeds from Aaron's pony, Tornado, as he succeeds in bringing his knees and nose into pretty sharp contact with the ground. The "By Gosht!" it is almost needless to say, emanates from Aaron, who picks up the pieces, and, after an inspection, pronounces, in a tone almost of disappointment, that the brute's knees are all right. This performance was repeated, at intervals of about ten minutes, throughout the day; but the imperturbable Aaron kept his temper, as well as his seat, on all occasions. By the way, as this individual's sayings and doings may appear rather often in these pages, it will be as well, before we go farther, to give a slight sketch of his favourite expression, " By Gosht !" It is not to be found in any dictionary of any language. I think it has never been heard to proceed from any one but Aaron; therefore, we may reasonably conclude that to Aaron, and Aaron alone, is to be ascribed the proud honour of being its author. Like Mr. Pegotty's " I'm gormed !" it was supposed to possess an infinity of meaning, although that meaning had never, in the slightest degree, been fathomed by any mortal. By skilful modulation of the voice, accompanied by suitable pantomimic action, Aaron could convey to his hearers by means of it an expression of every mood of the human mind. When pronounced short, and accompanied by a grin of very broad dimensions, it expressed pleasure in the highest degree. This particular variation of it might be seen to perfection in the billiard-room, as he went round pocketing the ichiboos, after having cleared the table at pool. In the same locality it might be heard in its most terrible form, as it was thundered forth in anger, on its illustrious author having been fluked into the pocket by some beginner. To express astonishment, it was prolonged, as, " By Gorsht !" Pronounced in a slightly mincing manner, as, " Bay Gösht !" accompanied by a slapping of the right trouser with a small cane, it is known to have been used with great effect in some of the most fashionable watering-places. But perhaps the circumstances under which it bordered almost on the sublime, when it became, in fact, a brilliant accomplishment, something to be admired and envied, was when, with the fore-finger of the right hand applied to his nose, and with a wink of the eye, it was used to intimate to some sharp blade who was trying to get over him, that he—Aaron—was up to his little game, and that there was not the slightest use trying it on. On these occasions there was such an air of intense knowingness investing the whole performance, that the individual on whom it was brought to bear invariably collapsed before it, and gave up the project of trying to do Aaron as utterly hopeless and impossible.

About three miles from the Camp, just after we had passed a prettily-situated little tea-house, R—— pulled up, and pointing to a bridge, told us that it was the scene of the murder of a Frenchman about three years before. The facts of the case were never arrived at. He was out by himself, engaged in some scientific pursuit, and it was supposed that he was cut down by a party of two-sworded men, simply because he happened to be a foreigner. As is invariably the custom amongst the Japanese on these occasions, they attempted to justify the cruel and cowardly act of their countrymen by imputing their motives in killing him to pardonable feelings of jealousy, caused by his own conduct. But this, as in almost all other similar instances, was a base calumny.

"It is a shame!" remarked Aaron, on hearing this; "as if women had not enough to answer for, without sticking 'em in these kinds of rows. By Gosh!" he added, in a burst of virtuous indignation, "I believe if ever I'm cut down in this country, they'll make out that I've been spooning the Tycoon's favourite wife." Here Aaron displayed his white teeth from ear to ear, and winked his old eye, as much as to say that more unlikely things had happened, and might happen over again.

We all laughed heartily at Aaron, and resumed our way, quite forgetting in a few moments the melancholy fate of the quiet, inoffensive French botanist, who probably received his death-blow while stooping down to examine in ecstasy some plant which we would have thought nothing but a vulgar little roadside weed.

Our first halting-place was at a house about seven miles on our way, where we were received by roars of laughter from the old women, and a general "scuttling away" of the young ones. The reason of this was soon apparent. R——, who was well known here, was looked upon as a tearing wag in his way, and his appearance was hailed as the prelude to some exquisite joke which was soon to follow. His first little pleasantry after the storm of "Ohio donezan's!" &c. ("Good day, gentlemen!") was over, was to feign a burning and consuming passion for the old lady of the house, an old okami-san— married woman—aged about seventy; and when he brought this performance to a close, by pretending to give her a tender and impassioned kiss, he regularly brought the house down, the most demonstrative and noisiest in testifying their delight being the old woman herself and her husband: the latter was quite beside himself; and as he coughed and choked, he gasped out some words which we have not the slightest doubt were the Japanese for "Isn't this prime? Was there ever such a wag as this tojin yakonin? Oh my, if he doesn't stop this, I shall have a fit!"

From the old people, R—— soon turned his attention to the moosmies—unmarried girls—who had hidden themselves on his approach, and in a very short time four or five of them came tumbling in from the back yard, followed by R—— in hot pursuit, occasionally cracking his whip, or administering a playful slap on the plump little shoulders of one, as she tried to dodge past him towards her place of concealment again. This levity on the part of the young was reproved by the old ones,—funny old creatures! they themselves had been twice as frivolous and childish a few moments before, without the excuse of youth on their side,—and they were soon bustling about, handing us tea in diminutive bowls, and sweetmeats. This tea, as a rule, met with the same fate as the tea at breakfast; and a little weak brandy and water was found much more acceptable to most of the party. R—— said that we had better have a quarter of an hour's rest here; so, after seeing that our bettoes had washed the ponies' mouths out, we got our cheroot cases ready, and prepared ourselves for a smoke. These tea-houses are the picture of comfort and cleanliness. Let not their name impress you with the idea that only the "cup which cheers but not inebriates" reigns supreme: they possess licenses "to be drunk on the premises," both as regards human beings and liquor. Many a blear-eyed old *habitué* have we seen at these establishments, with a chalk against his name, that would have reflected credit on a Bill Styles at any of our village pot-houses.

They are generally built a little off the road, and the space in front is covered with low tables and benches, where the traveller can sit down and sip his tea or his *saki*, in peace and comfort, the while he enjoys the sunny landscape before him—we speak of the roadside tea-house—or amuses himself by taking stock of the passers-by : not that much opportunity is afforded him of enjoying this latter pastime ; for we don't recollect ever having seen a Japanese who had the heart to pass a tea-house. If he has any money, he will have a drink, either tea or *saki*, generally the latter ; if he has not, he will sit on one of the benches, and apparently derive much satisfaction from watching others engaged in their potations.

Our cigars being lit, we proceeded to enjoy ourselves after the manner of the natives by sitting outside. I don't think we talked much, although we were rather a noisy lot, but we puffed away in silent admiration of the scenery. Nowhere in the world is there such a diversity of colouring as in a Japanese landscape. One of the party, we recollect, who was a bit of an artist in his way, amused us rather by declaring that the best method of painting the view before us would be, just to draw the outlines of the hills, with a few thatched farm-houses here and there, and then to upset your paint-box promiscuously over the whole, taking care previously to extract most of the sombre colours.

That brute, Solon, the Aide's pony, who we believe was under the impression that his mission was to make himself disagreeable on every possible occasion, broke in upon our meditations by engaging in conflict De Tabley's pony; and the united efforts of the whole party were required to separate the enraged combatants. After this, the wretched Aide was made to mount Solon, and wait until the rest of the party were ready to start.

It had been noticed all the day that Spiro, generally the noisiest of the noisy, had been unusually quiet and subdued: perhaps coming events were casting their shadows over him, and filling his mind with dismal forebodings. It was observed, too, that as he passed Solon, on his way to mount his own steed, he shuddered visibly.

The lower orders of the Japanese are wonderfully inquisitive and observant. Our summer uniform differed from that worn by the regiment we relieved; and this fact was soon made the subject of endless inquiries. The next stage was the manipulating one, when we all had to submit to being turned round and round, and having every part of our dress examined minutely. They were particularly anxious to know who that *moosmi* was that some of us had on our caps,—the figure of Britannia, the badge of the regiment,—and were lost in amazement at the idea of a lot of yakonins—military officers—so far forgetting the respect due to their sex and calling as thus to pay homage publicly to a woman; to set her up, as it were, on a pinnacle of honour.

We were not sufficiently masters of the language to explain exactly who Britannia was; and we left them in a perplexing state of uncertainty as to whether the badge was meant for the Queen of England or the wife of our colonel. The former illustrious person's existence they had never heard of; and they laughed us to scorn when we told them that the ruler of our land belonged to the gentler sex. They thought at first that it was only one of R——'s wild jokes; but when we had convinced them that it really was the case, it was amusing to watch how the old women bridled up and looked at their lords, as much as to say: "Aha! you see there *are* countries where women are treated with proper respect. These tojins aren't such barbarians after all!" On the other hand, the men looked puzzled, and strove to enlighten themselves by asking questions. "Do your women, then, fight?" With one accord the whole party responded, "Rather!" the voices of the married men, of whom there were two or three amongst us, being particularly noticeable. Again the old women looked significantly at each other, and then at their husbands, who thinking, perhaps, that the subject, if followed up, was one which might convey a bad lesson to their wives, hurriedly changed it.

For the next few miles, after leaving this tea-house, we passed through a succession of lovely Devonshire-like lanes, with camellias growing luxuriantly on either side. The growth of the camellia tree in Japan is most wonderful. Let not the smile of incredulity light up the face of the reader when we state that we have seen some of them attain the height of at least forty feet. Many such as these we passed, and the appearance of them in full blossom may be imagined. Before we had seen this ourselves, we should have thought it about as likely a circumstance that we should one day sit under the shade of our own mignonette, as that we should ride for miles under camellia trees in full flower. Later in the season, when the camellias have ceased to bloom, their place is supplied by the azalea, which marks the hillsides with gaudy patches of crimson, and the landscape becomes more gorgeous than ever. With the barley and rice in full ear, nothing but a rich mixture of gold, crimson, and green meets the eye, which turns from this, as from too much of a good thing, with a feeling almost of relief and refreshment, to dwell upon the quiet, thatched homesteads, with their well-swept yards in front, where the children are playing, and the old women are sitting at their spinning-wheels. What an air of perfect peace and contentment reigns around! The rustle of the leaves as they shimmer in the sunlight, the merry shout of some little child at play, the bark of the *fukee* dog, as he sniffs the blood of the tojin—all is delicious! so delicious that we begin to wish that it could always be like this, and that we had never to go in-doors again, but that we could dream away the rest of our existence lying down in a shady glade, drinking in the lovely scene with half-closed eyes, and—shall we add?—a pipe or cheroot between our lips. We hope we have not spoilt the above picture by this; we do not think we have: the landscape will look all the softer seen through the haze of a good manilla. *Chacun à son goût.* Some would substitute for the pipe or cheroot the only girl he ever loved by his side. Another might say, "Give me the tried friend of my youth, one in whom I found a spirit kindred to my own, with whom to enjoy all this;" and we actually know of one stout old gentleman, a distinguished member of our regiment, who would be all in favour of a soda and B. We give in to all these diversities of taste, with the exception of the last-mentioned one. If we allowed this one soda and B., it would only lead to a request for another and another, and so on, until the scenery would indeed become more "truly rural" than ever. You will be introduced to this old gentleman in due time. His name is Captain Puffles!

Our next halting-place was at the top of Kanasawa hill, when R—— pulled up to enable us to look at the view, which is famed even in Japan for its beauty. Rather in the penny-showman style, he entered into an elaborate description of the different features of the scene, which we listened to attentively, until he came to "over there to the left is the village of Kanasawa, where we are to tiffin." At this every one is seized with a desire to push on; and Goths, Vandals, mere animals that we were, all appreciation of the beauties of nature vanished, and we clamoured to be led to our food. R——, cut short in his lecture, was nothing loath, and away we trotted for two miles, which brought us to the Kanasawa tea-house. Here, as at the other place, R—— was received as an old acquaintance in the same jocular manner. What was it, though, that wrought such a sudden change in his jaunty and jocose air, as he engaged the old woman of the house in conversation? There was no need for us to ask a second time. We knew it. We divined the cause at once, and we were prepared in a measure for the blow which fell upon us, as he turned round and exclaimed: "Here's a go! the grub hasn't arrived." A look of blank dismay settled on the whole party; but we brightened up a little as he continued, "But the liquor has come all right, and the coolies who brought it say that the other fellows will be here in half an hour." Under these circumstances we determined to go on to Daiboots after a short halt at this tea-house, and then return to it for tiffin. All the party got off their ponies and went into the house, with the exception of the Aide, who had to sit on Solon, like Patience on a monument, not daring to dismount, as his betto had not yet arrived, and he had no particular ambition to furnish in his own person a mid-day repast for his gallant steed. At last, to his intense satisfaction, the party emerged from the house, and we all once more proceeded on our journey, the Aide, as usual, following about thirty yards behind. It was just at this time that Spiro, prompted by the workings of an eccentric mind, or obeying the finger of destiny, which was beckoning him on to a cruel fate, turned Queen's Regulations round, for no earthly reason that any one could see, and, with his long arms and legs flying about until it made one giddy to look at him, galloped down the road towards Solon. In vain the Aide shrieked out a warning! In vain the main body of the party yelled at him! In vain even Solon added his voice to the general cry, and, with a shrill neigh, seemed to announce his intention of putting a stop to such a proceeding if it were persisted in! On came the devoted Spiro, shouting with delight at his own performance, and mistaking our warnings for applause—on he came to within five yards of Solon's nose. A bound! a shriek of terror! a roar of laughter from the party! and Spiro and Queen's Regulations lay rolling in the dust. With an agility which nothing but his terror of Solon could have induced, Spiro managed to extricate himself from his pony, and crawled to the side of the road, where he lay moaning, and gasping faintly that his leg was broken. Every one was really concerned on hearing this, and all crowded round him, profuse in their offers of assistance to get him across to the tea-house; but he intimated, in a feeble tone, that of the two he rather preferred being left alone to die by the roadside than endure the agony of being moved a single step. He had just finished this plaintive and touching remark, when the voice of the Aide broke upon his ear, as he yelled: "Look out, for God's sake! I can't hold him!" And Solon, having worried Queen's Regulations to his heart's content, came crashing towards the unfortunate Spiro. In less time than it takes to jot down one single word of this veracious chronicle, that much-persecuted individual hopped over the wall which bounded the road, and placed a good field between himself and his pursuer, who, thus baffled, again turned his attention to Queen's Regulations, who now seemed rather desirous of redeeming his honour; and, to the horror of the Aide, whose only safe place hitherto had been on Solon's back, the two engaged in deadly combat. Loud were his shrieks for assistance; and soon all the party were belabouring the combatants with their hunting-crops, bamboos, or anything they could lay their hands on. Belabouring the combatants we said; but we ought to have added, "and the Aide;" for—owing to the number of cooks, the general excitement, and the constant changes of position—that gentleman shared these little attentions with the ponies.

In the meantime a change had come o'er the spirit of Spiro's dream. Perched at a safe distance from the scene, on a wall, he loudly applauded the whole performance, occasionally offering the odds freely on his own pony, or beseeching the bystanders to "let 'em alone, and give 'em fair play, and no favour." However, to his intense disgust and the Aide's delight, Queen's Regulations, notwithstanding the encouragement he was receiving from his owner, suddenly came to the conclusion that he had had enough, and with a farewell squeal and a fling of his heels into the air, bounded down the road, and was soon lost to view. Solon was now at once secured by about ten sets of hands hanging on to his bridle; and the Aide, pale with excitement and apprehension, anxiously felt himself all over, to ascertain that there were no bones broken. After this examination he pronounced himself all right, and returned thanks for the timely aid rendered; but, at the same time, he begged to request, that should a similar occasion for their assistance arise during the remainder of the day, his friends would bear in mind that Solon's hind quarters, and not his, were to be the particular object for their cuts to be directed at.

Public attention was now turned to Spiro, who was suffering from lowness of spirits, consequent on the defeat of his pony. Deprived of his excitement, and finding himself the centre of attraction, he suddenly had a relapse, and again faintly announced his inability to move. With difficulty, we slowly helped him across the field he had traversed so quickly a few minutes before on the wings of fear. We laid him down on a Japanese mat in the tea-house, and proceeded to examine the broken limb, as he persisted in calling it. His legs were of that kind described often as being so peculiarly fitted for a top-boot, the same size all the way up; in fact, a fastidious connoisseur might have found fault with them on the score of being perhaps a trifle too fine; but notwithstanding their fragile make, they had proved pretty tough, and, with the exception of being very much bruised, they were passed as all sound. Their owner, however, was too stiff to proceed, and we left him reclining quite comfortably on his mat, after having taken the precaution of leaving his revolver by his side, and administering some Japanese tea to keep his spirits up during our absence.

There was now a council of war as to what was to be done about Solon; several of the party refusing flatly to proceed any farther with him. At last some one suggested that it would be all right if the Aide consented to his being shot immediately on his evincing any refractory symptoms: this his owner agreed to; but still smarting from the effects of the bad shots his friends had made before, he stipulated that he himself was to perform the office of executioner, should it be found necessary to adopt this *dernier ressort*. This point was ceded, and the Aide faithfully promised to do his duty, which we firmly believed he would on the slightest provocation, such was the hatred which rankled in his bosom towards the brute he bestrode. The object of all this hatred and mistrust, as if aware of the penalty of any practical jokes on his part, behaved tolerably well for the remainder of the journey.

It was when the scene was at its loveliest, the hedges at their greenest, and the sun at its brightest, that we descried coming along in the distance a laughing, merry group of Japanese. When we met them, they turned out to be a *troupe* of conjurers and top-spinners, on their way to Yokohama. Here was an opportunity of amusement not to be lost; and on the promise of a few ichiboos, they declared themselves ready to give us their whole *répertoire*. A shady, grassy spot, with a green bank for seats, and a level sward, was soon found just off the road, and after tying up the ponies, we sat or laid ourselves down to watch the performance. This was the first time they had ever acted before foreigners, and we seemed to be a source of infinite amusement to them; for their preparations, as they laid out all their paraphernalia on the ground, were gone through amidst much giggling and furtive glances at us. They performed the usual Japanese tricks, consisting of top-spinning in every variety, juggling, the butterfly trick, and many others, all of which we suppose are more or less familiar to our readers now; for *troupes* of Japanese conjurers have visited America and England since then. Indeed, several of the very party who performed before us in this shady grove have since made their *début* before American and English audiences. We met some of them in Yokohama a short time after this, just previous to their departure for America. It is no use describing the top-spinning, which was wonderful; the butterfly trick, which was pretty; or the tumbling: those who have not seen them at home have probably read or heard about them all, and we will content ourselves by saying that we had the whole thing to perfection.

After the performance we left one another on particularly good terms, principally through the ichiboo medium, and each party wended its way in its own direction. Their first interview with the tojin certainly seemed to have made a favourable impression, for they went off chatting and laughing merrily, and frequently, as the distance widened between us, they turned round to give us another cheery Syonara—good-bye—which we always responded to. We were just going round a bend of the path, and in another moment would have lost sight of them, when our progress was arrested by shouts and frantic gesticulations for us to wait. We accordingly did so with some little curiosity, which was soon satisfied on perceiving that the band, consisting of two drums and two reed instruments, was about to give us a farewell treat, and in a few moments the morning was made hideous with the discordant notes. It must have been a sort of "Auld Lang Syne," for the horrid air was accompanied all through by signals of farewell. We had the politeness to wait until they had finished, and acknowledged the compliment by taking off our hats, and both parties resumed their respective ways. We have seen in crowded assembly rooms, in gorgeous theatres, in drawing-rooms amongst friends, wizards of the north, wizards of the south, wizards of every point of the compass, "caressed of crowned heads," *et hoc genus omne;* but never have we enjoyed anything of the sort as much as we did that half-hour with these top-spinners, in that shady, quiet little glade, with its soft, grassy bank whereon to recline and smoke the fragrant cheroot, and its clear limpid stream, at which to slake our thirst.

About three or four miles from the village of Kanasawa we arrived at Kamakura, where we stopped, for the purpose of visiting the temples, for which this locality is famed throughout the length and breadth of Japan, and to which pilgrims flock from all parts of the country at certain seasons of the year. The temples, as regards general outline of form, are very similar to all other sacred edifices in Japan; but in size, costly carving, and number, they far surpass anything of the kind to be seen out there. The entrance to the sacred grounds consists of three arched stone bridges, very much in the willow-pattern style, over a moat which was covered with lotus-plants and water-lilies. So very arched are these bridges—very nearly a semicircle—that our passage over them was made holding on to the sides. Of course to the Japanese, with their straw, sandal-like shoes, it is all plain sailing.

We here found two adventurous midshipmen endeavouring to urge their ponies over a bar, which was placed at the highest point of the arc of one of the smaller bridges. The four-legged animals, however, showed that they possessed infinitely more sense than the two-legged ones, by declining to have anything whatever to do with such an absurd proceeding, notwithstanding a pretty liberal application of whip and spur, accompanied by many terms of endearment. How the difference of opinion ended we know not, as we walked on, leaving them to their own devices. Just outside a gateway forming a second entrance, we were taken to see two sacred ponies, who appeared to lead anything but a stirring, active life. Perpetually caparisoned in the most grotesque manner, they are never taken out of their stalls, nor even allowed to lie down, being slung from the roof of the stable. The object of this is, that they are supposed to be ready at a moment's notice for the god of war, in the event of that deity taking it into his head to ride abroad. We forgot to ask whether he was expected to ride them both at the same time, circus fashion. Of course, it is only amongst the very ignorant that this superstition obtains any credence. The old priest himself, as he told us it, grinned from ear to ear; and even the little boys laughed.

These ponies were both perfectly white; and one of them had pink eyes, which gave him an Albino-like expression. On payment of a tempo (about twopence), the traveller may purchase for himself the unspeakable honour of being allowed to present them with two or three little saucers full of corn, which they despatch with a relish that leads one to believe they are dependent on this sort of charity for their keep.

Notwithstanding, though, this somewhat precarious existence, they had both succeeded in running to flesh to a considerable extent. One of them, in fact (not the Albino), had particularly distinguished himself in this way.

The next step to take, if you wish to do Kamakura thoroughly, is to buy at the inner gate, from an old woman who is rather *empressée* in her efforts to effect a sale, a map or plan of the place, on which all the temples, shrines, and other objects of interest are marked, if not with accuracy, still with sufficient correctness to serve as a tolerable guide.

We do not recollect any *one* temple striking us with any very great admiration or wonder: it was only taken collectively that they assumed an appearance of anything like grandeur.

One particular object, however, we remember, which was worthy of notice, though it would be out of place to give more than a very cursory one in these pages. Suffice it to say, that it was a stone about four feet high, in the formation of which Nature seems to have been actuated by most improper feelings.

A visit to it, and the observance of certain ceremonies in connection therewith, are believed amongst the lower orders of the Japanese at once to confer on the female suppliant the blessing of an heir-apparent, however she may hitherto have hoped against hope.

It is the custom for every lady who has visited this peculiar shrine, and benefited in the way above specified, to plant near it a bamboo stick in the ground, with her name inscribed on a rag fluttering from the top, in testimony of its wonderful powers.

It is even whispered that there are instances amongst Europeans of its services having been invoked with success.

The priest who conducted us through the grounds, and gave us all this information, asked with an air of pride if we had anything like that in England; and on our reply in the negative, we appeared to fall very much in his estimation as a nation. He added that some French gentlemen, who had visited the place a week before, had told him—we suppose for fun—that there were similar things in France, and that he therefore concluded that the French were a greater people than the English.

We soon had had enough of temples and shrines, and pushed on for Daiboots. On our way thither, R—— pointed out the spot where Major Baldwin and Lieutenant Bird, both of the 20th Regiment, were brutally assassinated, on their return from a visit to Daiboots, a few months before our arrival in the far East.

The interest with which we looked upon the spot increased as R—— dwelt upon how popular they had been with both officers and men of the regiment.

There was a tolerably broad path, where we pictured them riding together, talking and laughing as two friends would; then the path came abruptly to an end, and there was a broad flat stone placed across a trench as a bridge. Just beyond this, there was a gnarled and knotted trunk of a tree, behind which the miserable assassins crouched, ready to spring on their victims. On the two friends must have come down the path side by side, until they came to the little stone bridge, where Baldwin most likely took the lead. Had they known that death was lurking on the other side, and had they felt it their duty to go on, there probably would have been a generous altercation as to who was to be the first to brave the danger. Probably the first thing that the foremost one saw of his peril was the flash of the bright steel, with a scowling face behind it. Whatever their thoughts may have been, they had little time for them; for these heavy two-handed swords, with their keen edges, make short work when used against men taken off their guard and unresisting.

By this foul and bloody murder the feelings of the regiment were wrought to such an intense pitch of excitement, that nothing but the iron hand of discipline could have restrained the men from taking the law into their own hands, and committing some frightful atrocity to avenge the deaths of their murdered officers.

We believe there was some idea amongst the civil and military authorities of marching the regiment out to the scene of the murder, and burning down the temples of Kamakura, as a lesson to the Japanese, and to make the Government aware that they would be considered answerable for these deeds.

Some decisive measure of this sort would have been the best plan to prevent the recurrence of these horrible events.

The above step was never taken, however, and the Japanese were brought to book by other means.

At the execution of one of the murderers some weeks after, the whole of the troops of the garrison were present; and an eye witness described to us, that as the murderer was led forth to meet his doom, the pale faces, fixed gaze, and compressed lips of our soldiers bespoke almost the desire of a wild animal to rend the cowering wretch who tottered before them limb from limb; and when, after the executioner's sword had done its work, and the headless trunk lay quivering, such a sound filled the air as is only heard from a crowd labouring under some intense and painful excitement. Not a roar, nor a murmur, but a gasping sound between the two. A sound heard perhaps once in a lifetime, and never forgotten. A sound which curdles and freezes the blood in one's veins, and gives one a choking feeling in the throat.

It speaks strongly for the discipline of the regiment that under all this, not a man stirred from his place, not an arm moved, but there they stood like statues until the word was given to march off.

A brisk trot of about half an hour, after leaving the scene of this tragedy, brought us to Daiboots, one of the most sacred edifices in Japan. Many a pilgrim has travelled hundreds of miles, footsore and weary, just to have one look at the huge statue; and to return to his home, in his own opinion, a wiser and a better man for having feasted his eyes on what he considers the greatest wonder of the world.

A few words of description may not be out of place.

We have been chary, as a rule, of inflicting many descriptions of places or country on our readers, and have entered on this field as little as possible, as we confess to having an abhorrence of anything in the guide-book style; and we are conscious of our inability to rise any higher in our descriptive attempts.

Daiboots, then, is a huge bronze figure, forty-three feet high, of a Buddhist god, who is represented sitting cross-legged and with clasped hands. The approach to it consists of a splendid avenue of trees, and the figure is seen to advantage from the end of this vista.

It has been photographed and sketched from nearly every point of view; but one of our party, wishing to be uncommon, climbed over a railing and took the venerable old gentleman in rear.

His appearance on paper, when thus taken, was anything but imposing, as he had two windows in the small of his back for the purpose of ventilating his interior, which, with its shrines, images, and general decoration, resembled very much a small Roman Catholic chapel. That spirit of Vandalism which is so rife amongst all tourists, and which we thought could hardly have penetrated to Japan, we here found flourishing in all its virulence, and to have left its abominably snobbish traces in the numerous inscriptions on the walls, showing how J. Smith and party had visited Daiboots on 19th October, 1865, and many other such horrid records.

We experienced some satisfaction, though, in observing that our countrymen were not the only offenders; for the autographs of J. Smith, Jean Le Brun, Karl Schmidt, and Phinehas Bunkum, of San Francisco, all rivalled each other as specimens of bad writing and taste,—and we were almost going to add bad spelling; but we will stretch a point and give these gentlemen credit for being able to spell their own names.

We are happy to state that on a subsequent visit to Daiboots—about a year afterwards—we found that these proud records had been obliterated by the whitewasher's brush.

After thoroughly doing the image, we were lounging quietly at its base, when a jolly-looking fat old priest waddled up to us, and greeted R—— as an old friend.

He was intensely obese, and as he clasped his hands over his ample stomach, he seemed to be hugging himself in unspeakable satisfaction at being the possessor of such substantial charms. He was Friar Tuck all over, produced from a Japanese mould. As R—— pointed us out to him, and explained that this was our first visit to Daiboots, he smiled cheerily, and bobbed his shaven head as low as his fat paunch would allow him. At last his eye rested on T——, the A.D.C. we have described as being slightly inclined to *embonpoint*—then there was a sudden change. The cheery smile became sickly and feeble, the polite bow constrained and faltering. In fact, so noticeable was it, that R—— remarked to us, that he could not make out "what the devil was up with the old cock." The "old cock," as he was thus irreverently termed, tried hard to appear at his ease, and to behave towards us with that winning politeness for which the Japanese ought to be distinguished above all other races; but in vain. His peace of mind had fled, why or wherefore none of us could divine. There was a silent sorrow which none of us could fathom, and which clouded his usually open brow, and cast a gloom over his soul. In vain R—— tried to dissipate the cloud by talking to him on subjects in which he was wont to take an interest, such as the price of rice and fish, or the number of foreigners who had visited Daiboots and had "tipped" him. But no, he refused to be comforted, and his replies were forced and constrained, while ever and anon he stole furtive glances at T——'s portly figure, after which he would survey his own with a troubled and anxious countenance. At last we comprehended the doubt which tortured his mind, the cause of his sorrow. He thought, and feared, that T—— was a fatter man than he was. Hitherto he had been looked up to and respected as the most corpulent man in the district; and yet here he was, as it were, the lion in his den, the Douglas in his hall, bearded by a tojin. Unable, apparently, longer to endure the agony of suspense, he measured his calf with a bit of string, and then advanced to T——, on whom he performed the same operation.

It was a trying moment for him, as with trembling hands he compared the two measurements. Oh, happiness! his was about half an inch bigger.

The gleam of delight which lit up his whole face was only momentary, though. Again was he troubled in spirit. *The great test had yet to be applied.*

With a sigh of doubt, he encircled his huge stomach with the same bit of string, which had to have another spliced on for the purpose; and again T——, with that good-nature which has made him a general favourite throughout China and Japan, submitted himself to the old priest's trembling hands and bit of string.

Oh, joy! triumph! the old Nippon was again the winner; *this* time by about two inches.

Smiling from ear to ear, and rubbing his hands, he

commenced a series of bows we thought were never going to end, which T—— responded to in true Japanese style.

We all crowded round the delighted old man, and proffered our congratulations, which he received as if he were quite aware that he had thoroughly earned them. He now conceived an intense liking for T——, whom he treated in an affectionate, but easy and familiar way. He had no longer now to fear him as a rival. He could extend to him the kind patronage of a great and generous conqueror over a fallen, but worthy foe.

A smart ride back to Kanasawa soon found us at the tea-house, where we had left Spiro.

We found that individual much recovered, and in very high spirits. He informed us that the luncheon was all right, and that he had passed the time while we were away very pleasantly, and hadn't found it at all slow; facts we easily accounted for, when we found out that there was a *pâté de foie gras* and a bottle of champagne deficient.

What a jolly luncheon that was! Unrestrained by empty conventionalities! that is to say, Spiro would make love to the pretty little moosmi who was waiting on us, and his example was followed by most of the party. Untrammelled by paltry usages of society! for behold, the bench on which the corpulent A.D.C. was sitting gave way with a crash under its frightful burden just as R——'s health was being proposed, and every one visited the unintentional breach of etiquette by shying something at the offender's prostrate form.

After this toast had been proposed, responded to, and in every way duly honoured, with the exception of the little irregularity on the part of the A.D.C. above recorded, we beguiled the time with song; and the country-people all crowded round, and stared at us through the windows, delighted beyond measure with the singing, and a view of the tojin as he appeared enjoying himself. How we made the rafters ring! and the paper windows flutter! and the yokels stare! and ourselves hoarse, as we gave the chorus of C——'s great Cornish song, generally commemorative of the glories of "Tre, Pol, and Pen."

This chorus was invariably a success, for we all knew it so well, as the song was a general favourite, and was called for on every possible occasion.

It owed the honour it thus received more to C——'s good voice and manner of singing it than to any merit of its own.

C—— was a Cornishman, and as he gave it, threw his whole spirit into the song; and when, in about the third verse, "Twice ten thousand Cornish men" are recorded to have arrived at the "Walls of London-town," to have there and then stigmatized the whole of the inhabitants of that city as "Cowards all," and then further to have tauntingly requested them to "Come out," C—— always looked as if he were ready to do battle single-handed with any number of these citizens, one after the other, who might accept this pressing invitation to "Come out."

Merrily the afternoon went, until the darkening shades of evening warned us that it was time to start home, and get over the worst part of the road before night closed in.

The ponies were got ready, stirrup-cups were imbibed all round, and away we started on the road home, through the same lanes we had traversed in the morning, up and down the same hills and valleys, and past the same farmhouses, outside of which we observed whole families enjoying, in the open air, their evening hot bath, which is taken altogether in a huge tub, while the water is kept almost at boiling heat by a charcoal fire in a small brick furnace at one end. Many a family, of all ages and sexes, we passed, simmering contentedly in these baths; and in return to our salutations, they bobbed their heads —the only part of them seen above the rims—cheerily at us.

One family we caught just in the act of leaving the tub, and they presented the appearance of boiled lobsters —perfectly red.

Some Englishmen are rather given to calling their countrymen the most "tubbing" nation in the world. We must really undeceive these individuals, and state that the Japanese are infinitely ahead of us in this respect.

Almost every coolie has his hot bath after the work of the day is over. Where will you find his prototype in England, or any other country, doing this? We can fancy Joe Buggins's contempt for any man in his own station of life who "cleaned hisself reg'lar every evening." If he—to leave Joe Buggins, and to return to the coolie—is in a town, he will patronise one of the lower bath-houses, where he can reduce himself to the state of a boiled lobster on payment of a few cash. If he is in a village, there are certain to be a public tub or two at the end of the street, where he can go through the same process at even a cheaper rate.

Nothing particularly worthy of record happened on

the road home, except a "spill" or two as the ponies got tired and careless.

Only one thing more remains to be told of our trip to Daiboots, the history of which we have spun out to such a length, that we are almost afraid of not getting a reader to accompany us through the whole journey. This one more circumstance we would feel inclined to suppress, were it not that we have made a point hitherto of giving you "the truth, the whole truth, and nothing but the truth;" and we will not now depart from this rule from mock motives of modesty.

About ten o'clock that night we were proceeding, rather sleepy with the events of the day, from the mess to our quarters. As we neared the gate, an individual in a long night-shirt, evidently under the impression that he was on duty, emerged from one of the huts, and addressed the sentry this wise :—

"I shay, shentry, ish't all right?"

"All right, sir!" responded the sentry promptly to this somewhat vague and open question.

"Oh, then *thatsh* all right," remarked he of the long night-shirt, drawing this conclusion with the satisfaction of one who congratulates himself upon having taken all precautionary measures, and that if anything *now* goes wrong, no blame can attach itself to him.

After murmuring the sentry's answer to himself once, as if to make quite sure there was no mistake about it, he retired, apparently greatly eased in his mind.

CHAPTER VII.

SCHOOLING THE GRIFFINS.

During the continuance of the hot weather but little could be done by the Holy Boys in the way of amusement, beyond the morning and evening rides, accompanying hounds in their exercise, or exploring the neighbouring country and seeking out its most beautiful views.

It is not every man who cares to go into ecstasies about, or can remain for hours entranced by, a lovely landscape; but coarse and uncultivated indeed must be *his* mind who cannot appreciate the beauties of nature, as seen in Japan.

They *must* appeal strongly to the most careless of ordinary observers; and how much more to the sportsman, to whom an eye for country is a necessity!

Equal charms have they—whether viewed in the early summer, when the endless mass of green might be monotonous, did not its tints vary from the deep, dark shade of the pine to the light and dainty colouring of the fairy-like bamboo; when, looking down, as you may do, from some wooded height over a wide stretch of paddy-field below, where the young crop shines with its peculiar brilliant verdancy, you might easily imagine yourself standing on the Hemplow Hills, hoping anxiously that one of Mr. Topham's particular "old *generals*" may break away over those glorious pastures for Stanford

Hall or Kilworth Sticks, and praying fervently that in that event you may—which is no easy matter—get a good start, and—what is still more difficult—succeed in keeping it; or whether, again, when the scenery bears a rougher and a bolder form, the brown hills but diversified by the evergreen firs and the changeless laurel, and the varied landscape stretching away sharp and distinct through the frosty atmosphere to the distant mountains, high above which towers the stately Fusiyama, now clothed to its base in purest white.

Every day and in every ride you could find some fresh view; and in the cool summer evenings, when the sun had lost much of its power and a gentle breeze fanned your brow, few things could be more enjoyable than to saunter slowly along on the back of an easy-going animal—revelling in the scene, as you puffed quietly at your cheroot, and for the moment felt in charity with all men.

During this season, though, we did not forget to look forward to the time when the Drag Hunts would bring more active exercise and employment; and, though but bastard substitutes for the noble science, would serve to awaken many a reminiscence that might otherwise slumber out its existence, and keep alive hopes and expectations that pointed encouragingly to our return home.

With a view to teach the ponies their business and render them handy for their future cross-country work, a piece of unoccupied grass land beyond the garden in front of the ante-room was converted into a practising ground by the erection of a couple of leaping bars, with the addition of a turf wall, water-jump, double fence, and thorn hedge with blind ditch.

For this spot, when the heat was not too great, the ante-room and billiard-room would often disgorge their contents, as the ponies were brought out for half an hour's "schooling;" and the summer-house overlooking the field served as a gallery for a sympathetic and enthusiastic audience, who were ever ready to applaud a successful jump, or cheer an unfortunate wight whose raw brute had lowered him to the dust. Of course, most of the "griffins" required a little lungeing at first; but it was marvellous how soon they learnt to pick up their legs, and take their leaps in something like proper form.

At this fun some of the younger lot were completely in their element, and threw themselves into it with every zest.

Many a good cropper have we had in this arena; but, though such casualties were neither few nor far between, we never saw any one meet with harm.

Often a wild, unbroken animal—purchased or on trial —that had never been backed before, was brought on the ground, and by dint of a strong hand and a liberal use of the persuaders, added to a yelling, flogging crowd behind, made to tumble in and out of the ditch or roll over the bar for the amusement of the bystanders.

Here are a lot just coming out; so let us take our places in the gallery. We shall very likely see some fun—certainly a fall or two.

The ball is opened by Mulvey, who has only to *show* the jump to old Ugly; for no sooner does he catch sight of the bar, than, taking the bit between his teeth, he races over it and across two fields beyond before he can be stopped.

The next to perform is Iona, who looks a little

stumpy about both fore-legs—the result of too much of the early morning "*exercise.*" He hasn't quite learnt the proper style yet, but bucks jerkily over—causing the Aide, who is riding him, to show rather more daylight than you are ever likely to see between himself and his saddle after a few months more of the continual rough riding of Japan.

"Mind yourselves!" cries Aaron, as he lifts an untutored griffin, which he has bought but a day or two before as a companion to Tom Brown, and pops him over the wall in good style. "By Gosht, he *is* a clipper!" adds the well-pleased owner; but, instead of being content to let well alone, he wheels round to return over the same place.

This time the mouse-coloured one—Titmouse by name—gets too close to his jump; and, catching his knees, gives Aaron a cropper that almost sends him to sleep with his forefathers.

The griffin is first on his legs again; and gallops off, leaving his chagrined rider to pick himself up and rub his shoulder at leisure. Aaron's mortified look draws forth any amount of laughter and chaff from the gallery, which is not much modified when he addresses them with wrath depicted on every feature: "My dear fellows, what are you laughing at? I am not angry: I am amused."

B. brings the Murderer out, and sends him at the bar, which he jumps both ways so creditably, that his owner quite makes up his mind he will win the next hurdle race, and tells a friend confidentially that he will train him "on the quiet, and run him dark. We might make a regular pot out of him, you know."

It is determined to make a jumper out of the Maneater, who, with his usual evil temper, shows a steady resolution to thwart the intention. Since we last saw him he has changed hands at a gift, by reason of his unmanageable temper. Tony is now riding him; and, following directions, puts him full split at the bar, which has been fixed so as not to give way if struck. The Maneater does not attempt to rise, and the two come down in a heap the other side—Tony receiving the consolation of hearing, as, in extreme terror of his life, he lies under his steed, "Never mind, old fellow! it will do him a power of good!"

Some ponies are now brought out to be lunged; and now Mr. Micawber may be seen to advantage. With a wonderful turn for acting, he is a bright planet lost to the stage. Equally at home when enacting the sublime or the ridiculous,—though, truth to tell, more often personating the latter,—he forthwith takes possession of a long whip; and, adapting himself to the character of a riding-master at a circus, struts up and down, and takes off the original with an absurd exactness that brings down the gallery. At the same time, he rather hinders than assists the efforts of the Child, who, with his long legs firmly planted about a yard and a half apart, holds the lungeing rein while several animals are put—or attempted to be put—over the bar.

Some little speculation, too, goes on about the performances of the various ponies, each owner appearing to think he is in possession of a second Chandler or Lottery.

Bockbier—a long, low, powerful animal, afterwards the winner of both hurdle and flat races—is now produced; and as many pairs of hands tackle on to the lungeing rein as if he were a mad bull—and, indeed, as far as sensibility of mouth is concerned, he might be one. At the first attempt he flies yards over the timber; but now comes the tug of war! A good pull, a strong pull, and a pull all together, are of no avail to stop him; and after dragging his followers head first down two or three banks, and knocking them against trees and posts, he finally rids himself of them one by one, and carries off the lungeing apparatus in triumph into the settlement.

This part of the diversion being put an end to, we look round for other means of amusement; and to our intense delight, Mr. Micawber is induced, after much persuasion, to mount Falling Star, and ride him over the bar—on the condition that it is to be fixed as low as possible, and so as to fall down at the slightest touch.

These terms being complied with, he goes gingerly up to the jump; and Falling Star, poking his nose down, puts first one foot and then the other over with wonderful delicacy.

Encouraged by his success, and proud of the mighty feat he feels he has performed, Mr. Micawber tries it again with more confidence. But this time a dozen officious assistants rush out to help him on, a dozen hideous yells echo in his ears, and a dozen whips descend simultaneously on the flanks and quarters of his pony. Paralysed with fear, he can only give vent to a dismal wail of despair, and, dropping the bridle, clutch Falling Star's mane convulsively, ere the latter—almost as terrified as his master—bounds madly over, pitching him some yards away, where, for some time, he lies in a heap, looking more like a bundle of old clothes than a human being.

When at last Mr. Micawber is convinced that he is still alive, it is evident that he feels the loss of his dignity more than any bruises he may have sustained; for he explains apologetically—" Why, it wasn't my fault! I was *bound* to go; I hadn't got hold of the reins. I give you my word, though, I will never get on that brute again; and he shall be fed on nothing but chopped straw."

CHAPTER VIII.

THE HACK HANDICAP.

ONE evening at the mess-table, after much chaff about the merits and demerits of the miscellaneous lot that occupied the Camp stables,—during which each manfully defended his own "moke," and strove to vilify that of his neighbour,—several sporting offers were made in the shape of backing one flyer against another, when at last some one proposed a Sweep, which should give all a chance.

The notion was received and carried with acclamation; and after a long discussion, which necessitated an extra hour's sitting after the cloth had been removed, and caused one unhappy youth to cut himself severely while shaving the next morning, the following conditions were drawn up:—

"The Race," fixed for that day week, was "to be half a mile on the flat;" and then came two antagonistic clauses, both of which were all but necessary in order to carry out the idea in its full force—"*handicap*," and "*owners to ride.*"

For a long time the difficulty appeared insurmountable; some of those likely to contend being big, heavy men, while others on better ponies were smaller and lighter. For, beginning with the heaviest man,—who would necessarily have to be put down as the lowest weight; and who, as is often the case, possessed a charger more fitted to carry a boy of fourteen years than a man of fourteen stone,—it would have required a ton of lead to bring on equal terms the best of even the bad lot opposed to him.

At last a brilliant idea struck one of the party, and was joyfully seized upon by the assembled council.

It was that the handicapping should be—*not by weight, but by difference of start;* and that, in order to arrive at a knowledge of the respective merits of the animals, a preparatory race should be run over the same course, in which, as in a donkey race (not an inapt comparison, you will say!), each horse should be ridden by the owner of another, and this would insure the most strenuous efforts on the part of all to place their mounts in as forward a position as possible.

The grand affair being fixed for the ensuing Monday, the Saturday preceding it was named as the day for the trial; and all entries were to be made on or before Friday. It was agreed, too, that none but the most second-class ponies were to start—those, for instance, who had ever run in, or were likely to be entered for, the Yokohama races, being excluded; and the task of determining this point, and drawing the line between bad and worse, was left in the hands of Aaron, who agreed to act as handicapper and referee, with the assistance of B., in the capacity of judge.

As may be imagined, the announcement of the intended event, when posted up in the ante-room, created much diversion and endless *badinage;* but having survived this, it was pushed on with great vigour, and one or two of the leading promoters went about canvassing with all the spirit, and as much scheming and persuasion, as a doubtful member before a general election.

On Friday evening the entries appeared as follows— each horse being allotted a rider whose weight was as nearly as possible the same as that of his master:—

OWNERS.	NAMES.	RIDERS.
Dr. Quock Wock's	Woffles	The Fenian.
Mr. Micawber's	Falling Star	Dr. De Pifet.
The Aide's	Muffin Worry	The Child.
Mr. Tony's	Ichiboo	Mr. Jolly.
The Fenian's	Man in the Water	Dr. Quock Wock.
Mr. Tweeker's	Pig	Capt. Cower.
Mr. Jolly's	Haw Haw	Mr. Tony.
The Child's	Maneater	The Aide.
Dr. De Pifet's	Black Prince	Mr. Micawber.
Capt. Cower's	Rubbles	Mr. Tweeker.

At four o'clock the next afternoon all the competitors paraded at the Rifle Range, which furnished a capital piece of turf, just the distance; and after some time employed in exchanging steeds, and the consequent altering of stirrup leathers—to say nothing of the delay caused by the nervous trepidation of one or two of the party at the awkward sensation of a strange saddle—they were formed into a line and started.

By-the-bye, it is only now that Dr. De Pifet makes his bow before you; but as—like many another hero—he is best described by his deeds, we need say little more than Read On. Though one of those happy men who can boast of the possession of a tender, kindred spirit, with which to commune in joy, sorrow, health, or sickness, his ardent mind has yet prevented him from sinking—as too many have done before—into a social nonentity after the irretrievable plunge into the pool of matrimony;

and hence his present ambition to strike out into a new path, and take as leading a position on the race-course as he ever holds in the billiard-room.

It had been decided that the race should be run *down* the Range towards the Camp—the opposite direction to that adopted when, in the early days of the Yokohama turf, the Rifle Range served as the race-course. And the event fully justified the expectation; for, on the word being given, the ponies, many of whom would have obstinately declined to run away from home, on finding their heads turned towards the stables, went off at the best pace they could muster—a ready willingness that found anything but favour in the eyes of Dr. De Pifet and Mr. Micawber; whose feelings, as they lurched and rolled, but contrived by the most wonderful acrobatic feats to keep their seats, must have much resembled those of John Gilpin in his well-known ride, or Ingoldsby's Roving Rob during his trip on the witch's broomstick.

Flogging and spurring to the very last, the field came in in the most scattered order : Black Prince and Ichiboo well ahead; the Pig, Muffin Worry, and Haw Haw making a good fight for places; the others nowhere ; and the Maneater, to his owner's intense but silent satisfaction, fifty yards behind everything—having subsided into a trot on the first application of the spur.

De Pifet and Micawber were immensely delighted with the undoubted success of their first essay on the turf; and each talked loudly of what he would do on the Monday, when he " knew he could make his own pony go faster than the fellow who rode him to-day."

At tiffin, on the day appointed, Micawber, who had

been a little nervous all the morning, was encouraged in his determination of "steadying himself" with the juice of the generous grape. De Pifet also, who soon afterwards entered the ante-room, looking as if he did not care very much about the pleasure in store for him, was likewise plied freely; and the pair were induced to array themselves in breeches, boots, and silk (subscriptions from various wardrobes), by false assurances that the others would also appear in the orthodox costume.

Very proud were they of their borrowed plumes, as they gazed admiringly in the looking-glass, and strove to look as unconcerned and unconscious as if they had been born in them! After being assisted by officious hands into—and almost over—their saddles, the stirrup cup was handed up; and then, amid cheers from an admiring crowd, they were despatched as an advanced guard to the Rifle Range.

Rumours of the intended fun had got afloat in the settlement; and any source of amusement being at the time scarce in Yokohama, a crowd of carriages, people on horseback and on foot, had assembled to witness the sport.

We question if it was not the proudest moment in the lives of each of our friends, as—cigar in mouth, head erect, one hand placed in a *dégagé* manner on the thigh, or occasionally caressing the neck of his steed—he paraded up and down with an assumed indifference, that would have done credit to a Fordham or a Custance when about to ride for a £50 plate on which he has not a penny risked.

De Pifet's gentle spouse, who was present, shared—as became a dutiful partner—the feelings of her lord and master; and, as she followed him with her eyes glued to his figure, must have experienced the same emotion of admiring rapture, mingled with loving fear, that made the fair bosom of many a Roman matron alternately swell with noble pride and thrill with painful anxiety as she sent forth her life's protector equipped for the fray.

Presently the rest of the competitors arrived on the scene, accompanied by the whole camp *en masse*; and after a preliminary canter—dispensed with by Micawber and De Pifet for prudential reasons—the handicapper proceeded to clear the course, and marshalled his forces as follows:—

Dr. De Pifet's	Black Prince	Scratch.
Mr. Tony's	Ichiboo	,,
Mr. Tweeker's	Pig	10 yards start.
Mr. Jolly's	Haw Haw	12 ,, ,,
The Aide's	Muffin Worry	15 ,, ,,
Mr. Micawber's	Falling Star	20 ,, ,,
The Fenian's	Man in the Water	20 ,, ,,
Dr. Quock Wock's	Woffles	25 ,, ,,
Capt. Cower's	Bubbles	30 ,, ,,
The Child's	Maneater	40 ,, ,,

Now was committed a great mistake; for instead of adhering closely to the original conditions of the race, two post entries were allowed, one of which was taken by our friend Belleville, already well known to you.

But it was not so much in regard to him that the error we speak of was made, except in the fact of infringing the rules; for beyond adding to the beauty of the affair, and setting off its general appearance, the race was but little altered in character or result by his presence. At first it was made a *sine qua non* that if allowed to start, his whiskers should be plaited with ribbons in proper racing style. To this, however, he objected with so much vehemence, that the condition was waived, and his auburn tresses were allowed to float in unfettered freedom.

The other entry was made by a midshipman, mounted on a black, wiry-looking beast, of which nobody knew anything at the time, but which—though now little better than a bag of bones—was immeasurably superior to the wretched lot running, and afterwards turned out one of the fastest animals in Yokohama.

In spite of his present condition, his general appearance was sufficient to place him at the scratch in company with Black Prince and Ichiboo; but, as the sequel showed, he might have been put a hundred yards farther back without injuring his chance.

This same pony—he stood 14·3, with clean straight legs and strong springy pasterns—afterwards came into the hands of some of ours, under whose tuition he became the most accomplished steeple-chaser and safest jumper in Japan. Eventually we ourselves had the riding, and shared with Spiro the possession of him; and those who read " Bell " may have seen in the Chronicles of Foreign Racing how gallantly he could acquit himself. Poor dear old Boomerang! cross-grained and uncertain to all though you ever were in the stable,—ourselves, perhaps, a dubious exception,—you were honest and true to the backbone in the field; and when heart throbbed, and legs almost refused their office, you would answer gamely to the call, coming again and again, till sheer pluck would land you first past the winning-post.

Many an anxious visit to the stable, many a troubled night and thoughtful day have you cost us, when strain or overreach threatened to crush our hopes; to be well repaid when you would come out fit and well, and, without flinching, strain every nerve to win.

When, as on our last day in Japan, we bade you farewell in a stranger's stable, you nestled your soft muzzle on our shoulder, as if begging forgiveness for temper oft displayed against one who had ever petted and made much of you, and gazed on us with that big bold eye, as if entreating to be taken away, 'twas like parting with an old friend; and the "Good-bye, dear old chum!" came out thick and painfully from our throat.

We are getting almost maudlin in our recollections, so will hasten at once back to the point at which we turned aside.

The start was to be made from a stand, but some little delay took place before they could be despatched. Rubbles took it into his head to give vent to a horrible neigh, and attempted to seize on the "Man in the Water," which so terrified his gallant rider that he clapped spurs in and rushed wildly from the scene.

Peace being restored, Mr. Tweeker frustrated another attempt by discovering that he had omitted to rub the Pig's nostrils out with vinegar and water, after having brought a sponge with him for the purpose.

Then Mr. Micawber detained them by begging Aaron to come to his side for a moment, and asking him in a confidential whisper if he ought to spur before the saddle or behind.

Dr. Quock, too, who was dissatisfied with the amount of start allotted to him, complained that those in front got in his way. "God bleth my thoul! I haven't room." And then, in reply to a chaffing question as to his reasons for not having got himself up like his superior Æsculapian, he spluttered out the most extraordinary scriptural quotation we ever had the fortune to hear: "You fellowth alwayth make clean and platter the outthide of the cup, like an open thepulchre."

The other distinguished physician was all the time—in the pride of his youth and manly vigour—in a fever to be off, and besought Aaron to "let us buckle to at once."

At last the signal was given; and at the word, "Go," each one got under weigh as best he could; Rubbles, as he could *not*, or would not, remaining at the post; Micawber "wiring into" Falling Star, all legs and arms, with the impunity that that much-suffering animal allowed him; De Pifet jerking frantically at the mouth of Black Prince with one hand, and clutching hold of the mane with the other; his subordinate crouching over the head of his pony, and chirruping incessantly into his ears. Jolly roared in a deep bass at his steed; and Tweeker cursed at the Pig till his dictionary of epithets was exhausted.

The race was never a moment in doubt; for, from the start, Boomerang, with his light weight, rushed to the front and won in a canter; any feeling of annoyance that might have been experienced at his admittance without having gone through the preliminary trial being at once dissipated by the sight of his rider's happy face of thorough delight as he saw he had won.

Ten times more interest and enthusiastic applause, though, were called forth by the arrival of the second.

As De Pifet dashed past the post, triumphant excitement appeared to increase almost to delirium. Protruded eyeballs staring wildly round; the left hand, grasping the reins, held high and furiously waved above his head; the right still clutching the mane, though removed now and then, at imminent risk, to cut the air nervously with his whip; legs going in time with his arms, like a pair of huge tongs, opening and shutting on the saddle between them. Scarce did he resemble unto anything human!

As before the commencement of the struggle, one fond heart was sharing and revelling in the joy of her lord—one sympathetic breast beat in unison with his own; just as—to continue the previous allusion—a triumphal entry, given by a grateful country to a returning conqueror, might have crowned the hopes and rewarded the solicitude of the Roman warrior's wife. Rushing after the hero, she was in time to offer her congratulations—and from whom could they be so welcome?—as De Pifet lay exhausted on the neck of his steed, where the sudden jerk of stopping had thrown him.

Ichiboo was third; the Pig and Muffin Worry respectively fourth and fifth; the others all within a couple of lengths.

The finish having been so close among the others, it was unanimously agreed that—Boomerang being excluded—another sweep should be organised, and run under the same conditions, after a quarter of an hour's breathing-time had been allowed.

De Pifet was now quite difficult to hold, as the prospect of success appeared a certainty to his sanguine mind; and Micawber was eager and fierce as a tiger who has tasted blood.

Meanwhile, a slight variety in the afternoon's diversion is kindly provided by one who has not as yet had the honour of being introduced to you, our well-beloved patrons.

Got up in the tightest of breeches and oldest of coats, the Liver Cutter is mounted on a big Australian horse—a screw of the first water.

The history of that unfortunate steed would fill a volume of itself. Purchased, in the first instance, as a small speculation in the horse-dealing line from one who knew the full value of a horse, and had taken care to obtain it, he had gone through every grade of condition, from the fat state in which, on true selling principles, he had entered the Camp stables, to the present degree of fineness, which would be considered sufficient for a Derby horse. On first arrival he had been mashed and physicked (this operation being repeated at frequent and regular after-intervals), his venerable teeth had been filed, his dock shortened, and legs trimmed, under the impression that some one would be flat enough to reward his present owner by buying him at double cost price.

After careful walking, cantering, and galloping for months, he now appears fit to go for a week (though it is a question whether another animal could not be found to do the same distance in a day); but as yet no purchaser has come forward. Still, as the Liver Cutter sweeps past the admiring crowd, standing up in his stirrups and holding the screw well together, it seems quite on the cards that the *tout ensemble* of horse and man may beguile some unwary being to give way to his ambition and swallow the bait.

Little, though, does he wot—as he careers by in conscious pride, looking fondly down on the brightest of boots and longest of spurs, occasionally sitting down and "finishing" for fifty yards, then sailing along again on the even tenor of his way—how soon that pride is doomed to fall; how soon that spotless leather is fated to become unrecognisable with mire!

On one side of the Rifle Range is a well-known treacherous little spot—a deep black bog, that no draining or filling up has ever been able to remove.

Smooth and pleasant to look upon as a Jew moneylender, its hold, when once a victim is in its clutches, is as tenacious as that of the usurious Hebrew.

On come the gallant pair, secure in their fond forgetfulness of all trifles beyond their own present unruffled enjoyment, and stride after stride brings them nearer to a danger that they have oft evaded before.

If we remember right, Bunyan tells us—in the only Sunday book our anxious parents could ever persuade us, by coaxing or cuffing, to read—that when Christian approached the Slough of Despond, some one either went at it before him, or bade him charitably to "Ware Hole;" but, in this case, no one is at hand to arrest the progress of *our* pilgrim towards destruction. His first warning is a splash and a grunt, as he flies over the head of the "Waler" and plunges pitifully into the foul dirt.

Though soon rescued from his position, he bounded no more—for this day, at least—over the springy turf; but betaking himself in haste to the sea-shore, strove hard to get rid of the unsavoury overalls that clung so close to man and beast.

Whether this unfortunate accident militated against the sale of the horse we know not; but this much remains to be handed down to posterity—that after months more of physicking, training, and finishing, he was sent to a livery stable, and a bill for a few weeks' keep having been run up, was handed over in liquidation to the proprietor, the late owner declaring, with the most emphatic epithets, that "he would sooner be a dog and bay the moon than try to sell a screw in Yokohama."

You may wonder in what way the *sobriquet* of "Liver Cutter" came to be conferred on the gentleman in question.

On his first arrival in Japan,—horses having always been his one great taste in life,—he discovered that "finishing" was his especial forte; and, with a view to developing this talent to its utmost, he was wont to pay five pounds per month to be supplied twice a week with a "moke" for an afternoon's ride. Then, armed with a whip that would have raised wales on the flanks of an elephant, and spurs that would have brought blood out of a brick wall, he would sally forth with the avowed intention of "cutting" the poor animal's "liver out."

This process consisted in a series of most desperate hammer-and-tongs finishes—alongside another horse, if it could be obtained; if not, he would be content to set to and win by a short head from an imaginary opponent.

It happened one afternoon that he had been furnished, for the purpose of indulging in this innocent pastime, with a steed that in colour and peculiar elegance of make and shape strongly resembled the trusty charger of our revered chief.

By way of fortifying himself for the work in prospect, the Liver Cutter, after mounting at the stable, rode up to the mess; and, leaving his horse in care of his betto at the door—near which Flying Isaac also happened to be stationed at the time, in readiness for his master—attended to the comfort of the inner man.

Finding it was later than he had thought, he tossed off what he had called for, and hurried out again. Then, jumping into the saddle, determined to waste no further time, he proceeded forthwith to cut his horse's liver out in his own ingenious and systematic way: hustling his head tight up, driving in the "torturing irons," and curling the heavy whip two or three times round his body with a loud crack; at the same time bringing the most withering objurgations to bear on the unoffending beast.

Sharply as the feelings of Flying Isaac must have been wrung with surprise and pain, his amazement could not have been as intense, or his agony as bitter, as that of the Chief, who arrived on the scene just in time to see his unlucky favourite borne off to a fate to which death itself was almost preferable. Fortunately his orderly was close at hand; and, after a long, stern chase, part at least of poor Isaac's liver was saved; and, with flanks bloody and heaving, he was brought back to his not unnaturally mortified owner.

So thoroughly was the nervous system of the veteran charger upset by this adventure, that for days he hung his head listlessly—caring not for his modicum of corn, nor his *im*modicum of chopped straw; refusing to be comforted.

As for the poor animal for which he had the misfortune to be mistaken, his glassy eye and tottering step, as he was led back to his stable, almost justified the uncouth attempt at a joke that happened to reach our ears. It proceeded from the mouth of a soldier-groom, who, with a grim smile, watched him staggering off. "A *liverce* 'oss, is 'e ? Poor devil, not much *liver* 'e 's got arter the Capn's bin at him ! "

There is no doubt, though, that this continual " finishing " practice had some good results ; for on one or two occasions the final " wire in "—invariably gone through, whether first or last—was the means of enabling him to snatch a race from an unwary jock cantering too confidently in.

Somewhat silent and reserved is the Liver Cutter, happy only when riding his hobby or his horse ; for though seldom, if ever, entering on any other subject of conversation, on his one particular topic he is as energetic as eloquent. His lofty soul would appear to soar above the vulgar herd of nonconformists to the theory that " Horses in the stable and in the field " should be the sole study and occupation of a man's life ; for he is never known to encourage strangers to enter into conversation with him, or on the other hand to take the initiative himself.

Of this last rule, though, there are exceptions on record, when a convivial evening has sufficiently warmed his heart.

He then commences by putting two questions—and provisionally a third—to the favoured listener.

Q. 1. " Can you ride a four-mile steeple-chase ? "
Q. 2. " Can you give a horse a ball ? "

His auditor invariably being the most *un*horsey, as well as the most mild and inoffensive-looking man in the room, is generally obliged to confess an ignorance of these two great accomplishments ; and an answer in the negative brings down a concentrated body of pitying scorn in the third question :—

"Then what the devil's the good of you, sir?"

Returning to their former positions, the competitors were once more despatched to a good start. This time the Child kept his pony on the fidget; at the word, was off like a shot; and though soon caught and passed by half the others, the Maneater's condition—added to the pluck generally accompanying a bad temper—served him, and he landed the dollars by a short head from Muffin Worry, Ichiboo being third, and Falling Star fourth.

Where is our friend De Pifet? you ask.

Alas! saw ye not that riderless steed flying past the winning-post alone? Heard ye not that shriek of agony that rose loud and distinct to the heavens?

Look back; and ye may even now see a prostrate form, girded with yellow and black hoops, grovelling on the ground like a huge hornet!

Approach him; and ye may recognise, through the coating of mud that covers the features of the fallen hero, the grief-stricken face of Dr. Pierre De Pifet!

His feelings more hurt in a mental than a physical sense, De Pifet slowly followed his steed back to Camp; threw his colours, that had so nearly borne him to honour and distinction, into the fire; and, abandoning all hope of reaping laurels on the turf, retired into the bosom of his family, and from that day to this has never been on the top of a horse.

No sooner was the race over than Mr. Micawber was seen to ride back with a face distorted with anger and disappointment, and accost an individual half-way up the course.

On inquiry, we ascertained the man to be his servant, whom he now accused of being the cause of his failing to win, by standing close to where the struggling horses passed: "You red-headed beast! you know you give him carrots every day; and of course he thought you had some for him now."

The servant, evidently used to such outbreaks, appeared to care but little for Micawber's wrath. Some time after, when his master had gone back to England on leave, and while cutting an officer's hair,—for he united the profession of barber with that of a son of Mars,—he described him as a "gent I used to think was dreadful fierce at first; but, lor' bless you, sir! when you comed to know him, he was as harmless as a lamb."

Soldier servants comprise in themselves a curious section of the *genus homo*. Get a good one, and he is worth his weight in gold—more valuable than a dozen of the powdered and pride-inflated lacqueys of civil life, though we are bound to admit that many of them are uncouth and clumsy in the extreme.

Exempli gratiâ.—A certain captain, formerly of ours, being in want of a servant, promoted to that distinguished office a man of his company, noted for steady good conduct, if not for brilliant talent. He took to his new work with the greatest interest, studying the wishes of his master with the utmost care and attention; till M——, who was a man of refined tastes and most particular in every point connected with personal comfort, began to congratulate himself on his choice.

At length the day arrived when his new servant, arrayed in spick-and-span new livery, made his first appearance at the officers' mess-table. Knowing little or nothing of what was expected of him in this new line, he thought he could not do better than remain close to and look after his own master.

M—— was blessed with a very fair appetite for the enjoyment of the good things of this life, and on this particular occasion a hard day's shooting had rendered him unusually hungry. As he turned round now and then to order something fresh, the faithful domestic was prompt in supplying his wants. One thing after another disappeared, and, in proportion, did the laudable anxiety of the servant increase, till his excitement got beyond all bounds; and, seeing the plate he was watching for one moment empty, he shouted out, amid an unfortunate pause, "Arrah, captain! and what'll ye be at now?"

M——'s disgust may be easily conceived; and it is needless to state that the unfortunate offender was never again seen in plush.

CHAPTER IX.

VISIT TO THE TYCOON.

In our first chapter we alluded to the mystery in which Japanese politics are shrouded; but, at the same time, we promised the reader that we would take a timid dip into the subject.

We now falteringly proceed to keep our promise.

We say falteringly, because we know that it is a theme on which many abler than we have attempted to treat; and when, as they thought they had succeeded in mastering it in all its intricacies and complications, and have published the results of their labours to the world, they have found themselves utterly at fault, and obliged to admit that they have not only been misled, but have misled others.

For instance, what individual at home, until very lately, thought—if he thought anything at all about it—that the Tycoon was other than the supreme monarch of Japan?

It is only recently that it has been generally understood that he is simply the external representative of the Mikado, who is the real head of the empire; but who, from the seclusion he is forced to live in,—being too sacred an object for the eyes of his subjects to rest on,—is incompetent; in fact, is not supposed to act personally in any of the affairs of state.

All edicts, though emanating—that is, *nominally*—from him, but *really* from his advisers, are carried out by the Tycoon; or, to give him his more correct title, the Shogoun.

As Tycoon, though, we will continue to speak of him, as it is doubtless a name more familiar to our readers.

He combines in himself, besides other offices for which we have no equivalents, the position of our Prime Minister and Commander-in-Chief.

The Tycoonate can—or rather could, for it is now a thing of the past—be held only by a member of one of five families.

It might be supposed that on the death of a Tycoon, the members of these families would engage in such hot competition for the coveted honour as to lead, not only to family dissensions, but also to civil war; but this is avoided by the law, which empowers the reigning Tycoon—we must speak of him as reigning, for his powers are all but regal—to nominate his successor. This selection has rarely, if ever, been disputed.

The last Tycoon was known generally to Europeans under the name of Stots-bashi, which was quite erroneous: Stots-bashi is simply a title which is borne by the chosen successor to the Tycoonate. It was therefore about as correct to talk of Stots-bashi, Tycoon of Japan, as it would be, when the Prince of Wales ascends the throne, to speak of the Prince of Wales, King of England.

The first official visit to the Tycoon was paid by the English Minister in March, 1867, at Osaka,—a town almost equal in size and importance to Yedo.

A brother officer of ours had the good fortune to be

VISIT TO THE TYCOON.

one of the party accompanying our Minister; and the description he gave us may interest many.

The party consisted, besides His Excellency Sir H. Parkes, of all the members of the British Legation, a few naval officers,—principally those in command of the vessels of war at Osaka,—and the officer in command of the Legation guard and mounted escort.

They all met at a temple occupied by Her Britannic Majesty's Legation; and thence, accompanied by their guard and escort, proceeded to the Tycoon's Castle, which was built on an elevation commanding the town, and surrounded by a moat of the width and depth of which some idea may be formed from a remark made by the captain of H.M.S. *Sylvia*,—nearly 1,000 tons,— that his ship could lie comfortably in it crossways.

The height from the surface of the water to the crest of the wall on the town side was about fifty feet, and to the top of the castle wall about one hundred and twenty-five. It was most solidly built: the scarp and counterscarp being faced with huge blocks of stone, fitted into each other as nicely as a Chinese puzzle, no mortar or cement being used.

This moat was crossed and divided by causeways, built in the same massive, solid way, leading to the principal gates, which were of great strength and height, made of the hardest known Japanese wood—the Ki-ya-Kee—and studded with iron bolts.

These gates were never opened except to admit officials of considerable rank, a small wicket being used as the usual mode of ingress and egress.

On entering, they found the road suddenly turned at right angles to the entrance, while facing them was a wall about forty feet high,—not visible from the outside, —composed of most enormous stones, two of which measured respectively thirty-six by twenty-six feet, and forty feet by eighteen.

Passing through another large gate, they found themselves in a spacious quadrangle, along two sides of which the road ran by the edge of another moat of smaller dimensions than the outer one. Surrounding this place were buildings used as stores, barracks, &c., all scrupulously clean.

No Japanese—excepting the guard of honour furnished by them for the Minister—were allowed inside these inner gates.

Again turning to the left, they passed through a third gate over a dry ditch, the walls on the side of which commanded the space they had already passed, and entered the grand square, in which was the entrance to the palace.

The palace is built—or rather was, for it was destroyed by fire in March last—in true Japanese style, and in a way which excited the admiration of them all. The beauty of the interior, though, even surpassed what they had been led to expect from the exterior.

When the Minister dismounted, the guards, Japanese and English, presented arms, and the officers, naval, military, and civil, formed in procession, and entered the palace.

After ascending a few steps, they arrived at the hall of entrance, in which were seated about one hundred Japanese officials, who touched the floor with their heads on the appearance of the Minister.

Several of the higher officials about the palace met

them here, and conducted them through a long corridor, remarkable for nothing but its height and breadth.

As they passed through this, Japanese soldiers, who lined the way on either side, presented arms in an amusing variety of ways.

Leaving this corridor, they were ushered into a reception-room, which was furnished handsomely, and almost entirely in European style. The screens which divided this apartment from the hall were beautifully painted, each in itself being a work of art. The blinds were made of very thin slips of bamboo, gilded and painted, with silken tassels of different bright colours—red, blue, and green.

For the first time, most of them now saw the full Court dress, which consisted of the robes usually worn, but made of more costly material, and capes of stiffly-starched muslin, or some such light fabric, projecting about six inches or more beyond each shoulder like wings. The Ha-ka-ma, or trousers, are made about three feet longer than necessary, and trail on the mats behind the wearer, who is obliged to shuffle along in anything but a dignified way, to avoid the catastrophe of being tripped up.

The origin of this preposterous fashion is, that formerly any one approaching the presence of the Tycoon, or even the apartment of the Mikado, had to do so on his knees. This sometimes entailed a walk, under these trying circumstances, of thirty or forty feet; and, being found inconvenient, a modification was allowed. The trousers were made long, to give to the wearer the appearance of being on his knees.

In this room, while waiting to be ushered into the presence, the Minister and party were regaled with sponge-cake, tea, and cigars—the latter European (unmistakable cabbage).

They were shortly summoned, and passed down an open corridor, or rather verandah, the panels along the side of which were covered with gorgeously-painted representations of cranes, falcons, peacocks, &c., while the ceiling was divided into squares, each enclosing a beautifully executed piece of mosaic work.

They had hardly time to bestow the amount of attention this deserved, when they were opposite the audience chamber. Seated in the middle of the room, on a peculiarly shaped chair of very old and valuable lacquer, sat a grave, quiet-looking young man, not more than thirty years of age, with a very pleasing expression. The self-possession that he maintained struck them forcibly. This was the Tycoon.

The room was divided in the centre, the floor of one half being raised a foot above the other. On the raised portion sat His Highness.

The floor was covered with the finest mats, whitened to a snowy tint with rice-powder. The partition screens were of a gold ground, with birds, trees, and flowers, done in the best Japanese style; while the wood carvings between the grooves the screens worked in, and the ceiling, were beautiful in the extreme.

This room looked out on a large square, where the attendants were waiting.

On their entering, the Tycoon rose slowly, while Sir Harry Parkes, with his interpreter, approached and made his speech in English, which was translated into

Japanese. During all this time no change of expression whatever was visible in the face of the Tycoon.

After a pause, in a low, soft, and particularly musical voice, he made his return speech, which was also translated for the benefit of the English Minister.

These speeches were merely complimentary, and consisted of mutual congratulations on the intimacy existing between the two nations, and hopes for its continuance.

The members of the party were then called up in succession and presented, their rank and names being translated to His Highness, who returned their salutes.

After each had been presented, he retired backwards for a few paces, as is customary when before royalty on such occasions, and joined the rest of his party.

The Tycoon was splendidly and becomingly dressed, with perhaps the exception of the state cap, which was a most peculiar shape, made of paper; it rested on the very summit of his head, and was kept in its position by strings, which fastened under his chin.

His outer robe was of rich white silk, ornamented with medallions in mauve colour, and his stockings also white silk.

Behind him stood his sword-bearer, holding his long sword; in rear, again, knelt several attendants.

It is against etiquette for a Japanese, no matter how high his rank, to wear his long sword in the presence of any one he may visit, it being the weapon of offence or attack; and it is invariably laid aside in some anteroom before entering; the short sword, with which the act of *harakiri** is performed, only being worn.

---

* The Japanese name for the act of disembowelling oneself, called very often by the English "the happy despatch."

After the ceremony of presentation was over, the Tycoon retired, but shortly reappeared in another dress, consisting of a black silk jacket, or *háo*, trousers of dark blue silk with a gold pattern running through, and a rich *obè*, or belt, in which a handsome short sword was thrust. In both dresses he was photographed by Mr. Sutton, R.N., of H.M.S. *Serpent*.

We had almost omitted one peculiar circumstance. A short time before they were admitted to the Tycoon's presence, a sound of hus-s-s-s-h pervaded the whole place, which they were at a loss to understand; but afterwards were told that it was used to warn every one of the approach of His Highness, when all had to kneel down and remain prostrate until he passed.

Strange to relate, hardly a year had elapsed when all this state and position were upset by a revolution, in which the Tycoon was deposed, forced into retirement, his states partly confiscated, and the splendid castle at Osaka, with its beautiful carvings and paintings, its massive walls and handsome palace, burned and razed to the ground.

CHAPTER X.

THE DRAG.

> "Lydia, dic, per omnes te deos oro,
> Sybarin cur properas amando
> Perdere ? cur apricum
> Campum oderit ?" &c.

THUS, to his own immense satisfaction, the Child bawled out one of the few scraps of the classic authors that he had not succeeded in erasing from his memory during the few years that had elapsed since he found himself released from scholastic bonds, and which he flattered himself was peculiarly adapted to the question he now proceeded to put to Aaron, whose sanctuary he had penetrated about eight one morning in the early autumn.

"What's the row with you, Aaron? Has some fair enchantress got you in her clutches? or the governor stopped supplies? You haven't been out of bed before nine o'clock for the last week."

"By Gosht, my dear fellow," answered Aaron, who looked somewhat pale and yellow, "I wish my liver was sound as my heart. To begin with, what do you think my female population," as he was in the habit of denominating his female relatives collectively, "would say if I was to get spliced out here?"

"Well, Aaron, you must manage to buck up a bit, for it's time we had a drag. We took the little dogs out for exercise this morning, and the country is now almost free from crops. Why not advertise one to come off this week?"

The effect of this conversation was, that a notice appeared, which gave forth that, "On Thursday next, and on each Monday and Thursday until further notice, the Camp beagles will run a drag. The first meet to be on the Rifle Range at 2.30 P.M."

Before we get too far away from the subject, a word or two about the Lydias of Japan. By this term we refer, not to the transplanted flowers of dear Old England, who, in every clime under the sun maintain their country's prestige for the loveliness of its daughters. To borrow the expression that Colonel O'Kelly is said to have used, when he predicted of his horse, with a confidence that well deserved its success, "Eclipse first —the rest nowhere," they may truly be placed with regard to all rivals, "English women first—the rest nowhere." The fair ones themselves must pardon the horsey parallel; for, as the sailor, when parted from his love on shore, turns to the object he adores next best in the world, *his ship*, and while absent consoles himself by personifying the one in the other,—so we are apt to connect continually in our mind the two works in God's creation we love best; not dragging the more highly gifted down to the level of the lower nature, but rather raising the grandest of dumb nobility, till it stands inferior only to the brightest masterpiece of His handiwork.

Say! can anything approach nearer to perfect consummate loveliness than a beautiful woman on a beautiful horse? and here we appeal to the entire body of male humanity—be they enthusiasts, who will endorse our sentiment whole and undivided; or be they cynics, who, while sneering openly at our "ecstatic absurdity," are fain to give an unwilling concurrence.

The only men who can have the slightest excuse for not ranging themselves on our side are some very rare specimens of the class called Benedicts, who will tell you that—

"Sunshine and smiles
Are merely a part of those innocent wiles
Employed to entrap "—

during the needful antenuptial practice of courtship. But take these grumbling ingrates away from the blessings they so little appreciate, and they are the most miserable beings in existence—missing and pining for their daily domestic skirmish as an inveterate smoker, who has the misfortune to be staying in a house where cigars are tabooed, yearns for what has grown to be a necessary of life.

Certainly we are humble followers of the opinion expressed by him whom we look up to as a kind of patron saint; whose intimate acquaintance with what was hitherto considered the unfathomable depths of the feminine mind—equalled, if not surpassed, by his thorough knowledge of our other idol—leaves us lost in respectful admiration, as he describes a characteristic vagary of the one, or seems to carry you in person to the scene of some thrilling display of the prowess of the other. E'en though he leads you a willing captive to the feet of Kate Coventry or Parson Dove's daughter, he holds that the fair being, whose supple little fingers control with ease the exuberant spirits of a thorough-bred in the Row, appears more in her proper place than the bolder Amazon in shorter skirt, who—the most charming votary of Diana—edges keenly up at the earliest whimper to the most likely corner; and, once away, can take her own line, and keep it with the best men that Melton or Harboro' can produce.

A similar view of the question must have occurred to a certain gallant colonel—*absit (n)omen*—who, essaying to give his better-half a lead over some stiff post-and-rails in the grass country, was brought abruptly to the ground. " Lie still !" cried the lady; " I can clear you both !" and as the fallen warrior cowed down in no enviable state of mind, she sailed over horse and man without a touch.

We were about to speak of the native beauty of Japan —and who that has been there will deny that it *has* its beauty?

Fair-skinned almost as their sisters of the West; small but neatly—nay, sometimes faultlessly—shaped; their flowing robes displaying in its own gracefulness the model that Nature has adopted, and which none of the meretricious deceptions of civilisation can improve upon; with pretty captivating manners, and a language musical and soft as Italian, the laughter-loving nymphs of the Rising Sun have many and powerful charms.

At the same time we beg most emphatically to protest against the ridiculous raptures some writers on Japan feel themselves justified in indulging in, when treating of the fairer portion of its inhabitants. But a few days ago we picked up a standard work on the subject,—containing much true and carefully-gleaned information on other points,—which, after a short description, drawn chiefly, we imagine, from the fancy of the author, who

was evidently an ardent admirer of the sex generally, (and for this who shall blame him?) goes on to say that "the ladies of Japan are, in refinement of manner and elegance of deportment, fit to hold their own in any Court in Europe." It may be so; but we cannot help thinking that the style of compliment in vogue,—frank, eminently to the point, and leaving so little to the imagination,—with which it is the custom to seek the grace of the said ladies, would be thought somewhat out of place at St. James's; and it would certainly take the world rather by surprise if these *belles dames* acquired sufficient influence over their English sisters to induce them to adopt their plan, so exquisite in its naïve simplicity, of taking their daily baths in the street outside their doors. *Honi soit qui mal y pense.* And if the writers in the leading journals and periodicals are to be believed, the fashionable maids of the Upper Ten are rapidly nearing that happy consummation, when for evening costume the milliner's art will no longer be required, and Nature shall reign triumphant in undisputed sway.

But, on the other hand, the wanton freedom that other authors connect with social intercourse among the Japanese is extremely and wilfully exaggerated, even if it is not altogether a myth. The rules in force among themselves are most strict, and the punishments for infringing them most severe.

This is not a dissertation upon "laws and habits," so we will enter no deeper into the subject; only adding, that, though the most marked politeness is observed by one individual towards another among all classes, yet even in the Court of the Tycoon, we have *been informed,*— and of such princes as Satsuma and Oowazima, the former of whom might now be styled the king-maker, we have *observed,*—the same candid but peculiar way of "calling a spade a spade" is in fashion.

The announcement having gone forth that there would be a drag in three days' time, caused some little stir among the sport-loving portion of the community,— civil and military,—and each one busied himself in the numerous preparations necessary before a first appearance.

Breeches were looked out and cleaned, tops polished, and the state of the gear generally—and girths particularly—as carefully examined as if for Kirby Gate.

Let us suppose it to be 2 P.M. on the day before the fixture, and accompany B., Aaron, Bones,—for a sketch of whom we must again beg you to turn to page 210, —and a few other kindred spirits, in a stroll down to the stables, where they are going to smoke their after-tiffin weeds, and glance over some of the lot that will come out to-morrow.

The stables are long, irregular buildings, chiefly divided into loose boxes; and by dint of careful boarding, flooring, and roofing, the horses seem, in many cases, to be better off, as regards lodging, than their masters.

Aaron's pair are first visited, and both appear in good fettle—Tom Brown putting his head out for the usual crust, while Titmouse snaps at the hand like a terrier; indeed, when the latter afterwards changed owners, and became Mulvey's property, he succeeded on one occasion in breaking the forefinger of each of his hands as he attempted to get hold of the bridle previous to mounting.

Aaron thinks Tom Brown's tail should be shorter,

and accordingly sets to work in person to cut off another inch. B. is to ride Titmouse to-morrow, and gives orders that he is to be carefully muzzled to-night to prevent his eating the litter, of which, being sweet rice-straw, the horses are particularly fond.

Old Ugly presents much the same appearance as when he first obtained his name, but is in good hard condition, and will go better, when his joints are warmed,—and other more taking animals are beginning to tire,—than at starting.

"Holloa, Micawber!" says Aaron; "Falling Star has got an over-reach!"

True enough, he has got a slight cut on the heel of his off-fore; but Mr. Micawber, not quite catching the remark,—or, what is more probable, not understanding it,—replies with animation: "Over-eats himself! I should think he did! You should see my forage bill!"

As we never did see the forage bill, but only the animal in question, it has been ill-naturedly supposed by some that such a thing could have had an existence only in Mr. Micawber's imagination; for Falling Star's two great ragged hips stuck out so that you might have hung your hat on either.

Tweeker is discovered in the act of painting over two bare patches on the otherwise spotless coat of the Pig with a piece of burnt umber, and the Child is raving savagely at his betto for allowing the cold bandages, on which he had relied for Iona's having a clean pair of fore-legs on the morrow, to get dry and hard.

The Maneater, the Aide's mount for the coming chase, has to be approached cautiously; and, it being found requisite to look at his feet, a running noose has to be passed over the side of the stall, and slipped round his neck. When he has been half strangled, he becomes more tractable, and allows a bridle to be put into his mouth.

Pericles looks very much as if he had just come in from grass, which is explained by Bones, on the plea that he " likes to keep 'em low between the races."

All the others are visited in turn, and various remarks —not always the most complimentary—passed on their looks. Jolly has invested in another pony, but this time has been even more unfortunate than before; for, since his purchase two months back, the beast has only been twice out of the stable, having fallen dead lame a week after. As far as to-morrow is concerned, we are not quite sure that Jolly is not rather rejoiced than otherwise at the prospect of having to stop at home.

The following morning a strong drag—consisting of an old shot-bag filled with red herring and aniseed—is prepared in Aaron's room; and Aaron himself issues forth, stinking like a badger from contact with the unsavoury mixture, and fully qualified to run before the pack in person.

At 1.30 P.M. the horses are brought round; and soon all are mounted, with the exception of Mr. Micawber, who keeps the party waiting while he endeavours— amid a shower of kind suggestions, all intended to mislead—to fit a spur on, with the buckles previously fastened, by passing the strap over his toe. At length, goaded to madness by failure and bad chaff, he condemns us all as "a pack of fools," and shies his new spur at one of the party, who bobs, and allows it to disappear into one of the waterbutts, standing, for use in case of fire, at the corner of each hut.

Being joined by a couple of civilian friends, we jog on to the kennels, and thence towards the meet.

Of these two—both foreigners by birth, but Englishmen by taste and naturalisation,—he on the chestnut is one of the chief supporters, if not the mainstay, of the Yokohama turf. Spending much money—though, in truth, he usually manages to reap as he sows—on the pursuit of the sport, he has the best lot of animals in Japan.

It is a matter of difficulty to determine which is the better kept,—his table or his stable. At both everything is turned out as it should be; though, if the head of the latter establishment could borrow from the *chef* of the *cuisine* some of his marvellous lightness of hand, there would be as many good mouths among Rudolph's stud as there now are shining coats and sound sets of legs.

He is riding a stout-looking animal, who has already scored two wins over hurdles, with twelve stone seven—the welter weight—on his back; and he will have to stretch himself to-day, for Rudolph knows no shirking, and will be "there or thereabouts" when hounds are running.

The other is His Most Faithful Majesty's Consul, and though a keen promoter of sport in any shape, is too bulky—so he says—to ride across country.

Lothario shines more on the carpet than in the field, and 'tis there his doughtiest deeds have been performed.

Hoc tu Romana caveto! Few of the frailer sex have been long in the neighbourhood of those killing eyes and classic features, and taken their departure unscathed!

The personification of obliging good-temper, he is nevertheless a fire-eater when roused. Ever ready at the call of unprotected loveliness, he is willing at a moment's notice to face at ten short paces the traducer's pistol, as if it were a popgun.

The kennels are soon reached; and the clamorous pack rush out in frantic delight, baying and frolicking round the horses they know.

Aaron has with some difficulty been persuaded to dispense with his horn, which arrived from England some little time back. For a week after he first received it, the most awfully discordant sounds were heard to proceed almost day and night from his quarters.

Having at last, as he imagined, attained a proficiency in the use of his new weapon, he fixed upon the hour immediately following tiffin for introducing it to the darlings. Accordingly, at the appointed time the beagles were brought by his aides up to the lawn, where Aaron, with the horn in one hand and a large dish of scraps in the other, was waiting with nearly every member of "ours" to receive them.

"Who Hoop!" screamed Aaron. "Yoi, Worry, Worry!" and the little ones crowded round and gave tongue vociferously.

This prelude being continued till the hounds were worked up to the proper pitch of excitement, the longed-for delicacies were thrown into the air, and the usual scramble ensued.

"Yoi, Worry, Worry!" yelled Aaron again; and, seizing the favourable opportunity, put the horn to his lips and blew a blast loud and prolonged, in the identical key in which he was in the habit of playing most of his variations in "Woodman, spare that tree."

The effect on the pack was perfectly electrical. In mortal dread of their lives, one and all dropped the tit-bits they held, or were struggling for; and tucking their tails in between their legs, joined in the general stampede.

Had Old Nick appeared among them with *his* horn, and laid about him with his pitchfork, they could not have been seized with a greater paroxysm of fear than now, when hearing for the first time that thrilling note —or rather, we ought to say, a burlesque on it—that with a quick, hurried "Huic Tally-ho! Huic Tally-ho!" we used to hear Charles Payne bring the spotted beauties flying to him over gorse and thorn, in the days when the Pytchley had (this all will allow) the quickest huntsman that ever got his pack clear of a Leicestershire crowd, and when we used to pray that it might some time be our luck to attain to anything approaching that delicacy of hand and firmness of seat that kept him ever close-glued to his hounds.

With a simultaneous howl of fright, they took to their heels and scampered off to the kennels; whence, on Aaron following with anything but blessings on his lips, and amid yells of laughter from the bystanders, they dispersed in all directions over the country—sneaking back one by one in the course of the night.

After this Aaron was wont to take a camp-stool every morning, and, sitting down in the kennel-yard, from which there was no escape, treat the unfortunate beagles to an hour's music; till at length they got so far accustomed to the horn, that they were content to put up with it as an unavoidable nuisance,—much as a charger may be induced to suffer a drum to be beaten on his back,—though they never paid much attention to it in the light of a summons.

CHAPTER XI.

THE DRAG (*Continued*).

"The Hunt is up! The Hunt is up!
Now must we sing, The Hunt is up!"—*Old Ballad.*

WE now move on towards the meet, the order of the procession being as follows :—

B. is leading the van; then come Aaron and the hounds, with the Child whipping in; and after them about a dozen representatives of the Garrison—including the Aide, Bones, Tony, Mulvey on Ugly, Fenian, Bobby, the Liver Cutter, Belleville, Dr. Quock, &c., &c.

Micawber is also of the party, and, with his usual generosity in that respect, affords us some little amusement on the way. As we trot pretty quickly along,—being a little behind time,—we pass one of the many Japanese houses with a garden in front and an open entrance into the road. Falling Star, who is not as keen in the matter of sport as his master, seizes the opportunity to leave the others, and turns sharply in. This move being totally unforeseen by his rider, naturally leads to a difference of opinion as to the direction to be followed—the pony making good his entry into the garden; while Mr. Micawber, inclining to the original road, pursues it alone, until brought up sharp by his head coming in contact with the ground. None the worse for his fall, though, except that his temper is slightly ruffled and his new coat considerably dirtied, he is soon in the saddle again, and has actually the effrontery to attempt to make us believe that it was a voluntary act!

"Why, I give you *my word!* I threw myself off to get away from the branch of that tree;" an assertion that, to say the least, it was most difficult for those to believe who had seen his despairing aspect as his right leg flew up into the air.

Arrived at the place of meeting, we find a fair number already assembled; and "among them we notice" (as they say in the newspaper reports) the Major and his wife, who, though he does not *intend to*, and she *may not*—much as she yearns to, on her little Arab—stick to the hounds across country, will, by taking advantage of short cuts and paths, and assisted by a hint as to the line to be taken by the drag, see pretty nearly all the run. There are also two or three ladies on foot, and another on horseback.

Of male equestrians from the Settlement there are many, and of pedestrians not a few. Among the former our old friend Jorrocks* stands out conspicuously; and with him are two or three who were always most regular attendants, viz., Alexander, who, cost what amount of time, trouble, or money it may, ever succeeds in bringing out the best griffin at each race-meeting; another who is his stable confederate; and the one in the hunting cap, who does the riding part of the business for the same establishment.

After all, the scene—though laid so many thousand

---

* Will the indulgent reader once again take a glance at our *chapter of reference* (page 207), where Mr. Jorrocks is duly presented to the public?

miles away from the old country—strikes many a familiar chord in one's heart.

The scarlet patrol-jackets,—for there has been a standing order ever since the murder of the two English officers before mentioned, that "uniform is constantly to be worn,"—and, in some cases, most careful "get up" of the military, present a thoroughly sporting appearance; and, blended among the black coats of the civilians, give the picture a variety of colouring, which, added to the presence of the ladies, the hounds, and the foot-people, brings one back in memory to many a well-known fixture at home.

The country, too, though it is never altogether wintry in its aspect, on account of the number of evergreen trees it produces, has a pleasant autumnal look about it, that, while it does not take away from the appropriateness of the recollection, is more agreeable to the eye than the hard, bare rigidity of an English winter.

Greetings having been exchanged, and the usual amount of light *badinage* sent flying about, Aaron announces his intention of laying the hounds on.

This is the signal for Mr. Micawber to light another cigar, and—but here we forbear, merely remarking that the said cigar was smoked to an end!

We must not omit to mention that, a little apart from the crowd, may be observed a pony-carriage, drawn by two well-matched greys, neatly handled by one of the fair occupants, and as well known at Yokohama as a certain exquisite high-stepping pair were a few years ago in the Park. At every meet of the Garrison pack may these bright-eyed damsels be seen, taking great interest in the sport, and possibly some little in one or two of the performers.

This last is, of course, nothing more than an impertinent conjecture of ours, though rumour goes so far as to state that nothing but the promise of gentle nursing, should he come to grief, has induced one of the party to risk his neck, or his *collar-bone*, in this his maiden essay with the beagles in Japan.

"Shy away your weeds, you fellows! It's time we were off. And, B.! keep old Bellman and Harlequin up with the rest, if you can!" says Aaron, as, after tightening his girths, he resumes his seat, and proceeds to shorten his stirrup-leathers a hole.

"Ah, Wah," drawls Bobby, "don't be in a hurry! I can't get on my brute." True enough, he is seen dancing in unwilling activity round a chestnut China pony, called Sweet William, who performed well in the last steeple-chases, and who now resists every attempt of his master to mount. In their peregrinations the two get close up to the Fenian's "Man in the Water," who resists the familiarity by lashing out, and all but catching the "middle-sized 'un" on the head. Bobby, in his alarm, lets Sweet William go; and another quarter of an hour is consumed in getting him back and assisting the rider into his saddle.

Meantime a shower of imprecations had burst o'er the Fenian's head, a storm of whip-lashes rained on the back of his steed; and, notwithstanding the indignant protestations that "Sure he's a poor gentle crayture!" both are banished from the immediate neighbourhood.

Now, to business! The hounds are taken a little off to the right, and thrown into a small copse, whence in a very few seconds is heard a single excited note, and then a general burst, as the unmistakable line of the drag is hit off. With a perfect storm of music they crash out into the open in one compact mass—even old Bellman in the midst with his deep bass note.

"Forrard! forrard!" from Aaron, who cannot refrain from the scarcely needful opening cheer; and, all lying well together, we settle down to work.

The country is in very tolerable going order; for, though nearly all arable land, it is light and level just after the removal of the autumn crop, and the ponies move well over it.

Away! over the hill; and the beagles here merrily forge ahead, till the down-slope beyond puts us on better terms with them.

Take a look at old Pericles while he is fresh, and the effect of the "low diet" has not begun to tell on him! There you may see the way in which a Japanese pony ought to go down his drops, and you may at the same time take a wrinkle from Bones as to how he ought to be ridden at them!

'Tis only from force of habit that Pericles can be called a pony, for he stands over fifteen-one. Somewhat long in the leg,—a fault we came, after a time, to look upon rather as a recommendation for this particular country,—he strides smoothly over the ground, sweeping grandly down the drops without a pause, and away again without changing a leg. The safest and surest animal in Japan at a big place, he carried Bones more than once down "Solon's Success,"—alluded to in Chapter XIV. as being a "drop of fully twelve feet;" but which has, since that was written, been measured by Bones' successor, and found to be thirteen feet six inches, with a slope of only two feet in that depth. We ourselves afterwards rode him down the same place; and, as rather an amusing—though at the moment somewhat alarming—incident happened on that occasion, we give it here.

Two days after our first drag hunt by moonlight we rode out with Mulvey, who was mounted on Titmouse, for the purpose of looking over some of the ground traversed on that occasion—this purpose being, possibly, as much an excuse for a lark as anything else.

Following the line, we found ourselves, after a time, in close propinquity to " Solon's Success," and turned a little out of the way to look at it.

"Shall we have a shy at it, Mulvey?" speaking, we confess, in the thoughtlessness of the moment, and without an idea that we should be taken at our word.

Mulvey, however,—who is fond of a jump, and when out, cares little if it is a precipice he is riding at,—responded, "All right;" and we found ourselves booked.

"Death being preferable to dishonour," we had no other course open but to take Pericles quietly up to it, leaving him well to himself; and, in his usual easy way, he landed us safely at the bottom.

Scarcely had we pulled up than we heard an agonised "Oh!" behind us; and, turning round, were just in time to see poor Mulvey, with arms outstretched before him, taking a header past the ears of Titmouse, who was in the act of jumping. It seems that, as he approached the edge, the pony had stuck his nose and fore-legs as far as he could down the bank, with a view of lessening the height to be descended. In doing this, however, he assumed such a vertical position, and hesitated so long, that Mulvey lost his balance; and flying head first from the saddle, with the cry of anguish that had reached our ears, dived down to plough up the earth with his head, Titmouse following, and dropping just beside him.

Most fortunately, the falling was soft in the extreme, or in all probability we should have had the doubtful pleasure of carrying our friend home; but, had he been killed on the spot, we could not have restrained the convulsions of laughter that the sight of his helpless, horrified face as he vacated his seat had thrown us into —to be renewed till it became absolutely painful, when, with deeply-plastered head and face, he rose to his feet, gasping open-mouthed for his breath; and the scene ended by our actually rolling out of the saddle, as a sense of his appearance seemed to strike him, and his begrimed features contorted themselves into a ghastly, but killingly ludicrous, grin.

No danger of any one riding over the hounds now; the little fellows are still keeping us at top pace, and, indeed, threaten to get away from the horses altogether; for, with the drag they are treated to to-day, there is no need for stooping or hanging.

The field is already becoming rather lengthened out, though there are a good many well up at present.

Jorrocks is better mounted to-day than usual, on a dark chestnut, with lots of power, but little pretensions to a mouth; and is in ecstasies as he hustles along, picking rather than shirking the biggest places.

"Look out, you fellows!" shouts B., as a hollow, overhanging bank gives way under his pony's hind legs, and he narrowly escapes a fall. Aaron pulls up into a trot and drops down safely, as also does Mulvey on

Ugly. The Child is next seen wakening Iona up with a cut down the shoulder, as he picks him off his knees and nose, and sets him going again. The Aide's hitherto brilliant career is here brought to an untimely end; for, after turning head over heels with the Maneater on the top of him, he has to take to his heels to avoid the enraged brute's onslaught, and the two return by different routes to the Camp—the Aide to strip off breeches and boots, and drown his sorrows in the bowl; the Maneater to seek out a fresh object, biped or quadruped, to devour. Belleville also kisses mother earth; but after ascertaining that both whiskers are still on his face, loses no time in renewing pursuit.

The others get either down or round without further casualty; and it is "forrard" still over a succession of nice little jumps along the brow of a line of hills— Jealousy and Wonder (the two representatives of the pack now on their way home to England with us) striving with Conqueror for a lead; while the rest, with the exception of Harlequin and Bellman, already beginning to lag, are lying close up in a cluster.

No lack of music is there, though they are going nearly their best pace; and the blood runs quicker, and the heart beats excitedly, as we catch up their enthusiasm.

"Forrard" past the race-course. Thank goodness, the man with the drag has considerately spared us the railings! for, though favourite objects for a lark, when looking out for a quiet jump or two in an afternoon's ride, the four feet of stiff timber would prove rather awkward after some time at a good pace over deep country.

A little further on the drag has been lifted for a short distance, and a most welcome check occurs.

Jorrocks gets off for a moment, turns his "Xerxes'" head to the wind, wipes his own cranium with a handkerchief that would have made a counterpane for anybody else, and observes that "it really is beautiful, though he would give five dollars for something to drink."

The Major, his spouse, and two or three others who have followed Abdul's pilotage,—for the latter, on account of a recently-broken limb, is now obliged to ride "cunning,"—are already on the spot before us.

The horses all seem glad of the chance to get their wind; and the hounds are allowed to work for the scent by themselves for some time, before Aaron takes them in hand to lift them forward.

"To him! To him!" as the two whips send them on to his holloa. Handmaid and Conqueror hit it off quickly; and the rest flying to their note, we are soon sailing away towards the valley below.

With a good jumper it is very pleasant work going smoothly down a nice succession of drops, as plateau succeeds plateau in different levels; and such practice ought to improve the hand and seat, and exercise the nerve—preventing the loss of all three, that residence in a hot climate is so liable to bring about.

With unabated chorus the pack crash into a small cover with thick undergrowth, which reduces the horses to a walk. A thick bamboo fence bounds the far side of the plantation, but B. carries enough of it away to let every one else comfortably through.

At the bottom of the valley is a strip of paddy-ground,

which must be crossed somehow. The deep boggy fields are separated by narrow turf paths, which are the only means of avoiding the treacherous surface.

Ugly and Pericles, as old stagers, know how to cross quietly. Aaron and B. dismount, and lead along gingerly.

The Child is succeeding capitally in his endeavours to steer Iona along the awkward causeway, till the Fenian comes rushing along, and all but precipitates the pair into the mud.

Virtue, however, meets its reward, and sin its wages. The lighter pair succumb, and the "Man in the Water" becomes a "Toad in a Hole."

As we passed by the spot on our return, about an hour after, the Fenian had succeeded in wading out of his ill-smelling bed, and stood on the bank mourning over his unlucky steed—still stuck fast. He had evidently resigned himself to the loss of the pony; for as we reached him, he observed mournfully : "Holy Nailors ! Sure he'll die ! "

The pace, though not as hot as in the early part of the run, is still quite as much as we can comfortably manage at this stage of the proceedings, and already a good many have been choked off.

Two or three of the black-coats are well to the front. Rudolph, though his animal's speed—or rather, the want of it—precludes his taking the lead at any time, has been going steadily and well, without accident ; and Alexander is still pounding along on his stout China pony, nothing daunted by the one cropper he has already received, and which makes up but half his quantum for the day.

Dr. Quock was last seen running after his pony, his saddle over his arm, with girths broken and dangling, and holloaing out in a voice rendered more unintelligible than ever from loss of wind and a mouthful of dirt: "I thay! I thay! Thtop my horth! God bleth my thoul!"—the last expression being represented by an inarticulate spluttering, and only recognised by his hearers from the fact of its always appearing at the end of a sentence.

"Steady there, gentlemen! Give 'em time!" but the warning is hardly needed; for in a moment little Jealousy—who seems to work quite independently, and when a difficulty occurs, is always first to solve it—throws her voice with the music of a pack in itself, and the whole body struck off sharp to the left.

"By Jove, B., he is going to give us the 'Selling Drop!' Never mind, I think we have got steam enough left to get over it; at any rate, let's give 'em a pull over the next two fields! There'll be some fun there."

Yes! without doubt there is the "Selling Drop," as it has been christened; and some good men have fallen there. As you approach, it appears nothing more than an ordinary drop, separating one level from another; and it is not till the unwary is right over it that he perceives that immediately under the overhanging bank runs a bridle road. This is also sunk below the level of the field beyond, which is in itself some six or seven feet below the height of the upper one.

Aaron, B., Mulvey, and the Child go at it as hard as they can "leather," and get safely over. Pericles is a bit blown; but Bones pulls him together, plies whip and spur, and the old horse covers it well.

Bobby puts Sweet William at it too slow, and the two

roll over together—the rider getting up with his foot twisted in the stirrup, but trying to regain the saddle without waiting to release himself. As the China pony is a known vicious one, and each ineffectual attempt throws Bobby again on to his back and close to the heels of the beast, his position is anything but pleasant, and everybody shouts to him to clear himself. Tony is particularly affected by the sight; and, mindful only of the danger his friend is in, stops not for choice of language, but yells frantically to him, " Bobby, you d——d fool, you'll be killed ! "

Poor Jorrocks wants not for powder as he charges it boldly; but the chestnut—apparently seeing nothing more than ordinary before him—gallops down it as he has done everything else, and the result is that the corpulent hero and his horse come down together on the hard ground with a fearful crash. Worse than all, Jorrocks is underneath; and the awkward accident keeps our poor friend in his bed for a week afterwards—to reappear at the next meet with undaunted pluck, and no less roseate complexion, to pursue his favourite sport.

This is the only accident of any consequence that we remember to have happened to any one, when out with the beagles, during our stay in Japan—with the single exception of that which befell Bobby, who once succeeded in breaking his collar-bone by larking on his way home after a long run. It is usually such soft falling that little danger is to be apprehended from a cropper, though many a run has been no less fertile in such than the one we are describing.

While pulling up to watch the casualties, the hounds have left us a little behind, and we have to put on extra steam to catch them, which we succeed in doing just as they are about to leave the ridge of high land, and plunge merrily down to the lowlands beneath. At this point a plain-looking hedge, with a deep hidden drop into sloping ground, rather takes the leaders by surprise, and causes several who have been riding very straight hitherto to diverge to a hand-gate and a path.

"Hold up, Tony!" shout two or three voices simultaneously, as the latter, who never turns aside for anything, is seen on the neck of his steed at the unexpected descent, but by help of mane and ears saves a fall.

Through the little village at the bottom, with a holloa or two that must have given the peaceful Nippons an idea that a troop of wild " foreign devils " were let loose to pillage and murder. " Forrard! forrard!" still, with lessened field, but undiminished ardour, over the plain of low country towards the hills beyond.

Now comes the "teaser" of the whole run ! A widish brook, with only one practicable place, at which not more than two can go abreast.

Aaron, in his capacity of huntsman, is allowed precedence; and, getting a clear run at it, finds himself safely landed on the other side. Bones goes at it next ; and, though Pericles just drops his hind-legs in, he is on the point of recovering himself, when Mulvey comes up with a rush on Ugly, and knocks him back into the water, where the four wallow promiscuously.

B. gets well over; and Iona—balking the first time at the struggling horses—when put at it again, stops, then makes a powerful standing spring, and with a flounder and a scramble just reaches the other side.

Rudolph and Bobby also negotiate it successfully;

while Alexander splashes in and out—an example followed by two or three others.

Bones and Mulvey are soon under weigh again, and doing their best to recover their lost ground. The latter has left both his stirrups at the bottom of the brook, and rides the rest of the run without them—no mean performance when the style of country is taken into consideration.

The pack present a much more scattered appearance as they toil up the steep ascent in front; but they are in good trim, and the little ones are not wanting in pluck.

"I shall get off and lead up this place," says one; and his example is generally followed—the exception being Tony, whose proverbial laziness here overcomes his humanity. He is very properly rewarded by finding himself left behind, completely done brown, three fields further on.

"For-rard, on there, Jollyboy! Ge-e-t away on there, Bellman!" screams Aaron, as he mounts again. "By Gosht," he adds ecstatically,—while a radiant smile displays a white and regular row of teeth in a symmetrical curve, bounded by an ear on one side and an ear on the other—"this is clipping fun! Tom Brown is carrying me like an English hunter." Hardly are the words out of his mouth ere the said animal—who is, not unnaturally, a good deal blown with the twelve stone on his back—puts his fore-feet into a small trench, that he either does not see, or is too careless to jump, and Aaron gets a view of the heavens through his own legs.

"This cannot, surely, last much longer," says Bones, who has already made up his mind that Pericles' ration of corn must be increased. A little farther, and Bobby's nag, who has been pounded along all the way with a loose rein, has *compounded*; and Bobby is fain to get off—this time without any fear of difficulty in remounting.

Just ahead are three well-known drops in immediate succession, with a grassy hollow below; and it is more than probable that the drag will be "run into" here. By this time all are pretty well baked, and not more than six or eight are at all near the hounds.

The first of the three drops is a fair open one of about six feet, and the leading lot all get safely down. Then comes one that must ever be most trying to beaten horses. It is about ten feet high, with stiff brushwood growing out of its face, and is not only perpendicular, but overhanging.

"Bellows to mend" causes a refusal on the part of the first two. Then comes Iona; but, though he faces it pluckily, tired nature can do no more for him, and he rolls over like a rabbit. Tom Brown manages to keep his legs; Mulvey comes down gallantly without his stirrups; B., also a light weight, follows in safety; but Pericles—good as he is—has not an ounce left in him, and with a melancholy grunt falls helplessly down, pinning Bones to the ground by his leg.

Rudolph, of course, has a shy at the place, but is numbered with the fallen ones. The others very properly take the state of their horses into consideration, and deem the longest way round the shortest way down.

The third and last of the drops is an easy one, and without further mishap all reach the bottom; where, as we anticipated, the drag has stopped, and the pack are even now baying round.

A "worry" has been provided; and with much screaming and extravagant gestures, Aaron goes through the ceremony.

Girths are loosened and damages ascertained. Cigars are produced; and Rudolph, as usual, bringing out flint-and-steel and a large flask of Cognac, is immediately the centre of attraction.

A short time spent here increases the number to fifteen or sixteen; and, after the ordinary amount of mutual praise, self-reflecting compliments, and inquiries after the missing ones, we move slowly off in the direction of Camp.

* * * * * *

Such is a fair specimen of one of our drags in Japan; and it may appear but a sorry apology for sport to those who have the opportunity of riding to a pack of well-bred hounds, on well-bred and finished hunters, and over a good country, be that country the shires or the provinces.

Still you must allow us this—that it is far better to work on rough materials, or, in other words, to make the best of a bad job, than to allow one's love of sport to cool down,—one's appreciation of pleasure to grow rusty, —or one's frame to become slack and enervated for want of that exercise in the field which gives a clear healthy tone to body and mind, and preserves the keen sense of enjoyment that English blood and breeding teach us to find in the exciting pastime of the chase.

CHAPTER XII.

THE ANNIVERSARY NIGHT.

That the luxurious pleasures of the table should follow in grateful contrast to the more laborious ones of the chase is a time-honoured and ever-pleasant custom.

With what happy anticipation does the wearied sportsman look forward to the convivial board that he knows to be awaiting him at home! And are not the delights of the day's sport enhanced doubly as he dwells on them with legs stretched comfortably under the mahogany—when good wine, light hearts, and good fellowship combine to give everything the rosy tint, which we are told it is the exclusive privilege of Youth to view as the pleasing mantle of reality, and of Old Age—in its unenviable far-sightedness—to see through as the gaudy mask of deception? We thank Heaven that as yet we are neither old nor far-seeing.

Then again, O goodly band of smokers, the calm enjoyment of the after-dinner cigar, or, if your taste leads you to prefer it, of the companionable pipe! For ourselves,—at home from motives of economy, and abroad from habit,—we rather lean to the latter, though a hot climate will not allow of too free an indulgence in it. Indeed, we have always borne in mind the spirit of a piece of advice given in our earliest smoking days by a classical cousin, who saw us labouring hard to darken a stubborn meerschaum, with every chance of colouring ourselves in the attempt:—

"O famose puer, nimium ne crede colori!"

Is it not always the case that in proportion to the goodness of the sport experienced—or more often, perhaps, to the success of their own share in it—are men inclined to estimate the company *and the claret* of the evening?

The man who has gone entirely to his own satisfaction in a trying and select thing is ever in the best of humours, and his well-pleased mind lends a reflective charm to all he comes in contact with; while he, on the contrary, who had the misfortune to get badly off at starting, or to be thrown out by a false turn,—thus losing what the other describes rapturously as "the run of the season,"—is at first inclined to be captious and unsociable. He must be of a bad sort, though, if he does not quickly find his spirits and his conversation with good cheer and boon companions to warm his heart!

We are speaking, of course, of bachelor parties, and bachelor parties *only;* and, in so doing, we are far from intending any breach of the unwritten rules of gallantry.

May we not be excused for saying that after a hard day in the saddle or the stubbles, the polite observances, at all times so necessary—at *other* times so delightful—to adhere to in the society of ladies, would *now* be found—(how can we, their most humble, devoted admirers, put it so as not to lose favour in their sight?)—not quite so eminently desirable—in other words, a slight effort to fulfil?

'Tis in these pleasant sequels that the sports of Old England assert their superiority to what are called the nobler ones of wilder countries. True! the actual game of the latter is grander by far, and nature may there be seen and enjoyed in all her primeval magnificence; but it may well be answered that we pursue not the fox for himself, nor do we look on the partridge as so much meat for the pot. The excitement of big game shooting is intense; but so, indeed, is the riding to a good pack of hounds with a warm scent; and the enjoyment of the latter is much more frequently attainable in an equal time than that of the latter.

But the point of comparison we chiefly wish to insist upon is—that whereas in the one case, after toiling for hours,—perhaps under a tropical sun,—you come back to a camp fire to cook your own dinner, and that probably none of the best; then eat it with a dirty hunting knife, like a savage; wash it down afterwards, if you are lucky, with some rum and water; and lie down to sleep exposed, according to the climate, either to the pitiless attacks of mosquitoes, or the no less cruel biting of the cold; in the other, you return after your day's work to bathe and dress like a gentleman, and find a recompense for the worst of sport in a comfortable dinner and agreeable society.

Passionately fond as we are of both phases of sport, as far as our present limited experience has taught us, we must confess that, were we to allow ourselves to conjure up wild and impossible *châteaux en Espagne*, they would assume the shape of a hunting and shooting box in a good neighbourhood at home, rather than, with commensurate means, of a quarter within reach of the best hill-country in India, of the fabulous game tracts of Gordon Cumming, or the boundless buffalo-covered prairies of the New World.

The evening of the occurrences related in the last chapter chanced to be peculiarly favourable for the banquet that it had been settled some time before should be held to celebrate our opening day with the beagles, inasmuch as two anniversaries also put in a claim for commemoration. One was that of the battle of Ferozeshah, which figures on our regimental colour; the other, and a no less important date in the eyes of him it chiefly affected, was that of the first entrance into Her Majesty's service of one who is known among the Holy Boys as "the Captain."

All of those who have been out with the hounds are present in the ante-room, and in high spirits; the unfortunate Aide alone being a little out of sorts at first, and inclined to resent, not only all affectionate inquiries after his own health and that of the Maneater, but even the oft and delicately-expressed solicitude as to the state of his "poor feet." Addressing the Child almost angrily, he inquires, "What the devil he had put him on that savage brute for?" But, receiving no other answer from that amiable infant than a hearty burst of laughter, in which all present join, he is compelled to call for a sherry and bitters, and pray for better luck next time—the Child considerately promising him the same mount again if he will but undertake "not to let him go running all over the country alone."

"Oh, here's Colonel Summers! How do you do, Colonel?" as a tall man, very young-looking for his rank, enters the room.

He is a member of the American Legation; which, at the time we speak of, consisted of two generals and three colonels.

Majors and captains of their army we have never met, though we presume they have such people occasionally.

"Quite well, thank *you*, gentlemen," replies the Colonel, who is known to most of us.

Dinner being announced, we are soon hard at work; and the amount of exercise lately gone through is a guarantee that full justice shall be done to the bill of fare, which, at this season of the year, is anything but a despicable one. During the winter months the Yokohama market is stocked with almost every variety of game—including venison, wild boar, geese, duck, teal, pheasants, quail, snipe, and woodcock, besides an occasional bear; and all who have been fortunate enough to taste it will speak to the rich and delicate flavour of a bear's ham.

From this long list you will be apt to imagine that Japan must be a paradise for shooting; whereas, as far as the foreigner is concerned—and the natives themselves always use the snare instead of the gun—the opposite is rather the case. There is, no doubt, a great quantity of game scattered throughout the country; but all the favoured spots are out of the reach of Europeans, who, by the existing treaty, are confined within the limits of a segment of a circle, whose radius is thirty miles, and the pig and deer are brought from the wooded mountains far in the interior. But of this more hereafter.

The conversation at table naturally turns very much on the day's sport; but, as no fresh light is thrown on any of the incidents already described, we need not trouble our readers with a repetition of what they have heard.

Mr. Micawber, at first in a pathetic mood, soon warms into a gay, and thence into a boisterous one, and entertains the company with the wonderful exploits that he wishes us to suppose he would that day have performed, "if that brute hadn't been so full of corn that he bolted with him."

"Well, Micawber, all I can say is, he must run to bone instead of flesh," remarks one.

"I say, I will give you two dollars for Falling Star for the kennels. He might be fit for the hounds in a couple of months," says Aaron, who has ever an eye to business and the welfare of the pack.

"At all events, Micawber, if you haven't got a good horse, you have a fine framework which you can build upon," adds Abdul, in allusion to the Star's attenuated appearance.

Poor Micawber, completely routed by this unexpected and ungenerous attack, contrives, with great presence of mind, to divert the channel of chaff against a new object. This is no other than Dr. Quock; and, after a sharp contest between him and Micawber about the relative merits of the two distinguished animals, Falling Star and Woffles, the others, swooping down like eagles scenting a quarry, join in baiting the luckless doctor, and soon effect their object, of "getting a rise out of him," by congratulating him on the wonderful tenacity of seat which had enabled him to ride down two consecutive drops while perched between his horse's ears. This he denies indignantly, but is unable to avoid the many generous congratulations on his own prowess across country under the saddle.

Such an incident, of course, gives fresh impetus to the

onset on Dr. Quock, who splutters and blusters in vain attempts to get rid of his tormentors. Never very quick at repartee, he now searches his brain without effect for weapons with which to demolish them, till, of a sudden, a bright idea seems to strike him, and turning on Abdul, who is one of his chief persecutors—with sparkling eye and eager, triumphant countenance—he crushes him with the withering speech :—

"God bleth my thoul! *you* look very well on parade!" then, finding his shaft of irony strike so true, he repeats it on the Aide, and annihilates him also :—

"Yeth, thir! and *you* look very well on a horth, too !!"

During dinner every possible subject is discussed; the main topic being, however, ourselves and our own doings.

As the wine goes round, mirth increases in proportion. Good stories abound—some of them bordering very closely on the marvellous; others, none the worse for being twice told. Every one is in himself a wit, and feels bound in honour to applaud every one else as the same. Jokes fly about in volleys; and the objects of them are ever the first and heartiest laughters.

We say it without fear of contradiction, or of being thought egotistical in our praises—and entirely without reference to the evening in question. For real conviviality and true good-feeling there is nothing like a military mess on a night when something out of the ordinary has occurred to give a fresh fillip to the spirits of those assembled, and an excuse for a little extra merriment.

On the present occasion everything combines for the encouragement of fun ; and, from Jolly's deep bass to the

Fenian's mournful treble, each one adds his voice to the almost continuous chorus of laughter.

The cloth having been removed, the wine is circulated, and the health of Her Majesty given in the usual loyal form by the Captain, who is sitting president.

While this is being generally responded to, we must take the liberty of drawing your attention to "the Captain," and in a few words introducing one more of the Holy Boys to your notice.

"The Captain," *par excellence*, among us,—this is the eighteenth anniversary of his entrance into the army and the corps he belongs to; but of this we need say no more, for he himself will presently address us on the subject.

Much beloved by the subalterns, he is one of them in all their tastes and pursuits. Like Daddy Goring,—and such a character could never have been a mere offspring of the imagination of the talented author of "Sans Merci,"—he heads our mess as he does our amusements. No party is considered complete without his presence; no scheme pronounced practicable without his approval; and if any one is in need of good sound advice,—freely given when asked for,—the first person he thinks of going to is "the Captain."

'Tis said by ill-natured people that he is slightly disposed to be hypochondriacal, and that the symptoms of his being under the influence of that feeling are discernible by a sudden rise in the thermometer of his moral condition. As an instance in proof of this, they are apt to relate how he was met one morning, when emerging with a most doleful visage from his hut— which, by-the-bye, he had an unaccountable fancy for keeping at a hot-house heat all the year round, by means of stoves and tightly-closed doors and windows.

"Holloa, Captain, what's the row? You seem very unhappy this morning."

"I'm very seedy, indeed," replied the Captain, in a voice that whispered scarce audibly from his chest—accompanying the remark with a most unwilling cough.

"Why, you are not looking amiss. What makes you fancy you are so bad?"

"I've got an awful pain in my chest; and *I've been thinking about religion all the morning.*"

Though possessed of a tender and susceptible heart, he has—wonderfully enough—not yet been drawn into the silken meshes of matrimony. That same tenderness of disposition evinces itself even in his treatment of the inferior animals. Thus, he could never be persuaded to part with a little Japanese toy-dog, even after she—for it belonged to the more uncertain-tempered sex—had bitten several of his brother officers. So attached was he to Omè, that he would believe no harm against his pet; and she continued, undisturbed, to take up her position every night, curled up in his easy chair, in spite of the allegations and complaints of which she was the object.

After a certain lapse of time, during which wine and conversation have continued to flow freely, and two or three of the seniors slipped quietly away, the Captain rises amid vociferous cries of "Hear, hear!" rapping on the table with knives, and a view holloa from Aaron, whose countenance already bears the honest flush of drink.

"Gentlemen! It is now eighteen years to-day since

I first joined the service, and became an ensign in this regiment." Before the speaker can proceed further, Micawber has mounted his chair, and given the time for " Three cheers for the Captain!" which are brought forth with an energy that threatens to lift the roof off the mess hut.

"I am not much of a hand at speech-making ('Oh! oh!' with much pantomimic action of hands and features, from Aaron), but on this—this—propitious occasion I feel myself bound to say a few words. This is the glorious anniversary of the battle of Ferozeshah (cheers). Harvey! put some more of the No. 1 claret on the table! and though it is so long since, that none of us here were present, when the Holy Boys helped to show the niggers what British pluck was worth, we have no less reason to commemorate the day. I myself, though a native of Ireland, was born at Cawnpore, and learnt early to take pride in the achievements of our countrymen in India."

After this last truly Hibernian sentence, the Captain sits down amid uproarious applause; and Ferozeshah must indeed have been a sanguinary battle, if the blood spilt on the field bore anything like a proportion to the rich, red stream that flows so copiously on this its anniversary.

Sitting on the right of the Captain is C——, preserving the same cool, unruffled face that has given us double confidence when awaiting, side by side, with rifles cocked and fingers on the trigger, the charge of a rogue elephant, as—yet unseen—he crashes down with a resistless fury that hurls the tangled jungle aside like straw. An unerring shot; equally good on the green cloth of the billiard or the whist table; and a proficient on the no less smooth and verdant surface of the cricket-ground—he owes much of his success, and the preservation of that quick eye and steady hand, to the careful following out of a precept which he who erst commanded the Holy Boys was wont to impress on his "youngsters."

When the old brown sherry had more than once wended its way round the table, and the story of "the bird that towered" had been repeated to an attentive audience, their well-loved chief would frequently give this piece of thoroughly practical advice to one or all of the junior portion of his listeners—the while he stroked his long moustaches fondly:—"Do as I do, my boys; *drink freely, but never exceed!*"

A hot discussion is now seen to be going on at the top of the table, which evidently concerns Captain Puffles, whose seat is on the left of the president, and who hitherto has been setting a meritorious example in the way he has directed a steady attack on the bottle. He is trying to leave the table, and several voices, not to speak of the two nearest pairs of hands, are determined in their efforts to retain him in his chair.

"Let me go, you fellows!" he entreats. "I'm on garrison duty; and it puffectly cert'n I *must* go! 'Ow am I to get up the 'ill later on?"

The last argument, so powerfully delivered, carries his point; and Puffles is allowed to buckle on his sword—after shaking out a reef in the already lengthy belt—on the express condition that he will rejoin the party after he has gone his rounds.

"Gentlemen!" begins Mr. Micawber, rising. "Gentlemen!" he repeats, when something like silence is obtained, "I have very great pleasure in announcing that Colonel Summers has kindly consented to favour the company with a song."

The individual named appears considerably surprised at the announcement, inasmuch as he is sitting at the end of the table farthest from the speaker, with whom he has never interchanged a word in his life. This is not, however, a time to stand upon ceremony; and, with obliging readiness, he prepares to carry out the proposition, while Micawber adds, as he raps loudly on the table,—

"Silence, if you please, gentlemen, for No. 21 in the books!"

As the Colonel trolls out one of those splendid marching choruses with which the Federal troops in the great American war were used to keep their ardour from flagging and their spirits from drooping; and as the refrain is thundered out after each verse—

> "Hurrah! hurrah! we'll sound the jubilee!
> Hurrah! hurrah! the flag that made us free!
> 'Twas so we sang the chorus from Atlanta to the sea,
> As we went marching through Georgia"—

it gives one some faint idea of the effect it must have produced when caught up by "fifty thousand" voices.

Men who served in that cruel war tell rapturously—as cheek flushes and eye sparkles, as if with the light of battle—how many a tired soldier, weary almost to death, seemed animated with a new life, and endowed with a new strength, as column after column burst forth in the soul-stirring war-song! How he would straighten his back under the heavy knapsack, and grasp his rifle more firmly, as he looked up to the starry banner he loved so well—pressing forward to the fight with renewed hope that he might still live to return to the dear ones he loved still more!

The Colonel's song is received as it deserves to be, and he is about to exercise his privilege of calling upon some other to follow his example, when one of the party, by name—well, never mind the name! it is not one of those who have as yet appeared before you—in whom the melody just sung has apparently worked upon recollections previously called up, till they can no longer be kept confined in his own bosom, gets on his legs, and with much emotion proceeds to give vent to his feelings as follows:—

"Gentlemen!" a dead pause. "Gentlemen!" he continues, in a key some two octaves higher, and giving the letter *s*, where it occurs, the true vinous pronunciation, "there'sh a fellow shaysh shomewhere—can't quite recklect where—'De mortuish non esht dishputandum.'" The first two words of this Dundreary-like quotation are delivered slowly, a syllable at a time, while the remainder are run over as if he were afraid they might give him the slip. "This, gentlemen, means—for perhaps you are not all as well up in the classics as myself"—and here a self-satisfied smirk crosses the features of the orator, giving him an expression irresistibly comic—"means that we must think no harm of the dead—something very much the same as 'Honi soit qui mal y pense.' But that wasn't what I was going to say;—I was going to—I was going to say——" and the speaker takes some little time to consider what he *is* going to say, while Aaron chimes in with, "Don't say Nay, charming Judy Callaghan!" and encouraging cries of "Hear! hear! Try back!" &c., &c., fill up the void. "Well, I was going to say something about Ferozeshah," a dreadful word for the poor man to pronounce; but which, when once mastered, seems to have a magical attraction, as he repeats it at every opportunity. "I wasn't at Ferozeshah myself ('Oh, nonsense! Yes! yes!' from all parts of the room), but I had a cousin, poor f'llar!" At this point emotion completely masters the eloquent youth, and he can only mumble "Poor f'llar!" and spill his claret down his shirt-front. At last he recovers sufficiently to continue, "Poor f'llar! my cousin was at Ferozeshah, and—and"— as the hot tears drip into his wine-glass—"he washn't killed himshelf, but he told me of sheveral poor f'llarsh who were. My toasht musht be—musht be—bumper. Here'sh health killed and wounded at Fosheshah!"

The unexpected finale to this speech fairly startles his hearers, whose feelings have been worked up to the highest pitch of sympathy by the eloquence of the speaker, the depth of his own emotion, and the heart-opening effects of their potations. Accordingly, a general outburst of wrath takes place, and the offending member is considerately helped to bed.

All of a sudden a voice is heard demanding an audience, and Aaron is seen addressing the assembly in indignant expostulation: "Stop a moment! I do wish to speak! There is some fellow in this room that is no gentleman! He is shirking his liquor and pouring it down my back!" And sure enough, his next-door neighbour, to whom he has been sitting with his back half turned, has contrived, while attempting to do justice to the last toast,—of which he had caught but a faint notion of the meaning,—to upset his glass between

Aaron's collar and neck. The anger of the latter, though at first considerably increased by the merriment consequent on his announcement, being at length appeased, a song is called for; and the following, which was produced during the voyage of the Holy Boys out to China in 1864, is the selection of the minstrel :—

THE FOX.

The fox, the gallant fox I'll toast,
  A bumper full we'll drink!
'Tis four years ere we sport again
  That glorious bit of pink.

CHORUS.

  So fill, boys, fill!
  To Reynard fill a stoup!
  And make the rafters ring it back,
    Tally-ho! Forrard! Who hoop!

He waits but for a single cheer;
  Then off and straight away,
With eighteen couple close behind,
  And a perfect scenting day.

He swings his brush, defies his foes,
  Then marks his point ahead;
He'll reach it now, or fail and die,
  And struggle till he's dead.

The "bullfinch" and the "oxer" too,
  We'll take them in our stride;
But steady at the "double," with
  A ditch on either side!

We'll skim the grass; we'll trot the plough:
  The water now is nigh:
We pick him up; now straight and fast!
  We've done it in a fly!

So join me all who love the hound,
  The fox, his mortal foe;
And make the walls again resound
  With one good view holloa.

Scarcely has the singer finished the last verse ere the door is burst open, and in rushes Captain Puffles, his eyes starting out of his head, hair dishevelled, and his usually rubicund countenance blanched to a greenish yellow—reminding one forcibly of the somewhat unique derivation one of the most learned and revered of the Rugby masters used to give of the word "crocodile," an animal old Herodotus evidently put on the same footing as we do the gorilla in the present day. "The name κροκοδειλος," he would say, "is compounded of the two words κροκος, *yellow*, and διιδω, *to fear*, because at the sight of the beast you are apt to become *yellow with fear*."

Rushing up to the president, Puffles bursts out with the inquiry, "Am I drunk? Say, am I drunk?"

One's first notion under such circumstances would naturally be that he *is*, or else that he has been seized with a sudden fit of insanity; but a second glance at his scared, terrified face and look of agonised horror quite removes the impression, and all expect that he bears the news of some fearful catastrophe. It requires little persuasion to induce him to tell his story, which comes out in quick, disconnected sentences—his rapid, vehement utterance bearing the plainest impress of truth.

"I've seen a ghost! He stopped me as I was going round the guards! I 'olloaed to him, but he never answered! I ran him through with my sword, but he never said anything!" and poor Captain Puffles seems on the point of swooning.

It was not till the next morning that any further particulars could be gathered from him; but that the affair bore a different light to certain free-thinking individuals than to him whom it more immediately concerned, is apparent from the following lines, which Abdul brought in and handed round at mess on the following evening:—

> As Falstaff as slender, as modest, as brave;
> As chaste as Miss Venus, who sprang from the wave;
> As sober as Bacchus; as Peony pale;
> There, the "'Ero" you 'ave of this 'orrible tale.
> For a more gallant soldier in vain you may seek,
> Though like a true Taffy he'll swallow his leek.
> His conduct when serving his Queen in Kotee,[*]
> Likewise in his *Tunic*, was brave as could be.
> He adored the fair sex as a true knight became,
> And for them "fiends of 'ell" was his playful pet name.
> One night at the hour that most people call dead,
> Because the departed then walk it is said,
> Our "'Ero" was making on duty his round,
> And cursing the darkness and roughness of ground,
> Being fully persuaded that 'tis not a story,
> That—"duty's path" often may "lead you to glory;"
> When all of a sudden !!!!! (the path was not wide)
> Close in front a tall figure in white he espied.
> "'Oo are you? 'Oo goes there? Do you 'ear me?" he cried;
> But the figure stood staring, and nothing replied.
> Then "'aving 'is 'and on the 'ilt of 'is sword,"
> He challenged again, but got never a word;
> And in cold perspiration he thought, "Oh, by Gum!
> "'Tis surely some spirit; I swear it is *rum*."
> Then his hair stood on end!!! for, Oh! HORROR to see,
> It vanished before him like—Soda and B.
> How our 'Ero got home 'tis not easy to say,
> Though 'tis thought he did *not* spend much time on the way.
> Then, with countenance paled to the hue of old port,
> To his comrades he made his most direful report.
> But his sceptical friends thought (unkindly, alas!)
> That his ghost was like Banquo's, just seen with a glass;
> And that one so familiar with spirits should fear
> A familiar sprite, seemed to them very queer:
> But he'd never have funked it, they're ready to swear,
> Had he found it in water instead of in air!

---

[*] One of the glorious actions fought in India, in which Captain Puffles distinguished himself.

This was not the first occasion on which Captain Puffles had been the victim of a similar hallucination.

Some eighteen months previously the Holy Boys had been dragging on an uncertain existence amid the heat and fever of Hong-Kong.

In this one season—certainly the most unhealthy on record—they lost nearly three hundred of their total strength: a large proportion by death, the remainder invalided; and many a fine fellow, who deserved a better fate than to wither and die of a sudden pitiless sickness in a land of strangers, did we lay in his last resting-place in what has been named with a terrible—almost sacrilegious—humour, the Happy Valley.

Never, as we passed under the entrance-arch of the graveyard—the thrilling wail of woe of the Dead March in Saul, human-like in its intense despairing anguish, ringing in our ears—could we repress a shudder at the fearful truth of its inscription, "Hodie mihi, cras tibi;" and, thoughtless and giddy though we may be, prayed that it might never be our lot to make one of those who slept under the ever-increasing cluster of unsodded mounds—so far from those who would have softened a painful illness or soothed a last hour.

Requiescant in pace! What right have we to speak on such a sacred subject here? And how can we straightway resume our flippant nonsense, with pen still wet from touching on the saddest memories of our stay in foreign lands?

Even as, returning from a funeral, the band would play its liveliest airs to raise the spirits of the party from the low ebb to which they had been brought by the mournful ceremony just witnessed—so may we be pardoned for turning at once to lighter themes.

It had been the regular habit of Captain Puffles during the hot weather to retire to his own room shortly after dinner; and, with doors and windows thrown open with a view to coaxing any slight breeze which might dispel in some degree the stifling closeness of the atmosphere, there to enjoy in quiet his pipe and the accompanying soda and brandy.

One night some discussion, probably on the subject of the fair sex—a topic on which he is ever most eloquent; more, 'tis sad to confess, to deprecate than to praise them—kept him in the ante-room, and induced him to break through his ordinary custom.

Meanwhile a crony of his, Joe Burly by name, who used often to drop in to cool his tongue with the iced drink, heat it again with the sociable weed, only to make the refrigerating process still more grateful, had strolled into the vacant room; and finding his host absent, had sat down alone to partake of the pleasant liquor laid out on the table, and await his coming. After a pipe or two he began to feel somewhat drowsy; but not wishing to leave without a chat with his friend, threw himself down on the bed, and was soon fast asleep.

Captain Puffles, returning rather late, found the lamp had gone out; and, giving up the idea of another smoke, felt his way into his sleeping clothes, and also lay down on the outside of the bed—getting between sheets at that time of the year being, of course, quite out of the question. In a very few seconds he was snoring in a way that must have been very annoying to the peaceful inhabitants of the Land of Dreams; and, could any one have seen them, it would indeed have been a touching sight to view these portly Babes in the Wood as—side by side, in sleeping innocence—they lay almost in each other's arms.

In the middle of the night, however, Captain Puffles moved uneasily in his slumbers, and his leg came in contact with a fleshy mass beside him.

Whether this incident chimed in with some horrid dream he was at that moment under the influence of, or was merely distorted by his half-awakened faculties, is not known ; but, with a howl of terror, he sprang out of bed, and rushed madly down the passages, crying out that "there was a *dead man in his bed!*"

The corpse, in the meantime, brought to life by the terrified yell of Captain Puffles, and thinking that if he stayed where he was he might very possibly be shot in the confusion, sloped quietly off, and betook himself to his own room.

Puffles soon had a strong party at his heels, and returned to drag to light the unwelcome intruder; but, naturally enough, no dead man could be found, though he pointed in triumph to the double impression on the bed, and insisted that it must have been removed in his absence. He failed, however, to convince his hearers that his lifeless bedfellow had any more substantial reality than the work of his own imagination, assisted by the last of the four B. and S.'s that he was known to have "stowed away" before leaving the ante-room; and three or four of the subalterns, in revenge for being awakened from their sleep, rose up in open mutiny, and administered a sound bolstering to their superior officer.

No persuasion, though, would induce Captain Puffles

to return to his couch; and for the rest of the night, armed with his black pipe and a thick bludgeon, he paced the verandahs, and mused over his terrible adventure: nor was it until some months after, when the joke had in a great measure passed over, that Joe Burly confessed to a select circle—amid the indignant wrath of Captain Puffles—the share he had taken in that night's alarm.

CHAPTER XIII.

ODDS AND ENDS.

ONE of the first things the new arrival at Yokohama does is to visit "Curio Street," which, as its name almost implies, is a street composed entirely of shops for the sale of Japanese curiosities. It is nearly half a mile long, and very broad. On either side, ranged temptingly in the shops, which are quite open to the street, with small verandahs in front, is every description of lacquer, bronze, porcelain, and ivory work. Here is to be seen and admired everything, from a little camphor-wood box or fishing-rod for two tempos each, up to a gold lacquer cabinet or antique bronze for two or three thousand ichiboos.*

As the would-be purchaser passes along, on the lookout for some article suiting his fancy and his purse, he is hailed on all sides by the inmates to come and inspect their wares; and many a chaffy remark they pass upon him as he proceeds on his way.

Some of "ours" became after a time such adepts at their vernacular that they were able to return this fire, and engage the enemy the whole way down the street with a tolerable amount of success, notwithstanding being exposed to a heavy cross-fire, and having to contend against an overwhelming superiority of numbers.

* A tempo is worth about twopence; an ichiboo, about eighteenpence.

The funny man, if he is out in Japan, and can talk the language, need never be at a loss for an appreciative and applausive audience. The slightest pretext for a laugh is seized on by the natives with avidity.

The more you chaff with this class of Japanese, the better you can get on with them. They themselves never think of going beyond a certain point, and know exactly how far a joke ought to be carried—a happy knack never to be too much commended.

A stranger may go into one of these shops, and after staying an hour, if he likes, looking at and examining every article, and turning the whole shop almost upside down, may go away not making a single purchase, without any fear of having even a rude or uncivil look cast at him. In return to his "Good day!" the "Syonara!" from the proprietor, and probably all his little family—they always have on hand a good supply of small children—will be as cheery as if he had bought a thousand ichiboo cabinet.

They will even probably, after he has expressed his determination not to buy, offer him a cup of tea.

How different from the bullying, "What's the next harticle, mum?" in our cheap shops.

We have several times made comparisons between our countrymen and the Japanese, always unfavourable to the former; and we are almost afraid that we may be laying ourselves open to the imputation that our proclivities are entirely with the latter.

If any reader has been led into this idea, let him at once disabuse his mind of it. At the same time, we are not so bigoted as some of our countrymen we have met in our wanderings, who can never bring themselves to admit the superiority of any nation over our own, even in the most trivial matters.

Very often in the mornings, when there happened to be no duty to be done, it was a favourite way of passing an hour or so before tiffin to ride down to Curio Street, and lounge about the different shops, inspecting any new article that had been received from Yedo or Osaka,—whether we bought or not, we seemed equally welcome.

One old couple, who kept one of these shops, we were on intimate terms with; that is to say, we seldom passed without a few words to them. One day, seeing the old woman by herself, we asked her where her husband was, and were told that she supposed " he was after the girls," after which she laughed, as if delighted at the idea of having such a gay old dog for a spouse.

It was evident this old lady's peace of mind was never likely to be attacked by the green-eyed monster.

The next time we visited the shop, we rallied the old fellow on being such a gay Lothario; but he did not seem as proud of the reputation as his wife was, and indignantly declared the aspersion cast on him to be totally without foundation. We were half inclined to believe him, and even now think that the old woman's statement may have only been a vain-glorious boast.

When any large ships of war, or the American packets from San Francisco were in, trade was brisk in Curio Street. Naval officers, American tourists, sailors, &c., crowded every shop, and of course prices ran up wonderfully. In this flourishing condition we leave Curio Street.

Within the last few years it has become the fashion

of the Japanese to ape the European in every way. One instance, which we know from personal experience, where the higher classes have proved themselves talented copyists, is the kindly way they have taken to drinking champagne. We know of one Daimio who had *delirium tremens* from indulging in an overweening fondness for this beverage.

They are beginning now to cast off their own picturesque and becoming garments, and to adopt the European style of dress in its place; and in Yedo and Yokohama, yakonins are to be met in every street attired in most villanously-cut coats and trousers; they have also a weakness for jack-boots; and their whole get-up is strongly suggestive of scarecrows.

Hardly a mail leaves Yokohama without numbering among its passengers several of these Japanese gentlemen on their way to London or Paris.

We were on board the "P. and O." steamer one evening before her departure, and were introduced to sixteen Japanese of all ages, from fourteen to thirty, all belonging to the same party, and all provided with note-books and pencils, sitting in the saloon round the stove, taking notes on everything they saw and heard, at a rate which threatened soon to leave them without a single blank spot in their books. They all spoke a little English; and, by way of opening the conversation with us, one of them remarked, evidently prompting himself from his note-book, — "Lon-don-is-a-ver-y-big-place, sir."

We allowed that, and informed them that it was as big as Yedo or Osaka. At this, they shook their heads incredulously, but thought it worthy of a note.

Another, the smallest and youngest of the party, favoured us with the following interesting extract from his note-book:—"We-are-go-ing-to-vis-it-the-fol-low-ing-pla-ces,-Shang-hai,-Hong-kong,-Sin-ga-pore,-Galle-A-den,-Su-ez,-Al-ex-an-dri-a,-Mal-ta,-Mar-seilles,-Par-is,-Lon-don."

Here was an opportunity not to be lost for the gentleman who had taken a note on the size of our metropolis, and had brought it out with such startling suddenness on our introduction; for when the other had ended his long catalogue of names with "Lon-don," he chimed in again with, "Lon-don-is-a-ver-y-big-place," and then looked round for applause. The remaining fifteen all looked at him approvingly, and then nodded their heads at each other in a way which said as plainly as words, "Observe the value of taking notes! See how well *that* came in!"

"What-are-its-chief-pro-ducts,-sir?" asked the little one of the party, who spoke like a young geography. It was on the tip of our tongue to enumerate a list of such articles as balloons, gig-lamps, chimney-pots—in fact, anything that occurred to our fertile brain; but a suspicion that this juvenile seeker after knowledge had already the proper answer down in his book, and was only asking us for the purpose of proving the correctness of his note, restrained us.

We soon had enough of them and their note-books, so wished them "good-bye and a pleasant voyage, which," we added, "was a long and very often a tedious one."

We left them all busily engaged, entering with great pains in their note-books, "The voyage from Japan to London is a long, and very often a tedious one!" facts they no doubt found practically exemplified before they were many weeks older, and were able to bear in mind without reference to their notes.

At certain seasons of the year kite-flying becomes the rage in Japan; and, amongst the lower classes, every man and boy provides himself with one of these articles.

No little vagabond is too poor to buy one with its modicum of string. They are to be had of all sizes and shapes, from a little one six inches square up to one almost as big as a house.

We have seen the sky almost obscured by the number of kites soaring above—in the shape of eagles, swans, warriors, and dragons; while the air has been filled with a humming sound made by them.

A Japanese will manœuvre his kite, and get it up to any height, without moving ten paces: when once up, as high as it is intended to go, it will remain quite steady and stationary.

We recollect once, we were presented by a Japanese acquaintance with a kite of huge dimensions, and we provided it with string to such an extent as nearly to empty our scantily-filled coffers; and, even then not satisfied, we committed a daring burglary on two Government offices, and abstracted therefrom two balls of twine destined for the purpose of tying up weighty " officials."

A distinguished company assisted at its first ethereal flight. There was present no less a personage than the Commanding Royal Engineer; besides whom, there were the barrack-master and a host of subalterns.

Our first attempt to get the kite under weigh was unsuccessful; it evinced a decided disinclination to soar into what ought to have been its natural element. First it plunged headlong into the stomach of the Commanding Royal Engineer; then it flapped harmlessly about the heads of the whole party; then it made a swoop on some windows, so as to elicit a cry of horror from the barrack-master; and then, finally, it dashed itself frantically to the ground in a way which made us tremble for its bamboo framework.

All this was very discouraging; but our Japanese grooms took the affair into their own hands, and soon we had the pleasure of seeing it floating gracefully in the pure *æther*.

It remained steadily at the extremity of its allowance of twine for three days and three nights. So liberal had we been in this allowance, that the kite was almost out of sight; but we could hear it very plainly, for it was "a devil to hum," as the gentleman who lived next door to us remarked testily the morning after its first night out.

We do not know to what cause to attribute the forbearance shown by some of our wild jokers in not cutting the string, unless they recognised in the fact of a kite flying from our quarters an appropriate and touching symbol of the general impecuniosity which characterised our establishment.

We got quite fond of this kite, and used to sit *almost* under its shade for hours.

What a picture of peace! Sitting under the shade of one's own kite! proudly feeling the tension on the string, and sending "messengers" up to it so often, that we were forced to commit another depredation on the aforesaid Government offices for more foolscap.

Alas! on the morning of the third day it came on to blow suddenly; and our kite found a last home in the branches of some far-distant trees.

Sometimes may be seen in a crowded street nearly every fifth or sixth person flying a kite, and yet never getting the strings entangled.

A party of us were riding through a village called Isibarra during the kite-flying season; and, while we stopped at a tea-house for a quiet smoke and a cup of tea, one of the party took a sketch of the villagers engaged in this pastime.

Another amusement resorted to later in the season is battledore and shuttlecock. The patrons, or rather patronesses, of this noble game are generally the young girls. It is played with a diminutive shuttlecock—a small piece of wood not much bigger than a pea, with one single feather stuck in it—and a flat piece of wood, about a foot and a half long, splaying outwards from the handle, for a battledore.

The players stand in a circle, and after the shuttlecock has been once started, any one trying to hit it, and missing it, receives a smart slap from all the players with their wooden battledores.

We have sometimes joined in the game when passing a noisy little knot of moosmies; and the way in which they visited on us any mistake on our part has recalled forcibly painful reminiscences of the days of our childhood.

A little later than the kite-flying season, as well as we can recollect, a curious custom prevails all through the country. Every Nippon, high or low, to whom a son has been born during the preceding twelve months, testifies his sense of the blessing by hoisting, on a bamboo pole, in front of his house, a huge paper fish, which remains in that position, flapping and fluttering, for the next three weeks, in proud testimony of the happy event.

Be it recorded to the honour of the Japanese ladies, hardly a dwelling, from a palace to a hut, is to be seen at this period without one of these monuments of the love they bear their lords displayed proudly outside.

Looking down on a town or a village from a hill, the curious spectacle is beheld of several hundred huge monsters of the deep floating in the air.

They vary in length from three or four feet up to twenty or twenty-five, and are wonderfully lifelike, both in form and motion.

All we know of the origin of this strange custom is, that centuries ago fishing was the most universal and honoured calling after that of arms. Indeed, it was a boast of the late Tycoon that his family had sprung from a race of hardy fishermen; and so proud was he of this, that every gift from him was accompanied by a piece of fish-skin, symbolical of his descent. A fish naturally became the emblem of the profession, as it was glorified into, and perhaps was displayed on these happy occasions to inspire the little stranger, even from its birth, with a laudable ambition to become a fisherman.

Whatever may have been its origin,—the above is only a surmise,—the custom is now adopted by all, irrespective of rank, profession, or calling, and was once even introduced into the English camp, as a delicate little attention, on the part of some of us, to an esteemed brother officer. He happened to be away on a shooting excursion, and during his absence we saw in the *Times* the announcement of the interesting fact which had made him a proud parent since his arrival from England. On his return from the chase, a fish of huge dimensions, —its exact size was twenty-eight feet,—floating conspicuously over his hut, proclaimed to the world and to him the joyful event.

It remained in this position for several days, an object of delight and admiration to the Japanese passers-by, who thought the whole thing an exquisite joke.

There is no lack of amusement amongst the Japanese. Besides top-spinning, kite-flying, wrestling, juggling, and many other minor sports, they have theatricals, of which they are passionately fond.

One has only to enter one of the large theatres at Yedo or Osaka, at any time of the day, and watch the faces of the crowd, to see how favourite an amusement this is.

A piece generally lasts throughout the day; and a regular Japanese play-goer will sit it out the whole time, having his meals brought to him. There is no tedious waiting between the scenes. They follow each other in rapid succession.

One stage we saw at Yedo was divided into different compartments by partitions radiating from the centre. On the completion of one scene, the stage revolved on a central pivot, disclosing the next compartment prepared for the ensuing one.

The gestures and pantomimic actions are so expressive, that the plot, which is invariably very simple, can easily be followed. In fact, in many cases we believe it to be quite *impromptu;* for we have known its course turned at the will of the spectators.

We were once at a large theatre in Osaka, sitting in a box belonging to some of Prince Chiosiu's officers, and looking at one of these plays.

A woman (this was the plot) had proved unfaithful to her husband, and had been sentenced to execution. Her pleadings were disregarded by the stern judge, and she was delivered over to the hands of the executioner, who stood glaring fiercely, and feeling the edge of his keen sword, which ghastly preparation she stood looking at with a terror-stricken gaze. A subordinate, now advancing, tied a rope round her waist, and dragged her to the centre of the stage. Here she was forced into a kneeling position, and the executioner advanced with uplifted sword, making extravagantly frightful faces.

The woman, as if unable longer to bear her agonising terror, jumped up, rushed frantically to the footlights, and wildly entreated the intercession of the audience.

So wonderfully well, and with such effect, was this acted, that the whole house "*rose at her,*" and with yells and shrieks demanded her immediate release. The judge remained firm for some time, as if determined to let the play go on in its proper course; but the audience lashed themselves into such a state of fury, that he at last signalled that she was forgiven. This was received with tumultuous applause, and the rope round her waist was untied amidst the wildest demonstrations of delight, which she acknowledged with bows and fascinating smiles.

Not content with cheering and shrieking until they were hoarse, numbers of the crowd stripped themselves of their girdles, or any pieces of finery about their dress, and flung them on the stage, as tributes to her wonderful powers of acting. Attention was now directed to the executioner, who finding himself an object of popular indignation, dropped his fierce looks and his sword, and beat a hasty retreat.

While all this was going on, we noticed several Japanese old gentlemen looking very grave, as if they thought it was inculcating a bad moral lesson, and was dead against the good old principle of virtue always being triumphant in the end.

We did not remain long enough to find out whether the heroine, profiting by the narrow escape she had had, turned over a new leaf and led a better life; for we were warned by some of the Japanese officers in our box that we had better retire, as they said that the crowd, after this extraordinary scene, was almost intoxicated with excitement, and that any slight incident might make us the objects of its fury.

As we were about three or four among as many thousands, and had noticed several glances at us from the crowd, which had made us instinctively feel our revolvers under our coats, we readily took the hint, and bade good night to the Japanese officers, who expressed over and over again their regret for the necessity—which they thought really existed—for our departure, and begged us to have before starting a little more champagne, of which they had a plentiful supply in the box.

A great many of these plays are founded on old legends and stories, the Japanese being particularly rich in legendary lore. In this way the mountains and forests are, many of them, inhabited as thickly by spirits, good and evil, as the Hartz Mountains and the Black Forest are believed to be by the German peasantry.

The mountain of O-yama, alluded to in our first chapter as one of the most sacred in Japan, is, on one side, the abode of an evil spirit with a long nose, whose name is Ten-jo. Abdul and Mulvey once started, on three days' leave, with the intention of climbing to the summit—not of Ten-jo's nose, but of the mountain; their principal reason for so doing being simply that they were told by every one that they had better not.

They first tried the ascent on the most accessible side, but fierce two-sworded yakonins jealously guarded it; and they were obliged to make the attempt on the other, which was almost inaccessible, and was Ten-jo's region.

The villagers at the base of the mountain begged them to give up the project; and one old man, a species of patriarch, reasoned with them.

"What are you going to do when you get to the top?" he asked.

Our two friends were forced to admit that their course *then* would be very similar to that of the King of France and his men—come down again.

The old man laughed pityingly, and said, "Well, go if you like; but, take my word for it, Ten-jo will do you an injury."

They asked who Ten-jo was.

"Why, Ten-jo," said the old man, "is an evil spirit with a long nose, who will dislocate your limbs if you persist in going up the mountain on this side."

"How do you know he has got a long nose?" they asked. "Have you ever seen him?"

"Because all evil spirits have long noses,"—here

Mulvey hung his head,—"and," continued the old man, not noticing how dreadfully personal he was becoming to one of the party, "Ten-jo has the longest of the lot. Did you ever know a man with a long nose who was good?"

"Come on," said Mulvey hurriedly to Abdul, "or the old fool will be making me out an evil spirit."

"Syonara!" said the old man as they walked away, "but look out for Ten-jo!"

After climbing hard for some hours, and not meeting a single human being,—not even the wood-cutter could be tempted by the fine timber to encroach on Ten-jo's precincts,—they reached the top, and enjoyed a magnificent view.

After a rest they started on their descent, the worst part of which they had accomplished, when, as they were walking quietly along a good path, Abdul's ankle turned under him, and he went down as if he had been shot, with his leg broken in two places.

With difficulty Mulvey managed to get him to the village they had started from, and the news ran like wildfire, that Ten-jo had broken the leg of one of the adventurous tojins.

"I told you how it would be," exclaimed the old man, "but you would go. Ah, Ten-jo is a dreadful fellow!"

All the villagers clustering round took up the cry, and shook their heads.

Ten-jo's reputation had increased wonderfully by this accident.

Poor Abdul was on his back for eleven weeks, and numbers of Japanese—for he was a general favourite amongst them—went to see him, and to express their regret and horror at Ten-jo's behaviour.

One of these visitors was an old man, who himself was at the time a victim of a popular superstition that the departed revisit the scenes of their life in this world in shapes of different animals.

We noticed that he was not in his usual spirits, and pressed him to unburden his mind to us.

He said that he had lost his little son Chiosiu, but that that was not so much the cause of his grief as the absurd way in which his wife, backed up by a whole conclave of old women who had taken up their quarters in his house to comfort her, was going on.

"What do they all do?" we asked sympathetically.

"Why," he replied, "every beastly animal that comes to my house, there is a cry amongst them all, 'Chiosiu, Chiosiu has come back!' and the whole house swarms with cats, and dogs, and bats—for they say they are not quite sure which is Chiosiu, and that they had better be kind to the lot than run the chance of treating him badly; the consequence is, all these brutes are fed on my rice and meat, and now I am driven out of doors, and called an unnatural parent, because I killed a mosquito which bit me."

We could not help laughing at the old man's tribulation, but gave him some sound advice, which was to clear his house of the old women, and that then his wife, removed from their baneful influence, would no doubt listen to reason.

He smiled at our inexperience, and said it was very good advice, but unfortunately it could not be followed, for we might just as well have told him to turn the redoubtable Ten-jo off O-yama as to expel the old women from his house; and as to his wife listening to reason on the subject, there was no chance of it, unless the mosquitoes were to bite her as they had bitten him, and he was afraid she was too tough for them.

Another grievance, which seemed to press sorely on him, was that the presence of all these animals, and the immunity extended to them, through their supposed connection with the defunct Chiosiu, did not add to the cleanliness of his establishment; and as every Japanese, no matter how low his station, or how small his dwelling, prides himself upon its exquisite neatness, this must even have outweighed his personal discomfort.

Everywhere is this cleanliness noticeable. The matting on the floors of the poorest habitations is scrupulously clean. The utensils, mostly made of wood, are scoured and polished perpetually, until they always look as if they had just left the hands of the carpenter.

We have sometimes stayed at farm-houses for a few days, and in the event of a scarcity of tables, we have not had the slightest objection to having our meals laid out on the floor, and partaking of them sitting *à la Turque*, or lying at full length, which latter position was only objectionable as being decidedly detrimental to digestion; however, that was a matter of little moment in those days of constant riding and hard exercise.

Certain curious ceremonies and customs, connected with this admirable quality, cleanliness, show how highly it is esteemed.

Some of us accompanied Sir Harry Parkes on a journey from Osaka to a place called Surina, when nearly the whole breadth of Japan was traversed.

All along the route, Japanese outriders preceded the British Minister and his suite, for the purpose of selecting the houses in the different villages where the party was to halt for refreshment and rest.

Outside each of these houses, on either side of the door, a pile of sand and dust, a pail of clean water, and a broom were placed, to show the guest that the house had been swept and garnished for their reception; and no mere empty form did this ever turn out to be.

Besides this, at every door of the village streets they passed through a broom rested, to indicate that should the party by chance wish to stop at any house, they would find it prepared and ready for them.

Of course such civility as this awaited not the ordinary traveller, and was paid to Sir Harry Parkes as being the guest of the Tycoon.

The inhabitants of the provinces they passed through had most of them never seen a tojin; some had never even heard of such a being; and the little band of Englishmen travelling through the midst of millions of these people was an object of the most intense wonder and astonishment wherever it went. A lady who was one of the party excited more interest and amazement than any one else, and though multitudes—so numerous that all round nothing was to be seen but a sea of heads surging and swaying about—thronged them on every side, eager to catch a glimpse of the tojin, still they were never obtrusive enough to impede the onward course of the party.

An official preceded them on horseback; and one single wave of his fan was enough to make the dense crowds crouch down and bow their heads.

Faces were to be seen surrounding them, some expressive of nothing but astonishment, some of hatred, and others, mostly amongst the women and children, of utter terror.

A different wave of the official's fan, which would have been obeyed as implicitly as the first, might have been the signal for the massacre of the hated and dreaded tojins, and not one of the party could possibly have escaped to tell the tale of treachery.

This was not by any means an unlikely contingency; for though, in our humble opinion, we believe that the Japanese are naturally the reverse of treacherous, still, so imbued are they with a fanatical love of their country, and so inimical to its prosperity do they believe the presence of the foreigner to be, that the end to be attained—namely, to get rid of him—justifies the means, no matter how foul and treacherous.

This feeling does not exist in places where the natives have had the opportunity of seeing how likely to lead to their benefit, instead of to their ruin, is intercourse with foreign nations; but in other parts of the country the assassin and murderer of a tojin is looked upon in the light of a patriot.

Very nearly the same party, at the commencement of this year, was attacked in a street at Kioto—one of the principal cities of Japan, and the residence of the Mikado—by a body of fanatics, who rushed upon them with their terrible two-handed swords, and, before they could be stopped in their murderous work, wounded eight of the mounted escort and guard.

One of these wretched would-be assassins was wounded and secured; and after remaining several days in charge of the medical officer of the Legation, he was handed over to the Japanese authorities, who executed him.

Before his death, he repeatedly expressed the greatest sorrow and contrition for his crime, not in any hopes of reprieve, but because, he said, he had learned how kind and good the tojins were; and had he known this, instead of believing, as he had been taught, that they were more devils than human beings, he would never have made an attempt on their lives.

Our experiences of Japan were by no means confined to Yokohama and its neighbourhood.

For this we were in a great measure indebted to the kindness of the naval officers on the station, who were ever ready to come forward with offers of passages and trips in their ships. In this way nearly every portion accessible to Europeans has been visited by us, and many pleasant days have we passed afloat as the guests of our gallant and hospitable brethren of the sister service.

We hope, wherever these kind friends are,—doubtless now in every portion of the globe,—that they entertain as pleasing recollections of our intercourse as we do.

It was on one of these trips that we became witnesses of how a complete cure for sea-sickness was effected; and, in a spirit of philanthropy, we publish it to the world.

Base indeed is the mortal who, cognizant of a method of lessening any of the evils to which his fellow-creatures are heirs, keeps it locked up in his bosom, and imparts it not for the good of mankind.

Let us not, then, be silent.

How many remedies have been confidently recommended for the cure or alleviation of sea-sickness, and how signally, when they have been adopted, have they failed!

We do not say our treatment is infallible, by any means; but we only state that we can vouch for the success attending it in the particular case we are about to cite.

We were proceeding to one of the northern ports of Japan in one of Her Majesty's ships.

The presence on board of one of the fair daughters of Eve shed, as usual, its refining and softening influence on all around.

Everything had been prepared for her reception with a scrupulous regard to the sensitive susceptibilities of the feminine nature.

Even the ship's dog, whose name we may describe as not being peculiarly fitted for polite circles, was rechristened for the nonce; and the sailors were particularly warned not to call him by his proper—or rather, his improper—title, on pain of having their grog stopped.

Everything, including the sea, went smoothly for the first day; but alas! on the second, our fair voyager succumbed to the dreadful malady, and we missed from the deck her fascinating smile and musical laugh.

Every plan that could be thought of was suggested, but the fair sufferer entreated to be left alone in her misery.

At last, her husband insisted on her coming on deck for fresh air, and she was supported, tottering and feeble, to an arm-chair on the poop.

There she sat, listless and weary, a picture of physical prostration painful to contemplate.

Alas! where is the slightly coquettish air of yesterday? Where is the jaunty little hat which—why, surely that can't be it? Yes; but oh, how unrecognisable as the jaunty little hat of the day before! Resting on the head, so as to obscure completely the vision of one usually—but alas! not now—bright eye, it bears unmistakable traces of having recently occupied a very cramped position between the fair owner's head and the pillow.

The whole figure, generally so natty and trim, surmounted by the battered little hat with its draggled feather, betokens an utter callousness and disregard to appearances.

Who can gainsay the power of sea-sickness, when it can thus crush out for the time the inborn love of admiration implanted in the breast of woman?

Don't think, fair reader, that we speak slightingly of the latter feeling. We find no fault with it—quite the reverse. Without it, where would be those little airs and graces which are so enchanting and captivating? Where would be those bright smiles, those soft glances, those winning ways—where, in short, would be everything which makes you—makes you—what you are?

Weaker and weaker the sufferer became, but she still persistently refused to try any of the many suggested remedies.

At last a brilliant thought struck one of the party, and now we are about to tell the secret, the disclosure of which is to confer a benefit on mankind.

A new medicine bottle was procured from the surgery, and into it a scientifically-mixed "champagne cocktail" was poured by one who had earned for himself an honourable and well-deserved distinction by the manufacture of this insinuating beverage. The bottle, after being filled, had the following direction labelled on it: "To be well shaken before taken. The dose to be repeated at intervals of one hour until relief is procured."

These directions being strictly adhered to on the part of the invalid, we had the pleasure in two hours of witnessing a perfect cure wrought.

The musical laugh once more struck pleasantly on our ears. The battered little hat was pinched and patted into shape, its feather combed, and its position rectified; and this happy state of things lasted for the remainder of the passage.

If the lady in question ever sees this, she will learn for the first time that "the horrid medicine, which, oh dear, she was sure she could never take," and which, after it had been tasted, was "not so nasty after all," was made up by a wild young naval lieutenant in the ward-room, and *not*, as she supposed, by a staid old medical officer in the surgery.

CHAPTER XIV.*

DRAG HUNT BY MOONLIGHT.

"Sic magnis componere parva solebam."

EVEN in this remote corner of the world we try to keep up in some shape or other the taste for sports instilled into us by our fathers in the old country. May it be long ere the force of their few, but honest old precepts, and better still, of their example,—straightgoing and no craning,—loving fair field and no favour,—cease to be felt by their Vagabond Sons! Who does not remember the time when, on one of those perfections of feather-weight hunters—a clever, well-bred pony—he first essayed to follow the governor—who, perchance in the excitement of the chase forgetting for the moment that he is giving his hopeful a lead, rides only for the hounds, till a yawner on the landing side makes him pull up short, and he looks round just in time to see the pony picking his hind legs out, as only a pony can do, and the young 'un scrambling back into his saddle after an agonising interval spent on the neck of his steed?

It is the memory of days like this, and its effects on our tastes and inclinations, that will always help to bear down the monotony, and soften much that is disagreeable in our foreign service.

* Reprinted from *Baily's Magazine.*

It is great presumption on our part thus to inflict our sentiments on our readers; but—had we the pen of a certain Colonel who holds as forward a place over the grassy slopes of Leicestershire as over the less stiffly enclosed fields of fiction, and whom for years we have looked up to with much the same kind of veneration as we can imagine the Greeks in the olden days to have entertained for their poet-warrior, Sophocles—then might we speak on this subject, and each of you would seem to see his own thoughts before him.

We suppose but few of "ours" can be heirs to "ten thousand" a year, or they "would take more care of themselves"—a theory so ably demonstrated to us the other day by Mr. Punch. When we say the other day, we forget that it takes two full months for anything in the shape of newspapers to reach us out here. Certain it is, though, that the suggestion that the next "chasse" should be by moonlight was seized and acted upon; and it was forthwith determined that a Drag should be run, weather and Dame Luna permitting, after dinner on the following guest night; it being expected, and, we think you will agree with us, with good reason, that a convivial evening and the music of the band would exercise a beneficial influence on any who might be wavering between the two rival virtues of valour and discretion, and bring many a doubtful recruit into the ranks.

Full warning of time and place was given to the civilians; and devout prayers were sent up that, on this occasion at least, the goddess of the night would deign to shine forth, and turn black darkness into light. The day preceding the eventful night was not a promising one, high winds alone confining the spiteful malice of the rain to fitful showers, and the sun went below the horizon without having given us even a glimpse of his face.

After dinner a general rush was made to look at the weather, when anything but an encouraging prospect presented itself.

The moon was just rising and struggling hard to peep through the dark masses of rain-cloud that obscured the sky, and rendered it impossible to see more than fifty yards ahead.

Fortunately, however, a strong wind still prevailed; and, as the moon got higher, the heavens began to clear a little, and objects became less obscure.

This raised many a sinking heart; and the good cheer and dry champagne having, as had been anticipated, their full effect on one or two who, when questioned beforehand, had looked the other way and answered, " I don't know; I shall see how I feel," but who now ordered their horses with the air of men determined to do or die, a good muster was expected. Indeed, several who had been foremost in scoffing at what it pleased them to call "a mad frolic," and had been casting forth bad jokes about "moon-struck idiots, &c., &c.—wit which enjoyed at the most but a one-sided appreciation —even these now went so far as to volunteer to "trot out and see what was going on."

Now let us get forward to the meet; and, taking advantage of the occasional bright moments, when the aforesaid goddess, womanlike in her fickleness, lifts her dark veil, and condescends to light up the scene, we will glance around and "take stock" of those already assembled.

There is a "goodish" field out, considering all things.

The Garrison show up well in point of numbers, and stand out in bold relief in the uniform adopted for the occasion, viz., nightgowns and nightcaps, knee-breeches and bare legs.

The moment you look at them, though, you cannot help remarking the absence of any and all that could possibly be classed under the denomination of "the Old Hands." It is curious, but no less true, that, on occasions like the present, they never do turn out.

They must be fully aware at what a dead lock promotion is nowadays, and yet they have not generosity enough to give us the chance of a single step. Most assuredly Her Gracious Majesty cannot complain that her old and tried warriors run any risk of depriving the country of their services! Perhaps if we were *all* field-officers, or, at all events, a grade higher than that of *subaltern*,—an epithet often bestowed on us by the evil-disposed with an air of supreme contempt, not unmixed with an affectation of benign pity,—then should we save our poor mothers much painful anxiety. Is it not possible that a deputation of these much and long suffering angels, acting on this hypothesis, might wait on the "powers that be" (whoever they be, whether at Horse Guards or War Office), and induce them to do something for us? Happy thought! Let it be tried!

To return: how proud should we be to see him who leads us on parade heading us also in the field—cheering us on to follow him, even as he did the gallant lot who swam the Taku ditch in the teeth of its barbarous defenders! He has the reputation, too, of being the owner of a Flyer. However, let us pass on, as we hope he will should this meet his eye.

We miss, too, that dauntless brave, the nearest objects to whose heart are his Queen and Country, and who is never so truly happy as when celebrating those two great anniversaries—the memorable occasion on which he took the shilling and the oath to serve Her Majesty and St. Patrick's day.

To leave the Major, and turn to a minor celebrity,— where is that gallant Captain, well known on the Yokohama turf?—and he, too, hails from the green isle of Erin—one whose manly voice may ofttimes be heard discoursing holy maxims to the unenlightened minds of the naked savage bettoes, making their conscience prick their souls even as does the sharp rowel of his spur their ———. They wear no trousers, gentle reader. However, if we get into personalities, we shall also be getting into hot water; but whoso the cap fitteth, let him put it on, and, as far as we know, he will hardly lose by the transaction.

Turning from those who are not here, let us look at those who are.

From the following descriptions you will not be likely to pick out the writer of this talented chapter. His own portrait is not painted by himself, and thus he need feign no self-flattering mock-modesty; nor, on the other hand, can he indulge his conceit by dubbing himself a hero.

Still, so flattering do some of our artist's remarks appear, that we should fully expect them to be followed by a modest request for the loan of some " ready," did not the state of our finances utterly preclude the possibility of his doing so with any chance of success.

First of all, we note a distinguished staff-officer, who occasionally, when forming part of a brilliant suite (or *suit*, as one thoroughly good sportsman, who would have been hunting the hounds for us to-night, had not the fell climate of China sent him home a sickly invalid, expressed it), has performed a prominent, but unwilling, part in amusing a crowded audience. On field-days his spirited charger takes the first opportunity of occupying what he evidently looks upon as his proper place, and pushing himself alongside the Commandant's venerable quadruped, much to the perturbation of their respective riders, no power on earth will induce him to quit his position. A good rider, though, is the Aide, and especially good is he in a two-mile race if he has got a horse under him that can stay. Such a one had he once, and his name was Sea-gull.

Alas! it would grieve his fond parent's heart if she were to see him now! That worn-out night-shirt is but a fair specimen of the present state of the kit, which her thoughtful care had brought almost to perfection when the "Holy Boys" went first on foreign service.

Here is one, too, whom a long sojourn amongst the barbarians has affected strongly, but in a different way. Once an exquisite of the first water, he has gone down in the social scale, and grown rougher and coarser under what he has suffered, till here we find him, got up like a mountebank, about to ride to a drag by moonlight; those delicate lower limbs that it was once a pride to King Poole to show off to advantage, now actually exposed to the gaze of the vulgar, and to what is perhaps but little less disagreeable to his feelings—the bites of mosquitoes. All that now remain of his former grandeur are his flowing whiskers, and a strong smell of "the most delicious 'air oil."

In grateful contrast to the woeful habiliments of our last friend comes out the befrilled and embroidered garment of Belleville.

A cloud is passing over the moon.

Never mind! the Fenian's fiery cranium blazes out the more conspicuously in the darkness. Not a bad beacon to follow, either, for his heart is in the right place, and he will push along close to the hounds, or wherever the white China pony, who has about as much mouth as a tree, chooses to take him.

Then there is the hard-riding little medico, who objects extremely to being balked at his fences, hurling at the unfortunate culprit who has been guilty of such an act the awful, but almost unintelligible, expletive, "You *cwothed* me, thir!"

He bestrides a would-be steeple-chaser, rejoicing in the name of Pluck, so called on the *lucus à non lucendo* principle, for a more thorough cur never existed.

A little on the left, and in conscious superiority holding himself somewhat aloof from the common herd, stands the Pig. His noble proportions strike the eye at once. That unfortunate off-fore, though, has cost Tweeker and his groom many an anxious consultation. No pains have been spared to bring him out fit to-night; and, before starting, the doubtful limb was carefully bathed for seventeen minutes in one pint of hot water and two of cold. Much wholesome discipline is exercised in that stable; and the Pig knows right well that, should he misbehave himself to-night, his reward will be "a good licking" and "a dose of physic."

Before leaving the Garrison we must notice one more of its representatives.

A member of a Scotch regiment, Podgy has only lately arrived in Japan, and says he hardly understands the "dwops of this countwy" yet. We hope he may not buy his experience too dearly.

Now let us glance at the civilians. They have turned out in very fair numbers; but we can only see four who really look like going. Of the remainder, some mean to await the finish of the drag, which will be close to the meet; others, feeling safer in trusting to their own legs than those of their quadrupeds, intend to follow on foot. These four, though, are likely to hold their own. That one in the neat breeches and boots has long been known at Shanghai, and, if his reputation be a true one, there are but few amateur jocks in this part of the world who can beat him.

De Lis let us call him. Many will recognise him under that name. And his companion—who is he?

Why, surely that is Jorrocks personified! Have not that jolly round red face and good-humoured countenance been familiar to us for years? Yes; so striking is the likeness that he might have been the original model for poor Leech's pencil, dressed as he is, too, in pink and hunting cap. Jorrocks, though, if we remember right, used to wear a low-crowned, broad-brimmed beaver.

Another of the four is a resident of Yokohama, and he will try hard to *Cope* with the strangers, though he suffers terribly from *Corns*—so much so that at the very sound of the word he has been known to shake like an *Aspen all* over.

We have just time to see that a few more men on horseback, and a good many on foot—a great proportion of both being still in dining costume—make up the meet, when a rate and the crack of a whip—for in the Yokohama Hunt they act on the principle that noise covers a multitude of sins—announce the approach of the hounds, and presently the forms of two horsemen loom through the uncertain moonlight.

They are considerably behind their time; for when about half-way to the rendezvous, they crossed the fresh trail of a fox, and breaking away, rattled him about the hills, making the silent woods ring with their melody. It was not till their two attendants had holloaed themselves hoarse that they succeeded in getting the truants back, and then with the loss of a couple and a half.

But how is this? Where is our worthy master?

Let me answer your question with another. Think you that if you or we were blessed (as a rule, *is it* a blessing?) with a help-meet for us, that she would allow us to be risking our necks—born to bear meekly the conjugal yoke—while she lies waiting for us to be brought home on a shutter? Moreover, *here* she would scarcely have even this poor consolation, for the country-people have not yet arrived at an appreciation of the luxury of shutters, though civilisation has already made so much progress that on a recent occasion an unhappy friend of ours succeeded in getting himself conveyed home in a *wheelbarrow*, insisting all the while that

" that confounded leader *would* keep looking him in the face!"

We miss, too, our indefatigable first whip, with his ready smile and his familiar "Yaup, yaup!"

It is certainly not faint heart that keeps Mulvey away to-night, else would he not so often have won fair lady. To-morrow he will lark over some of the biggest jumps in the line; nay, he *may* even try a "header" down "Solon's Success!"*

Who, then, are bringing up the pack?

First, let us take him on the big but rather leggy-looking black.

Even in his present costume there is a decided "hossey" look about him, as he sits easy and at home in his saddle. His trim little whiskers cut off square with the corners of his mouth, and round close-cropped head, would admirably become one of those gentry peculiar to the great stables in the shires, whose only ostensible occupation, after attending to their own personal comfort and appearance, would seem to consist in "looking out two to send on for the guv'nor to-morrow."

Ruff's "Racing Calendar" and Baily's "Guide to the Turf" have stood to him much in the light—though hardly, we will hope, in the place—of Bible and Prayer-book since he first learnt to read; and his highest ambition in life is to be able to tell you without hesitation the name of the grandam of the horse that ran third for

---

* Supposed to be the biggest and most trying jump in the neighbouring country, being an overhanging drop of fully twelve feet in height. It is so called from the fact of its having been first negotiated by a pony called Solon.

the Chester Cup in such-and-such a year, or who rode that filly by Orlando in her maiden race.

It is an edifying and instructive study to watch him, on the arrival of each mail, clutch at "Bell," and choosing some quiet corner, settle himself down to enjoy it. He eats not, neither does he drink, till every word of its contents is mastered; when he rises with a weary sigh, like a boy who has feasted on plum-pudding till he can stow away no more, then spits and begets himself to his ordinary vocations.

If you want a pilot to-night, you cannot do better than choose little B. How he came by that *sobriquet* is not generally known. Some say that in the early part of his education he had the greatest difficulty in mastering his A B C, and for a long time stuck half-way. It may be so; but we fancy we have heard another story which, if true, would make him out to be an object of intense admiration and endearment to the British soldier.

The sight of the black reminds one of the absence of his late owner, who so often steered old Pericles to victory. A member of a *scientific* corps, Bones' great aim and business is to master the *science of riding;* and, as far as steeple-chasing is concerned, we fancy he has succeeded pretty well.

Tough as leather and full of pluck and keenness, he would have been the first to promote a lark of this kind. An accident, however, prevents his appearing on the scene to-night; and B., who is glad of the mount, has been delegated to represent him on Pericles.

There is only one more to be "told off," and then we will lay the hounds on, or the scent will be cold. Him, we mean, on the chestnut, whose flowing mane and tail give him the appearance of a lady's horse rather than of the sort of animal for this rough-and-tumble country. Still, when the hounds are running, you will see Iona going as strong as a little elephant, and the whole heart and soul of "the Child"—under this *nom de guerre* many will recollect his bare-faced cheek (N.B. this is a goak)—in the fun.

Rather a good specimen of a child, you will think, as there is about six feet of him, and every bit as hard as nails, from his recent training for the Yokohama Spring Meeting. His old governor, of whom, as a true sportsman, he is justly proud, has evidently brought him up on the principle of "sparing the (Nim)rod and spoiling the 'Child;'" not that he seems to have done that altogether to the exclusion of other things, for the Child occasionally mounts the winged steed, and sitting down on old Pegasus, sends him along with as good a will as he does the chestnut, in both cases, perhaps, occasionally coming to grief in trying too big a leap.

We are all here now, so let us make a start before that big black cloud gets over the moon.

A lantern has been hung up on the top of a building named as the trysting-place, and will serve as a beacon to guide us in at the finish. The above building is a straggling Japanese house, built in the usual way of wood and paper, and aspires—so proclaims a large white board over the entrance—to the title of COFFEE-SHOP. A rather good-looking moosmi does the honours of the establishment, which, as far as one can perceive, consists of about a dozen old bottles arranged on a shelf in company with five or six cups and saucers, a long table, and two wooden benches. What honours there are to do we cannot guess. That they do not sell coffee we know; for in a moment of weakness we once asked for some on our way out for an early ride, when we were answered by a merry cackle and a "no got." Certain it is, though, that it is a favourite resort for the soldiers at all hours.

"Well, come along; we must idle no longer; so put 'em down to the left, it was somewhere about there that the drag should have started."

A cast of a couple of hundred yards in this direction produces no result beyond the discovery that it is very blind going; for already there are several scrambles, but no falls. We then proceed to try on round to the right.

The little fellows scatter themselves well and work hard, in hopes of getting hold of something. "Give 'em time; we shall hit it off directly. Look out! that is an awkward little drop;" and the words are scarcely out of our mouth when we hear that delicious identical "'Old Hup"—you all remember it?—and looking round we see Jorrocks's burly form flying over the head of his steed, himself wallowing in the plough. It would want a strangely strong and straight pair of fore-legs to bear up against the weight of fifteen honest stone when landing from the top of a five-foot bank. Never mind; it is soft falling, and no one will be able to see to-night that the pink has been dirtied. Our obese friend picks himself up apparently none the worse; and, after muttering an incantation over his pony's eyes, that he possibly imagines may have some effect in making him see better in the dark, rolls himself into the saddle. This little catastrophe will, we hope, teach the bay to be careful, and in future to creep a little more at his drops.

A few more jumps enable the ponies to get the measure of their leaps better, and they soon begin to calculate their distance and take off almost as surely as in the daytime.

Now old Comus feathers a bit with his unnaturally big stern; at the same moment Wonder drops his nose and starts off in that dot-and-go-one, hesitating sort of canter that seems to be the natural pace of a hound during the first few seconds of a find, when, as it were, fearful of over-precipitancy, he still cannot repress the thrill of delight that urges him on. Another moment and they close up together and are off, throwing their tongues as merry as school-girls. The moon shines out beautifully just now, and we may shove along safely.

One advantage of drag-hunting—at all events on our limited scale—is that every one gets a fair start. We go away at a good pace over the road and up the hill, and by the time a few enclosures and their attendant obstacles have been crossed, the field begins to spread a little.

On the right is B. with Pericles, evidently just enjoying himself; and immediately inside him is De Lis, going as straight and cool as if he knew the country perfectly, whereas he has never crossed a yard of it even by daylight. Lying close up are the Child and another night-shirt, whom we will call Fish, well carried by the winner of the Ladies' Purse at the late meeting.

On the left the Aide's mouthless brute is tearing ahead almost on the top of the hounds. Holloa! he is down! No; a strong haul has pulled him off his head again, though the amount of mud he carries in his nostrils ought to steady him a little. The Fenian is flashing along like a meteor, and Belleville is going the pace as if he were on a well-waxed floor with the band playing the Hilda, his long whiskers flowing over his shoulders like the pennants of a man-of-war. Poor Jorrocks is beginning to lag a little, and is already bambooing his steed lustily. This "throw up" will help him. No; a quick turn to the left and they are off again, running nearly parallel to the road.

Now the pace becomes really good. The ground is awfully deep, but we *must* go to keep 'em in sight; so catching fast hold of his head, we cram along.

Down a gentle incline, in which all the jumps are drops, on to a small extent of level bottom, where a small "grip," difficult to see, causes several stumbles, and turns the "flat-racer" a complete somersault. Fish sticks tenaciously to the bridle, till, the cheek-strap breaking, it is left in his hand, when he throws it and the "curse of Cromwell" after his departing steed. The pony takes advantage of his liberty to do a little hunting on his own account, only the object he chooses for his pursuit is the unfortunate Pig, who, going along well within himself, wists not of his danger till of a sudden he feels his tail gripped as in a vice. The pain and fright extort an agonised scream from him, and after trying in vain to rid himself of his tormentor by kicking and plunging, he bounds off frantically, dragging the other, nothing loth, after him.

As we said before, the pace at this moment is quite as good as we care about; but fast as it is, the Pig tears along faster. Tweeker evidently feels the horror of the position quite as much as the more immediate sufferer; and as he passes us in his mad career—with his terror-stricken countenance looking still more ghastly in the moonlight, his anguished gaze turned behind him, and his flowing white garment streaming in the wind—we are irresistibly reminded of Tam O'Shanter and his nocturnal ride. He lashes round with his whip in the vain hope of loosening that bull-dog hold. As well might the oft-quoted horseman expect to free himself thus from *atra cura* when she has once taken her seat behind him; for, beyond a tighter clenching of the relentless jaws, not the slightest effect is produced. At last, in sheer despair, he drives the spurs deep into the sides of the Pig, and the two disappear down a steep place and are seen no more.

By this time we are rising the opposite hill, and turning a little to the left, circle the brow for some distance. Here they overrun the scent and give us a moment to breathe, till Jealousy—one of the missing couple and a half, but who has now come up again—lifts her silvery voice, and dashes straight down the hill, through a cluster of trees veiling two awkward-looking drops.

The Aide charges boldly at the first with the courage of Quintus Curtius; but his animal is apparently not endowed with the same desire for self-immolation as the steed of that bold Roman, for he refuses resolutely.

"Que diable!" exclaims his rider, for from long practice he speaks French like a native, though the polished gesticulation with which he usually enhances the charm of his well-turned phrases must, for obvious reasons, be dispensed with on this occasion. So saying, he turns him round, and gets down at a second attempt. Meantime the Fenian and the Child have dived down, into the darkness, and the others follow, all feeling much the same sensation as one experiences on entering after dark into a room with whose interior arrangements one is totally unacquainted.

On reaching the bottom the hounds veer off suddenly to the right, just avoiding a narrow little stream, which would inevitably have proved a floorer to most, if not all, of those out. Well do we know that treacherous little brook, and to our cost! Feasible-looking enough, there is a deep boggy landing in which few horses can keep their legs.

Along the valley the hunting is slow and uncertain, and the field collect again, allowing even the runners to get on better terms. At last it becomes evident that if we mean to have any more fun we must do something for ourselves; so we throw 'em forward, and in another moment they hit it off and are going like smoke.

By Jove! this is awkward! They have breasted the hill, and on a sudden we find ourselves in a regular trap.

The moon has taken refuge behind a cloud, and objects are now disagreeably obscured. One can just distinguish a huge black-looking bank, rising round three sides of the enclosure, the only exit from which appears to be by the way we entered. It may be like riding at the walls of the Bastile, for all we know; but at any rate it won't do to stop here, and we ram the spurs in, and shove at it, in hopes there may be some little slope to give us a foothold. The Aide tries it in front; but he hasn't got pace enough on, and, after an ineffectual struggle, horse and man roll back together. Pericles attempts it with better success; though, as he gets his fore-legs on the top, and balances himself for a final effort, it seems any odds on his following suit. The strong little white China pony scrambles up after, and two others take it to the left, where it happens to be considerably lower, though perhaps more perpendicular.

The men on foot shout "Well done!"—for to them, standing above, it looks little less than like jumping out of a dungeon.

"Forrard" again, as we get to the hounds. Alas! we need not hurry ourselves, for from this point we can only potter along slowly. It is evident that the scent has been badly laid; and this we hardly wonder at afterwards, when, on our return, we find the man who ran the drag, and was to have waited at the finish to give the hounds a "worry," sitting in a kitchen, and soaking in helpless imbecility over his beer.

All that can be done now is to pick up a cold scent, which leads us back in the direction of the coffee-shop. Still an occasional "stiff 'un" is encountered, which in the present dim light is anything but easy to negotiate.

The proceedings are also varied by the performance of one of those who patronised the sport on foot, which, if gratifying to the spectators, could hardly have been so to himself.

The ponies will see their way pretty clearly when the light is so bad that you can perceive nothing but a dim waste before you. In this way our friend knew not that he was approaching a steep descent till he found himself flying through the air. He opened his mouth to entreat some one to stop him; but by this time he had plunged into a soft, deep bed, and all we could hear was a half-choked spluttering. "*Pooh, pooh!* he can't be hurt," was all the consolation he received.

Very nice had he looked when he left the dinner-table —the peach-bloom tint just deepened on his cheek; his embroidered shirt-front without a crease; and an ardent admiration of sport of any description, but more especially in the shape of drag-hunting by moonlight, suddenly developed in his bosom. Hardly so pleasant a companion did he appear an hour or two after. His own mother would scarcely have known him; and if she had, we doubt very much whether she would have remained in the same room with him.

One of the mounted party also creates some little diversion. The white China pony, of whom we have spoken two or three times before, is seized with a sudden idea that the fun is getting slow, and accordingly he pokes his head down and carries his rider, *nolens volens*, into a thick wood, which clothes an almost precipitous descent into the valley beneath. A shrill brogue, proclaiming "Be Gorra! he is off now!" is the last we hear of the Fenian as he disappears to meet his fate like a man. We needn't stop for him; he is sure to turn up again shortly. He is used to such little eccentricities on the part of his steed, and is prepared for every emergency.

At last we come in sight of the lantern on the coffee-shop, at the distance of about a mile; and leaving the hounds, who are now doing little or nothing, we start for a "scurry" in. By this time the moon again gives a better light, and each man taking his own line, there is a regular race for it. A cropper or two on the way, but no one hurt, and in a few more minutes we have arrived at the place we started from.

You ask, "Who got the best of the run in?" Well,

perhaps the Aide did; but he owns, like an honest man, that he "couldn't turn the brute's head off that path for the last few hundred yards;" and as we look up at the coloured engraving which hangs on the wall before us as we write—it is No. 1 of Ackerman's good old sporting series, entitled "The Grand Leicestershire Steeplechase, March 12th, 1829"—we see old Nimrod, in the queer high "stick-ups"* and enormous white choker of the period, reading out, "Any one opening a gate, going more than a hundred yards along a road, &c., &c., to be distanced."

Next in order are the chestnut with the mane, the China pony and the light weight—we told you he would soon be "all there" again,—and Pericles, with two or three others close up.

After a short halt to collect stragglers, we all adjourn to the Camp, where, over anchovy toast and etceteras, we discuss the events of the run.

One more word: Mr. Jorrocks *was* a little shaken by his fall; but he is not a bit discouraged, and still swears "there is no sport like 'unting, and no 'ounds like those of the Yokohama 'Unt."

* * * * * *

This Drag Hunt by Moonlight was pronounced such a success, and produced so much amusement, that another was organised a month or two later, which went off as well as its predecessor. Of this we merely subjoin the following poetical account—also by our old friend Abdul:—

---

* This was written before the re-introduction of the present cauliflower leaves.

> "I pedes quo te rapiunt et auræ
> Dum favet nox . . . . ."

'Twas at her full, the winter moon
  On Yokohama shining;
And *full*, as well, were all the lun-
  Atics, for they'd been dining.

So being under influence
  Of Bacchus and Diana,
With brains not overcharged with sense,
  But fumes of mild Havanah,

Each one felt ready for the sport
  For which they were preparing,
Which must be fishing, for, in short,
  'Twas hunting a red herring.

The fish was gone, the *meet* came on;
  The coffee-shop being chosen
As rendezvous; and every one,
  In night-shirt, came half frozen.

The pack of dogs was rather small
  In numbers and in breeding;
But this fact mattered not at all
  With liberal aniseeding.

So off they go, the echo rings
  With shouts. No one is thinking
That drops at night are dangerous things,
  For they've a drop been drinking.

I don't mean they'd a drop too much,—
  Let me not be mistaken,—
But only just a *little* touch
  Of jumping powder taken.

Some on their heads their nightcaps drew,
  And some they wore bell toppers;
And as the crops they gallop'd through,
  They naturally had croppers.

First of the train of horsemen white
  (He's never lost I own), a
Boy as wild as elfin sprite,
  Spins onward on Iona.*

---

* The Child.

DRAG HUNT BY MOONLIGHT.

A little cove* who rode a *hoss*,
   Tom Thumb, had five mishaps there;
Another nag play'd *Pitch* and *Toss*
   With the gentlemanly sapper.

Upon Black Prince a rider sat
   Who in for every sport went,
And always showed himself thereat
   A model of deportment.

A little nag (they called him Eggs),
   He would have gallop'd faster,
But for the weight, so lost his legs,
   And then he lost his master.†

But what's this dragging on the ground?
   I surely must be erring;
'Tis red, but 'tis too large and round,—
   It *can't* be the red herring.

'Tis Mister Jorrocks, so they say,
   Has tumbled off his racer,
The sporting gent that's from Shanghae,
   The mighty steeple-chaser.

Look out ahead, the paddy's near,
   Or you will soon be trouble in:
The Paddies are most dangerous here,
   Just as they are in Dublin.

There's one‡ with brilliant head (*outside*),
   Though, must not be forgotten,
Who cares not if the ditch be wide,
   Or if the banks be rotten.

No check on banks he shows until
   The field is getting thinnish,
When he presents the little Bill,
   The second at the finish.

Others were there; but why should I
   Go on the field describing,
Or give a separate history
   Of all the feats of riding?

---

* B.   † Belleville.   ‡ Fenian.

Some kept their seats in saddles light,
  Though others—'twas unlucky—
Show'd here and there too much moonlight;
  But all, at least, rode plucky.

The sport being over, each one owns
  A most successful meeting;
And though there were no broken bones,
  They had some grill'd for eating.

CHAPTER XV.

THE WRESTLERS.

"Come and have tiffin with me!" said Charley Pope, as he met three of "ours" one morning strolling through the Settlement; "and we will go and see the Wrestlers afterwards."

There happened to be a gathering of these men at Yokohama at the time; and as two of the three addressed had not yet seen an exhibition of the kind, it required very little persuasion to induce them to accept the offer. They were soon, therefore, seated round Pope's hospitable table, after having been treated, as a kind of necessary preliminary, to a very pleasant mixture—yclept *a cocktail*—first introduced into China and Japan by the Americans, but adopted and maintained in its present position "as an indispensable anteprandial appetiser" (*sic* a Yankee friend) by the foreign community generally. To those of our readers who have come across it in their travels, there is no need to explain what it is; and to those who have not, we can only say, Take the first opportunity of making a practical acquaintance with it.

After tiffin, the three referred to, viz., the Aide, Belleville, and the Child, accompanied Pope, A—— (his fellow "business-man"), and two or three others to the scene of the wrestling—wading, in their long boots, ankle deep through the sea of mud, into which the rainy season always turns the settlement of Yokohama.

A quarter of an hour's walk brought them to an immense amphitheatre built of bamboo, and just sufficiently covered to keep out the sun and rain. Flag-staffs rose above it at intervals, bearing banners on which were written the names of the chief wrestlers, their prowess, &c., &c.

Having paid an ichiboo each,—being considered, as foreigners, to be fair game, and consequently charged six times the entrance for a Nippon,—they were admitted, and ushered into good places among the raised seats.

The performance had already commenced, and they found that Bobby, Jolly, and two or three others had also put in an appearance.

The arrangement of the inside of the amphitheatre was very much like that of a circus at home.

Round the outer circle were seats raised in tiers one above the other. Below this was an inner circle—the pit, in fact—with one side kept clear for the wrestlers to dress and undress, sponge themselves between each round, &c.; while in the centre of all was a raised mound of earth, on the top of which was a round space, some fifteen feet across, where the wrestling took place.

As they entered, two burly fellows had just stepped into the arena, and were walking round,—each with the swagger of a cock on his own dunghill,—stretching their arms and legs, and showing their muscle to an admiring and applauding crowd, who, with eager, excited faces, were backing their fancy, and shouting as loudly and determinedly as the ring men on a Derby day.

They were very tall for Japanese—one of the two being

fully six feet high—and enormously fat, with huge bellies, but sadly deficient in real hard muscle. Stripped to a cloth twisted round their waists, you could see plainly the masses of blubber that hung loosely about them. This is to be accounted for by the fact that weight is the greatest possible desideratum in their principles of wrestling, inasmuch as being pushed out of the ring counts as a fall; and, in consequence of the space being so narrow, as a rule not more than one tussle out of every three produces a fair back-fall.

Having swelled about to their satisfaction, each took a pinch of salt from a cup handed to him, received a final sponging over from his attendant, and then proceeded to *challenge*.

This consisted in placing a hand on each thigh, just above the knee; then, stooping slightly, lifting each leg in turn, at the same time raising the hand, and replacing it with a loud smack, as the foot came sharply to the ground.

In this way they went on slowly and deliberately in front of each other for about a minute. Then, keeping their hands still on their thighs, they squatted on their heels face to face, and about a foot apart.

Standing just outside the ring was the umpire, who also acted the part of herald, proclaiming in a loud voice, as each pair of combatants appeared, their names, place of birth and residence, previous performances, &c. He was a rather showily-dressed individual, and carried a rod in his hand, with which to signal to those engaged to stop or go on, or to pronounce a fall.

The men are supposed to begin by mutual agreement; and if the umpire considers that they have started with an equal chance, he signs to them to continue; if not, he stops them, and they resume their position.

The match that our friends were about to witness was evidently one which excited much more interest than common. The two wrestlers were the champions of their respective districts; and, as both were strongly represented among the spectators, the house seemed to divide itself into two parties, and the betting was spirited in the extreme.

After gazing on each other for some time, one of them springs up; but, having anticipated his adversary, the umpire's wand interposes, and they both rise to walk round the ring, refresh themselves with another pinch of salt, rinse their mouths out with water, and go through the challenging process as before.

These false starts, with the subsequent swaggering, are gone through two or three times, until it becomes rather wearisome. But at length they make up their minds to business, and buckle to in earnest, giving forth short, quick shouts as they struggle for a grip. The chief aim of each, though, in addition to obtaining and preventing a hold, is to push the other beyond the confines of the circle, and they shove and butt at each other for some time before getting together. At last they are locked in a close grasp; and as they sway backwards and forwards, round and round, the party spirit becomes uproarious, and the pit shout lustily to their champions.

For a time it looks as if the bigger man will force the other down by sheer weight and strength; and at one moment he has all but got him in his power, when, with a quick effort, the latter releases himself, throws his weight in with a sudden push, and his adversary's foot goes beyond the ring.

The unexpected turn in the tide of battle is received with the most enthusiastic applause from his party, though the foreigners would naturally have preferred to see the fall fairly contested according to their own received ideas of wrestling.

Some time is consumed in preparing for the next bout; but when both are ready, after the preliminary "challenge," they settle down almost immediately to their work, and quickly getting a mutual grip, a good struggle results in the larger man "grassing" his former conqueror with a fair cross buttock, amid the encouraging cheers of his friends, who back him with renewed confidence.

The other gets up smiling, and his admirers are no less sanguine of success.

The third being the deciding fall, they take even longer than before in their preparations, and it is not until the second call to time by the umpire that they again take their places in the arena.

The excitement is now tremendous; and it seems as if, whichever man is victorious, the whole affair will end in a free fight.

The party feeling is almost contagious, and the members of the group of foreigners are backing their opinion freely among themselves. Bobby, as is but right, puts his five dollars on the smaller champion; and, to judge by appearances, the chances are slightly in his favour, for the other is blowing rather heavily.

This time they observe the greatest caution in opening the ball, and it is not until after two false attempts that they are up together, and the umpire bids them "Go on."

Their blood is now thoroughly up, and they close at once without shouting, for neither can afford to lose any breath. Twisting and writhing, they struggle from side to side—first one obtaining a momentary advantage, then the other. Now the taller one all but succeeds in repeating the cross buttock of the previous round ; now, in his turn, he is all but tripped off his legs ; and now, without relaxing their grasp, they stand motionless for some seconds.

The heavy weight, though, is too fat to last, and each effort blows him more and more, till his wirier antagonist, getting a good under-grip, doubles him over his leg ; and the giant staggers and falls, the other on the top of him.

At this juncture it seems as if one half of the assembled multitude had gone mad. Yelling, dancing, and singing, they testify their joy in the wildest conceivable way. Scores of coats, *obis* (the long silk girdle that the Japanese of both sexes wind round their waists), and shoes are cast in to the conqueror—one man actually stripping himself to his waistcloth to swell the list of gifts.

The victorious hero himself seems intoxicated with his success, struts about the ring, "challenging" fiercely an imaginary adversary, slapping his thighs, arms, and breasts, and behaving altogether like the barn-door warrior before alluded to when he returns triumphant from the fray.

When Bobby, with his accustomed assurance, strolled into the magic circle, to feel him over as he would have done a horse, he seemed highly flattered by the attention, though still more pleased by the present of an ichiboo, which accompanied the inspection.

Several more matches then took place—none of them, though, exciting anything like the same interest as the one described, though they afforded opportunity for enterprising speculators—both among the Japanese and foreigners—to risk their money.

After the active part of the performance was finished, a grand procession was formed of all the wrestlers, who, with hair carefully dressed, bodies cleaned and oiled, and with handsome embroidered silk aprons of various colours round their loins, as in the accompanying photograph, paraded in a body round the inner circle.

We—for, incorporating ourselves with those of the Holy Boys present, we will again use the first person in speaking of their further movements—we now sought out the head man of the party, and, by the aid of an interpreter, invited him to come up to Camp, and bring two or three of his friends with him.

This was done with the view of getting them to try a fall with some of "ours;" and the unsuspecting men, thinking themselves highly complimented, fell readily into the snare, and promised to come the next day.

On emerging into the street we found a lot of "kangoes"—the palanquins of the country—standing for hire; and it was proposed and carried that we should save our legs by giving them a trial.

These kangoes are anything but suited to the convenience of foreigners, though the Japanese, who squat in them with their legs under them, seem to ride very comfortably. They consist of a mere seat with a back and cover, made of the ever-useful bamboo, and slung on a single pole, each end of which is carried on the shoulder of a coolie. The subjoined illustration will give not only a good idea of what a kango is, but also of the way in which a fair native accommodates herself to it.

Bobby managed to tuck his little legs into it pretty well; and, as he puffed contentedly at his cigar, vowed he was never more comfortable in his life.

Jolly and Belleville—after several ineffectual efforts to stow themselves into the "cramped-up concern"— gave up the attempt in disgust, and preferred to walk home through the mud.

The Aide and the Child made the best of a bad job, and were carried along, with their legs dangling one on either side.

Every two or three hundred yards the bearers would stop, place a stick under their respective ends of the pole, and change shoulders, at the imminent risk—so it seemed to their terrified burdens—of dropping the kango bodily into the mud.

"Holloa! mati! mati! (stop! stop!) Here's a bath-house. Let's go in and have a look!"

Accordingly, the whole party, leaving their kangoes to await their return, entered a house from which voluble chattering and clouds of steam were issuing.

Do not, we pray you, gentle reader, at this point close the book in alarm! We are really not about to enter into minute details of what we saw.

You have probably read and heard often of a Japanese bath-house, and of the "disgustingly immoral practice of men and women bathing together;" but allow us to assert, without any reservation, that there is nothing whatever immoral about it.

We do not mean to say for a moment that such a custom might with advantage *be introduced at home*, and

become in time to be looked upon as no breach of delicacy —albeit it might lead to a desirable fondness for the bath among the youth of both sexes; and, after all, the line is but a narrow one between it and the style of sea-bathing at Boulogne and elsewhere. We dare say no more on this subject, or we might draw down the wrath of every guardian paterfamilias, and every prim mater*ditto*, on our irreverent heads.

Believe us, the Japanese see no more harm in taking their baths than their meals in company; and, as regards the latter, we know that the men of some Oriental nations would never dream of sitting down to eat with women.

Nor did our entrance in any way disturb the occupation of those engaged in their ablutions; for, after just noticing the arrival of the "tojins," they went on without paying any further attention to our presence.

Young men and maidens, old men and children, were mixed up promiscuously in the scene before us, each with a small tub of hot water before him or her, with which they employed themselves before entering the general bath. *Jam satis*—suffice it to say that you go away so thoroughly impressed with the entire absence of anything approaching to the sensational, or even the picturesque, in this incongruous mixture of youth and age, beauty and deformity, that a second visit is seldom desired.

The next morning half-a-dozen of the wrestlers made their way up to Camp, and, after being plied with cherry-brandy,—liqueurs being the particular fancy of both Chinese and Japanese,—submitted willingly to, indeed evinced great pride in, being examined.

On being asked if they would wrestle with some of

those present, they consulted together with much laughter, —evidently in derision at the temerity of the untaught foreigners, who dared enter into the field with them,—but made no objection to the proposition.

Taking them on to the lawn, the Child, as being one of the youngest, and in pretty good fettle, was told off to represent the "tojins;" and, throwing off his coat, he prepared to do battle for his cause, strutting about and "challenging" vigorously, to their intense amusement.

Their chief signed carelessly to one of his subordinates to go and demolish the rash foreigner; and the man advanced to do his bidding, without taking the trouble to strip.

Both he and his associates seemed much surprised when the other, wasting no time in preliminaries, rushed in, and getting a good hold, gave him the back-heel almost before he was aware of the attack. He appeared somewhat disconcerted as he rose; and the champion of the party was directed to strip, and avenge the defeat of his comrade.

The Child, too, seeing that they meant to pursue matters in earnest, took the precaution of doffing everything to the waist, so as to give away no advantage with regard to obtaining a grip.

Seeing the two together as they stretched and "challenged" in front of each other—for the "young 'un" went through every form carefully—it seemed any odds on the Japanese. Standing, as near as possible, the same height, the professional must have weighed more than half as much again as his whiter-skinned opponent, whose hard training (for he was even now almost wound up for riding) had left hardly an ounce of flesh on his body.

Squatting down, they eyed each other for some seconds—the one determined to reverse the result of the last encounter, while the other felt fully the necessity of keeping out of any position in which his burly antagonist could bring his great weight to bear.

Now they are up and at work; the native shouting lustily, and endeavouring, while he contrives to ward off his opponent's first attempt at getting a grip, to knock him over by sudden rushes. In one of these his tough head comes in contact with the Child's nose, causing him to see stars painfully, and slightly raising his dander.

From this kind of "butting" the ears of a professional wrestler will be found, on examination, to be battered down to shapeless masses of gristle.

For some while the Englishman is baffled in all his efforts to grapple with advantage—the slippery, greasy flesh offering nothing tangible to his grasp; however, he has got wind and condition on his side, and can afford to bide his time. At last he gets within his adversary's guard, and succeeds in slipping his arms round the bulky waist he can just clasp. At first this seems likely to avail him but little; for his enormous opponent raises him clean off his legs, and the unfortunate Child remains hugged in unsavoury embrace up to the portly stomach. Still, his long legs are free; and he resists all attempts to put him down, though compressed as in the arms of a bear.

"The fellow certainly did squeeze me precious hard," he said afterwards, "but I wouldn't have minded that, if he hadn't smelt so strong of his infernal oil."

Once set down again, he adopts the offensive in his

turn; and pressing his chin on the other's chest, throws all his strength into a haul at the backbone.

Now does the metal forged by good beef and beer tell against the soft untempered stuff induced by rice and *saki*. To his astonishment he feels the huge back gradually yield to his pressure; and a slight twist with the heel is all that is required to bring the weighty champion to the ground, to the surprise of his own party and the delight of the military.

The latter crowd round the Child, who is going through a fac-simile of the triumphal performance of the conqueror in the arena of yesterday, and—swelling with conceit—is "challenging" and swaggering with all his might. They feel his arms and legs—expressing their wonder loudly that there should be strength enough in those almost fleshless members to overthrow a trained wrestler and a Nippon!

Bobby now expresses his desire to have a "wire in" with one of them; and the smallest—but, to all appearance, the toughest and most muscular—of their number is chosen to try conclusions with him.

Bobby himself is as strong as a bull-terrier, and active in proportion.

The pair are well matched; a capital struggle ensues; and the first two falls are undecided—both being down, side by side. As before, condition at last prevails; and at the third attempt Bobby throws his man well.

After this one of the soldiers came up, and asked to be allowed to try his skill against the Nippons; and the last wrestler declared himself willing to accept the challenge. Time having been allowed him to recover his wind, he prepared to commence, as usual, by squatting down in front of his antagonist. The soldier, however, not understanding that this was but a preliminary position, and not the attitude of attack, rushed at him, picked him off the ground as he sat, and threw the astonished native over his head. He put up with this—to him—extraordinary proceeding with wonderful good temper, but took care not to give the chance a second time.

When they close, the European, though a stout, powerful fellow, proved not to be quick enough for his practised assailant, and had to succumb.

The same fate awaited two or three others of our men, who, being chiefly Irish, are, though formidable fellows in a row, not much skilled in the art of wrestling. Such a thing as a West Countryman there is not in the regiment, or he would no doubt have been able to give a better account of men so inferior to a trained Englishman in real power and muscle.

Our friends were now treated to more refreshment, and took their departure with many bows and polite speeches, evidently carrying away with them a more respectful opinion of the "tojins" than they had hitherto possessed.

Wrestling is a very popular amusement all over Japan, and is practised universally throughout the country.

Curiously enough, just as in the churchyards of most villages in the south and west of England a space used to be set apart in which the young men could practise the exercises of wrestling, backsword, and quarter-staff, so in Japan, wherever a village or district can boast of a temple, a portion of its grounds is devoted to the promotion of single-stick (with a heavy bamboo to represent the two-handed sword) and of wrestling.

'Twas but the other day we were discoursing on this very subject with Abdul, who is a native of Somersetshire, and, as we said before, as staunch a Conservative as ever breathed. Dwelling sadly on the manly contests that used to take place in those parts at the yearly "revels," or gatherings, he added mournfully, "But all that is changed now. The revels are still held; but the Reform Bill and the "march of intellect" have so improved the people that now, instead of wrestling, they get drunk. The cant expression is "elevating the masses," and literally they *do* get *elevated*."

The highly conservative opinions held by the aristocracy of Japan naturally recommended themselves at once to Abdul's favour, and he was ever loud in praise of them. During the whole time of our service in that country he always had two or three officers of high rank from the courts of different princes, who came to him to pick up some notion of the English system of drill and discipline. These men were remarkably quick, both in learning to speak English and mastering every sort of movement in the field. They would ask, too, all kinds of searching questions about interior economy, the composition of our army, &c.; but one point, in particular, they could never understand clearly.

With them, every person in trade is called by the general name of "akindo," or merchant, from the man who sells a farthing's worth of rice in the street, to him who transacts business with our own merchant princes. The highest of them are only allowed to carry one sword, and are ranked far below the yakonin, or two-sworded officer, who is qualified by hereditary right for the profession of arms. Thus one of Abdul's pupils, in his peculiar, slow, distinct, and almost ultra-grammatical English, put the following questions to him:—

"Speak without hesitation! Can the son of a merchant be an officer in your army?"

Abdul answered that he could, at which they appeared much surprised, but went on to ask:—

"But if the son of a merchant be an officer of high rank in the army, and have under him the son of a noble, shall *he*, the son of a merchant, though he be poor and mean, have honour among men?"

When told that in his official capacity he would have equal honour as if he were of the highest birth, they seemed doubly astonished at the Republican notion, and were apparently impressed with a very low idea of the general standard of officers of the British army.

CHAPTER XVI.

GREAT SPORTING EVENT.

In one of the previous chapters occurs the following sentence: "You will be introduced to this old gentleman in due time. His name is Captain Puffles!"

We are now about to fulfil this promise.

Reader, you are going to be introduced to Captain Puffles.

There are more stories told, more verses written, more riddles made, about Captain Puffles than about any man in the regiment—we may safely add, in the service.

The number of nicknames which have been conferred upon him, and to all of which he answers, passes all understanding.

As a rule, these names may be objected to on the score of personality, as all, more or less, contain a pointed satire on Captain Puffles's figure, which is not quite as slim as it used to be. In some of them the allusion is conveyed in a delicate and humorous way, but others are couched in particularly plain words, which admit of no doubt whatever as to their meaning.

Any passing event—a picture in *Punch* of a fat old gentleman in difficulties—anything of the sort furnishes matter for a new *sobriquet*. Puffles is, however, the most generally used one, and under it we present him to you.

Were this introduction personal, we are afraid Captain Puffles's first remark would be, "'Ow are you?" This little weakness of dropping his h's has only been contracted lately. When we first knew him he had no such bad habit. He attributes it to a very sharp attack of bronchitis he once had; but we are of opinion that in most instances the letter is omitted—this sin of his is only one of omission—simply from want of time; for Captain Puffles's tongue is going all day long on all subjects, and he is always in such a hurry to get the words out, for fear of some person by chance getting *one* in, that we believe the h is dispensed with as an economy of labour and time. His favourite topics are—India, where he has served many years, and about which country his tales are marvellous; and women, whom he professes to hate—in fact, the whole of them he includes under the term of "Fiends of 'ell"—— Now please don't, gentle reader—that is to say, if you belong to the sex we madly adore—please don't throw this volume away in disgust, and call Captain Puffles "a nasty, great, horrid, old thing!" Wait and read how we go on to state—there is nothing that he enjoys more than being in their society, and nothing can be more courteous than his manner towards them, when he finds himself thus agreeably placed.

To hear him talk about children would drive the fond father of a youthful family to exasperation, and yet we have seen him play for hours—when he thought he was not observed thus unbending—with troops of romping little boys and girls, who did just as they pleased with him.

He professes to hate animals of the lower order; yet dogs, cats, and monkeys make friends with him at first sight, and take boundless liberties with him with impunity.

His language is at times, when under excitement, as strong as his brandy pawnee,—and we can really think of no stronger simile than that,—yet he knows his Bible almost by heart, and could "pound" any of us in a theological argument, were any of us bold enough to enter the lists with him.

All clergymen are with him "Swaddlers,"—a term, like Aaron's "By Gosht," without any known origin, but with a great deal of latent meaning,—yet when in their company his behaviour to them is courteous and respectful.

We have his word for it that he is possessed of great personal bravery; yet he has been known on an occasion —duly recorded elsewhere in these pages—to beat a hasty and ignominious retreat before an imaginary ghost.

Of such a mass of incongruities is Captain Puffles made up; but we think that the good preponderates, and we hope, on a closer acquaintance, you will like him as well as we do.

We are sure he would scorn the act of telling a lie, as fully as any honourable right-minded man would; and yet we state without hesitation, and at the risk of having a quarrel with him, that his Indian stories bear not the stamp of truth; although, out of justice to him, we must add that we are of opinion that he implicitly believes them himself.

From the constant habit of telling them, and at each narration embellishing a little, these wonderful structures of fiction have grown little by little to their present gigantic proportions—quite imperceptibly to him, though—and he now recounts them in the firm belief that they are simply mirrors of facts, and that he has added nothing to them since the days when they were first told in all their pristine truth and purity.

In their relation he takes a high moral position, and brooks not contradiction. Any expression of doubt is invariably met with, "''Ave *you* ever been in India?'"

His rejoinders to the answer of this question, according as it is "Yes" or "No," are: "Then you must 'ave kept your ears and eyes in your breeches pocket;" or, "Then what the devil do you know about it, sir?"

With us, who know him well, all his statements on Indian subjects are received with caution; but strangers, who have never visited this quarter of the British possessions, are liable to be taken in by his honest, rubicund, old countenance and earnest manner,—particularly when backed up, as it were, by the portly figure, which always sheds such an air of intense respectability over its owner,—and to go away labouring under the conviction that India is a kind of fairy-land, in which Captain Puffles had been for some years a species of Jack the Giant-killer. We have seen some of these weak and deluded mortals leaving the Pufflesian presence, idiotically pondering over these tales of marvel, and trying hopelessly to make out how it was that he had never heard of Captain Puffles before, and why his fame had not totally eclipsed and thrown into the shade that of Napoleon or Wellington.

With a blush, we acknowledge that we must count ourselves, on first joining, one of this credulous lot.

To such an extent did our faith carry us at one time, that we have wondered why the many authors of books entitled "History of British India," did not add, "or, The Biography of Puffles."

Yes! when the down was springing on our upper lip; when its growth was watched for with such anxiety, that we perpetually wore a diabolical squint, in the fond hope of being able to catch a sight of it without the aid of a looking-glass—— Ah! proud moment, we recollect it well, when with such horrid contortions of mouth and eyes, that we wonder now those features ever returned to their natural state, we caught, for the first time, a glimpse of one single hair, and although our eyes ached, and we were conscious of being observed, we were not able to withdraw our fond gaze from the dear object. When our jacket was of a spotless red; when our shirts, just fresh from the inspection of a fond mother, had not shed a single button; when, in fact,—to cut short these recollections which crowd upon us quicker than we can write them down,—we were very young, and very inexperienced, and very confiding, we accepted Puffles at his own price.

Often, when we were in this green stage, have we, after having sat next to him at mess, retired to our bed, and dreamed through the night of jewelled Begums in the embrace of Puffles, Puffles in the embrace of tigers, and then the three in the embraces of a boa constrictor, until the whole formed such a confused medley, that it generally ended in a frightful nightmare, and our awaking, clutching our pillow, not quite sure whether we had got hold of a Begum or a boa constrictor.

These stories of Puffles—we speak of them, not as

they influenced us in our youth, but as we found them in Japan—became rather a nuisance; for as he hardly ever stirred out of Camp, he was always in or about the ante-room on the look-out for a listener, and any one going to read the papers was pounced upon and made the unwilling auditor of hair-breadth escapes, romantic adventures, and wondrous feats.

This reached such a point, that it was at last proposed, and unanimously carried, that Puffles was not to open his lips on the subject of India until the cloth had been removed from the dinner table; the penalty of any allusion to his adventures in that country being a fine. Puffles's remonstrances were at first dignified, then pathetic; but we were inexorable, and he had to succumb: we ceded one point, though, the following—on two days during the year, the anniversaries of the Battle of Pegu and Surrender of Kirwee, on both of which occasions he performed prodigies of valour, we allowed him the privilege of talking as much as ever he liked on his favourite topic, untrammelled by any restrictions.

There is one in the regiment who has attempted to follow in the footsteps of Puffles in these bright paths of fiction. His scenes are laid in the West Indies; and in this field he revels in the marvellous, as Puffles does in the East. His stories, if a total disregard of probability or possibility be their object, are a decided success; but, if anything higher is aimed at, we must say they are a total failure.

We think, though, that he is as implicit a believer in his own stories as we have stated Captain Puffles to be in his. This old gentleman's name is Mr. Pop. It cannot be a matter of surprise that two such bright stars as Captain Puffles and Mr. Pop could not shine in the same firmament without the lustre of the one dimming that of the other; and between the two there existed a jealousy, which found vent in frequent altercations and many challenges to trials of mutual skill.

Notwithstanding the repeated occurrence of these little passages of arms, and the appearance of both being always thoroughly in earnest, neither had ever come up to the scratch except on the occasion we are about to chronicle.

When we were all at mess one evening, a conversation on racing and gentlemen jockeys was started, during which Captain Puffles and Mr. Pop engaged in some sparring concerning their respective performances in the saddle.

Each declared himself to be moved to extreme mirth at the bare idea of seeing the other riding a race.

Old Mr. Pop got the worst of it, slightly lost his temper, and, goaded on by several near him, actually challenged Captain Puffles to ride a mile on the flat for twenty-five dollars.

Puffles was aghast at such temerity, and his reply was faltering and evasive. However, we were all determined not to let the matter rest. Pop was applauded on all sides, and dark hints were thrown out in stage whispers that we thought he had got the best of Puffles *this* time. These were seen to be doing their work, slowly but surely. "Why, Puffles," said Tony, "don't you recollect? You told us the other night how you used to ride races at Bangalore, and how your services as jock used to be retained months beforehand."

Puffles smiled feebly. At any other time this would have been quite sufficient an opening for him at once to have launched out into his favourite topic; but now, as we have stated before, he only smiled feebly.

"Take him up, old fellow," continued Tony, who was now in his element, as he was generally the leader of all the mischief plotted against Puffles; "take him up!"

"But I've got no 'orse," said Puffles, brightening up, as he looked upon this as a loophole through which he could effect a sure and honourable retreat.

This difficulty was at once overcome. A dozen steeds were proffered on all sides; and, at last, the Captain's "Black Bob" was selected by the company as the best weight carrier, and the most fit to be matched against Mr. Pop's "Bouncer." There was no escape. Captain Puffles, after a short muttered conversation with Tony, who was evidently egging him on, poured himself out a glass of sherry, drank it off with a gulp, and looking fixedly across the table at Mr. Pop, said, in a tone of fierce desperation, "Done!"

A roar of laughter followed this, as the President informed the two old gentlemen that, in accordance with an old mess rule, he fined them both for making a bet before the cloth had been removed, and that the after-dinner wine would be drunk at their expense.

Great was Mr. Pop's horror at being thus taken up, first by Captain Puffles, and then by the President.

To make a long matter short,—for much time was wasted in settling the conditions, owing to the constant efforts of each to back out without loss of honour to himself,—it was at last agreed that the race was to come off at two o'clock the next day on the Rifle Range race-course.

As the evening wore on, the two rivals, regarding the coming race from a post-prandial point of view, actually began to look upon it as rather a lark than otherwise, and one of them even went so far as to say that he wouldn't mind if it were over the steeple-chase course.

The next morning arrived, and with it a great change seemed to have been wrought in the opinions they had held after dinner the night before, as to the race being such a capital bit of fun. The whole forenoon both appeared constrained and uneasy.

Puffles sought relief in gentle stimulants. Pop, under the superintendence of the Liver Cutter, who kindly volunteered his services, busied himself in preparations for the coming struggle, which were carried on in this manner :—

"Now," says the Liver Cutter, "this is the way to give you a clip of the saddle;" and, balancing himself on one leg, he bends his knee, getting lower and lower, until he proudly holds the other leg straight out parallel to the floor, at a distance of a few inches; he then rises slowly: this he does two or three times on one leg, and then gives the other a turn.

"There now, try that!" he says encouragingly. But, by way of implanting a laudable ambition in his pupil's breast before beginning his lesson, he holds out his leg, and requests him to feel *that!*"

Pop pokes his forefinger about the Liver Cutter's leg, as if he were saying "Ketchee!" to an infant.

"Damme, man!" roars the latter, "that's not the way to feel a man's muscle. Catch hold of it like this;" and Pop's leg is seized in a grip which makes him quiver all over, and plead for mercy. "*Now* feel that!" again says the Liver Cutter, planting his right leg rigid as a bar. Pop stoops down, and feels it after the orthodox manner he has just acquired, while its owner's face wears a pleased expression, the whole thing being very suggestive of a cat being stroked the right way.

"Well?" asks the Liver Cutter, looking down and expecting a compliment.

"Well?" says Pop, looking up, not quite certain what to say, as he wishes to offer up his tribute of praise in free and easy sporting language, and does not quite know how to do it.

"Well, what do you think of it? Is it *hard* or is it *soft*, eh?"

"Precious hard!" replies Pop. "As hard as nails."

"Aha! I should rather think it was; but when a man goes in for what *I* call *riding*, he must be as hard as nails. Now, you try letting yourself down and getting up on one leg."

They both stand *vis-à-vis* on one leg each.

"Now," says the Liver Cutter, gradually letting himself down.

"Now," says Pop, doing the same, only in a very jerking, wabbling manner, until all of a sudden the strain is too much, the leg gives way under him, and he goes down with a crash.

"It's uncommonly hard!" he remarks in his sitting position; "I'd no idea it was so hard."

"What is," asks the Liver Cutter with a demoniacal grin,—"the floor?"

"No, no, not the floor; the going down on one leg, you know."

"Nothing to the getting up," remarks the Liver

Cutter, proudly going through that part of the performance with a flourish. "Now try *that!*"

Upon this Mr. Pop is put and trussed into an unnatural crouching attitude on one leg, the discomfort of which is amply portrayed in his expressive countenance.

"Now get up," says the Liver Cutter.

Pop gives a little bob of an inch up, and then an inch down again into the same position.

"Try again," invites the Liver Cutter.

Another little spasmodic bob is the only result of a second trial.

"Do it g-r-a-dually," says the Liver Cutter soothingly.

Mr. Pop tries hard to follow this advice. He becomes purple, his eyeballs seem starting from their sockets, and he grinds his teeth savagely; but, beyond giving himself the appearance of a hideous Chinese idol, or a bull-frog about to go off by spontaneous combustion, he arrives at no result, not even one of the little bobs he executed before. This state of things cannot last long, and with a groan of exhaustion he rolls on the floor.

"No go, I'm afraid!" says the Liver Cutter, giving his fallen pupil a hand. "But I'll tell you what I'll do. I'll teach you how to flog. I suppose you wouldn't like doing the horse?" he asks, looking up from a chair, which, in the event of a refusal to this mild request, is to supply the place of that animal.

"No," replies Pop, "I'd rather not."

"All right," says the Liver Cutter kindly, giving in on this point, and settling himself down to his work. "Now, whatever you do, don't flog like this; if you do, you'll hit your horse all about the kidneys, and play the devil!"

"Oh!" says Pop, "I never knew that."

"Well, you know it now," returns the Liver Cutter. "And now that I've shown you how *not* to flog, I'll show you *how*. This is the way;" and the Liver Cutter commences an exciting finish on the chair—having previously obtained the bell-rope for the reins. "Now this is the dodge." On this the whip is whirled through the air, but instead of descending on the leg of the chair, and landing it cleverly by a nose, its downward course is intercepted by the head of an unfortunate mess waiter, who at this moment makes his appearance on the scene, bearing a foaming tumbler for Captain Puffles. This brings the lesson to an abrupt termination.

One of the conditions of the race, made the night before, was, that it was to be ridden in colours.

"Oh," said Pop, suddenly recollecting this, "who'll lend me some racing things?"

"I will," said the Liver Cutter; "at least, I'll lend you a blue jacket and cap. Yes! ride in blue."

"I'm afraid I shall; I shall ride in a blue funk," replied Pop, with a candour for which we have respected him ever since.

The Liver Cutter was so disgusted at this, that he retracted his offer, and B. placed his racing wardrobe at his disposal, while Tony did the same for Puffles; that is to say, as far as the cap and jacket went, for no pair of breeches or boots could be found big enough for him. At last a pair of both articles were fished out of the theatrical properties, and in these his short, stout, nether limbs were encased.

The coming event of the afternoon had got wind amongst the men of the regiment; and the whole morning, officers commanding companies were beset by privates under convoy of non-commissioned officers, all on the same errand.

"Well, Atkins, what do you want?"

"If you please, sir, I want leave off school and afternoon roll call."

"What for?"

"Well, sir, I want to see the race between Captain Puffles and Mr. Pop;" and a grin would steal over the features of the man, that even in the presence of his officer he was unable to control. There were so many of these applicants that at last general leave was given for the afternoon, and the greatest excitement prevailed in Camp.

The fame of it even reached down to the town; and numerous notes came pouring into Camp asking the time, place, and other particulars. The answers to most of these were invitations to come up to tiffin, and then proceed altogether afterwards to the course.

Tiffin time came, and with it a goodly company.

Puffles and Pop were at the table, but seemed decidedly off their feed, and paid more attention to the liquids than to the solids.

Both, in reality, looked upon riding a race as a feat to be attempted only by those reckless of life or limb; and each inwardly cursed his folly for having embarked on such a mad proceeding.

They looked so very unhappy that it was feared that if they got together, they would cry off by mutual consent, regardless of all feelings of shame. So Tony and B. were told off respectively to Puffles and Pop, with instructions not to lose sight of their charges; on no account to permit them to engage in conversation of a private nature; and further, to exert themselves to fan the flame of jealousy which existed between the two to the utmost.

Right well did these worthies, Tony and B., perform their duties; and at half-past two the four wended their way to the Rifle Range course, accompanied by the whole of the tiffin party, all riding.

The only two in the whole assembly who did not look light-hearted and merry were the two principals.

Bouncer, Mr. Pop's pony, having been scientifically prepared for the occasion by the treacherous B., was unwontedly frisky, and as he sidled along, he every now and then treated us to a faint and feeble imitation of a buck—a performance he had been believed thoroughly incapable of hitherto.

At every little exhibition of this nature, Pop's equanimity was sadly disturbed, and he clung with all the energy of despair by both spurs, which had been carefully put on the wrong way—another piece of the arch-traitor B.'s handiwork.

On the other hand, Captain Puffles bestrode Black Bob with a determined and martial air, which had its origin, there is not the slightest reason to doubt, in brandy and soda, and also in the fact that Black Bob appeared sobered to a mournful extent by the frightful weight on his back. The latter walked along sorrowfully, and "the burden laid upon him seemed greater than he could bear."

No unbecoming levity was there about Captain Puffles.

Once, and once only, when a more pronounced buck than usual on the part of Bouncer caused Mr. Pop to shoot up into the air, and then to come fluttering back into the saddle like a shuttlecock, he laughed in a pitying way, which awoke in his rival's bosom a determination to "do or die."

This last buck was certainly one which reflected the greatest credit on B.'s handiwork, and gave an opening for betting men to lay heavy odds against Bouncer and Pop arriving at the winning-post in company.

But no takers were to be found. The view of the beautiful landscape, as seen on the occasion between Mr. Pop's person and the saddle, might have had charms for a lover of scenery; but taking the thing apart from this, it was hardly calculated to inspire confidence in his backers.

Arrived at the course, we found that nearly the whole garrison, with a fair proportion of civilians, had turned out in high expectation; and the appearance of Captain Puffles and Mr. Pop was hailed with the utmost enthusiasm.

The former acknowledged this with the air of a conqueror (it was whispered that Puffles was "pot valiant;" but what great man has ever lived and died unscathed by the vile breath of calumny?); the preliminaries were gone through with despatch; B. and Tony each relieved his man of his overcoat; and as the two distinguished jocks burst upon the public gaze in all the proud panoply of racing, an admiring shout greeted them.

Mr. Pop's jacket, instead of being tucked inside his breeches, fluttered gracefully outside. His cap was tied nightcap fashion under his chin, which gave him a somewhat matronly aspect; and his whip was held in a manner which caused a doubt in the mind of the spectators as to whether its owner was under the impression that it was an instrument for flogging with, or an implement used for the purpose of catching fish.

Puffles was most gorgeous as to his cap and jacket, which were Tony's colours—orange and black; but there was a decided falling off about the breeches and boots, which had both, as we have said before, been obtained from the theatrical wardrobe, and which, to say the least, looked peculiar. The boots, in particular, smacked strongly of the stage.

"Now, then, get into your places," said a gentleman, known under the name of Smiler, who acted in the double capacity of starter and judge—the starting and winning post being one and the same.

"*Get* into your places," repeated this indefatigable and slightly irascible little gentleman, in a tone which, to Captain Puffles and Mr. Pop, carried with it the awful conviction that they were fairly in for it without a chance of reprieve.

"I say," inquired Captain Puffles, more with a view to postponing the awful moment than to gaining any information, "is it to be run in 'eats?"

"In what?" indignantly asked Smiler.

"In 'eats," repeated Captain Puffles.

"'Eats be blowed! In drinks would be more in your line, I should think," returned Smiler, who was one of a hasty and quick temperament.

Puffles looked severely at him, and was on the point of retorting; but there was a feeling towards the starter almost of awe, as if that individual, *ex officio*, held some mysterious sway over his destinies; and he refrained, contenting himself with darting several indignant glances at him.

With the assistance of Tony and B. the two were got up into line, and were directed by Smiler to walk up together to the starting-post.

"Come up together! Get back, Captain Puffles! Come up, Mr. Pop! Come up! Are you re-ady?"

"No, no!" exclaimed Puffles excitedly, just as the word "Go!" was on Smiler's lips. "No, no! 'Old 'ard! I want to speak to Tony privately;" and leaning over, he whispered, "I say, Tony, couldn't you, like a good fellow, get some water in your handkerchief for me to damp my knees with without any one seeing?"

"No, no, nonsense," replied Tony. "Was that the style of thing at Bangalore?"

Puffles gave in with a sigh. (Tony basely repeated the whole of the above private conversation at mess that night to an uproariously appreciative audience.) After this stoppage, the two turned round, and again walked up to the starting-post under the direction of the starter.

Again was the question "Are you ready?" asked by that official, and again did an agonised "No, no!" grate upon his ears.

This time it proceeded from Mr. Pop, who continued in feeble and apparently heart-broken accents, " Stop! I've got my reins wrong."

"I should rather think you had," said the ever-attentive B., who was at his side in a moment, picking up one of them, which was hanging in a graceful festoon over Bouncer's near knee.

"Thank you," said Pop, clutching the proffered rein, and, in so doing, allowing the other to droop in as graceful a loop as the first on the off side.

"Well, I'm blest!" said B., giving way to an uncontrollable burst of laughter, as he dodged over to the other side, and gave the refractory reins in a bunch to Pop, who received them gratefully, and immediately proceeded to get them into a hopeless state of entanglement with his whip. All these little incidents, and the delays consequent thereon, afforded the utmost gratification to the spectators, with the exception of the starter, who was beginning to lose his temper, and the Liver Cutter, who—notwithstanding his offers of assistance in the morning—surveyed the scene from a little distance with bitter scorn, and looked upon the whole thing as most wanton sacrilege.

The faces of the two jocks themselves were in woeful contrast to the general merriment. They bore unmistakable symptoms of the keenest apprehensions. Alas! the proud bearing and determined air with which we have related that Captain Puffles rode up the course, receiving the acclamations of the crowd, had almost entirely deserted him.

A change, too, had come over Bouncer. His air was dejected even unto meanness; and it was only now and then that he afforded any amusement by a stiff and laboured attempt at a buck.

These little ebullitions of spirit, though, had become so inane and weak that they ceased to be a source of any serious discomfiture to Mr. Pop, who, with some slight assistance from mane and rein, managed to stick on all right, and even almost joined in the laugh at them.

At the third attempt at a start, which was successful, very little ceremony was observed.

Tony and B., each armed with a heavy hunting whip, stood behind Black Bob and Bouncer, and as Smiler gave the word "Go!" a smart cut rung on the hind quarters of each of those persecuted quadrupeds, and the two were sent away well together, in spite of a faint "No, no; I'm not ready," from Mr. Pop, and a something between a bellow and a shriek to the same effect from Captain Puffles.

As pre-arranged, Tony and B. had each instructed his man to wait on the other; the consequence was, that after the effects of the cuts the two animals had received had died away, the pace got slower and slower, until, at last, as they approached the half-mile turning, it became funereal.

On their journey round this turning they crossed each other times innumerable, but at length the shouts of the crowd proclaimed that they had gone round all right, without any accidents or bolting, and were now on their way home.

Up the course again they came neck and neck, at a very slow canter. In fact, but for the colours, they might have been taken for two old gentlemen out for an afternoon's quiet ride. Pop sat crouching well forward, and bumping at every stride in a way which, though it might have been highly beneficial to the process of digestion, must have, in its after effects, brought to his mind vivid recollections of the race whenever he sat down.

Puffles adopted quite a different mode. Sitting as far back as the length of his reins would allow him, he seemed to have given himself up to circumstances, and to have prepared himself for the worst.

Somewhere near the distance-post Tony and B. were stationed—both mounted; and now ensued the most extraordinary finish that we have ever witnessed.

Neither of the jockeys could spare a hand to flog with, only having two apiece, and those being already fully engaged with the reins, not so much for the purpose of guiding or restraining as of holding on by.

Had they been provided with three sets each, they might have treated us unassisted to a most vigorous finish; but Nature not having made any exception to her general rule of two per mortal in their favour, Tony and B. supplied the deficiency.

Once, indeed, Pop—incited thereto by an excited shout of "Let 'im 'ave it, sir!" from his groom—made an effete and aimless cut into the air with his whip; but the sudden and dreadful way in which this affected his equilibrium warned him not to repeat the attempt.

No such wild freaks did Puffles indulge in. He marked how nearly attended with disastrous results had been poor Pop's attempt to flog, and he effectually debarred himself from following his example by dropping his whip just at this juncture, either from accident or in a spirit of caution, the object being to put temptation out of his way.

As they came up at a sober pace towards where Tony and B. had stationed themselves with their hunting whips they divined what was impending; and, with a look of blank dismay, each cast an eye expressive of the liveliest interest and concern in the movements of their backers, who were now, to their horror, seen to be getting the lashes of their whips into readiness in the most business and workmanlike manner.

Too true were their conjectures.

Scarcely had they passed the distance-post when the cracks of two whips fell on their ears, and they felt themselves borne on at a pace which made them giddy, as Bouncer and Black Bob, finding themselves thus unjustifiably assailed in rear, strained every nerve to get away from their persecutors.

On they came faster and faster, B. and Tony belabouring with all their might, amidst deafening applause, which soon took shape in shouts of "Bouncer wins!" And so it was—the frightful weight of Captain Puffles was beginning to tell against Black Bob; and Bouncer, forging gradually ahead, eventually won by about a couple of lengths. Although both had now passed the judge, the great excitement had yet to come.

It so happened that the Rifle Range race-course at about sixty yards beyond the winning-post was brought to an abrupt termination by a sheer and precipitous cliff; and it was on this fact that the spectators grounded their hopes of seeing some fun, when Bouncer and Black Bob would be brought to a sudden stand-still by this obstacle after their exciting and vigorous finish.

On our two heroes tore past the stand, clinging on by every muscle to their steeds, who seemed to be possessed with a desire to dash themselves against the face of the cliff regardless of all consequences.

In this spirit of utter recklessness they galloped until within a few yards of the obstacle, when, as if suddenly brought to a sense of their danger, they stopped dead short, wheeled round, and then trotted past the stand.

This manœuvre caused Captain Puffles and Mr. Pop, one after the other, to quit their saddles, and to poise themselves for the space of some seconds on the necks of their steeds in a way which even the most sanguine of the spectators had hardly dared to hope for, and which elicited from all rapturous bursts of applause. By the time they reached the grand stand again, they had both —principally by means of the friendly mane, which, in fact, had been their mainstay throughout the whole of this trying occasion—managed to get back into their saddles, and were assisted to dismount by Tony and B.

Great was the satisfaction which beamed upon their countenances at finding their legs once more planted on *terra firma*.

They were both evidently greatly pleased with themselves. Pop's triumph made up for all he had gone through; and any pain Puffles may have felt in defeat was lost in his delight at having gone through his part without loss of life or limb, and he joked and chaffed in the highest of spirits, accounting in many different ways for not having won. He laid great stress on, and seemed very proud of, the fact of Black Bob's not bolting or showing any eccentricities; for he repeatedly assured us that he " 'ad 'im well in 'and the 'ole way."

Now, it was fated that Captain Puffles was not long to remain in this pleasurable state of mind; for Mr. Pop coming up just then flushed with victory, and prompted by those demons of discord, Tony and B., taunted him with having crossed him at the turning.

Then it was that Puffles turned upon his adversary, and delivered himself of the following ever-memorable speech:—

"'Ow the 'ell could I 'ave crossed you when I was a'ead?"

Before we go one single word further in the narration of these events, we feel that an ample apology is due to our readers for this intemperate language of Captain Puffles, and, on his behalf, we beg that it may, under the circumstances, be looked over this time, promising that it will not occur again.

It is not our wish or intention to defend for a moment the use of such strong expressions; but we do think there are some slight allowances to be made for the excitement under which he laboured at the moment, and the provocation he received in thus being publicly twitted by Mr. Pop, who ought to have shown more forbearance to a vanquished foe.

Now, this emphatic rejoinder of Captain Puffles—albeit it was plain and to the point—indicated that he entertained some most mysterious and vague notions of the definition of a cross. However, it seemed a poser for Mr. Pop, whose knowledge on the subject was about on a par with Puffles's, and the question, so forcibly asked, was unanswered.

Again, be it said to Puffles's shame, was it put in the same words, but this time accompanied with more vehement action and gesture.

Pop was still hopelessly confused.

"Answer me that," continued Captain Puffles, assuming a bullying air; for this old gentleman's pluck was of that description which rises not with danger, but quite the reverse. "Answer me *that*."

Pop looked at Tony and B., who had prompted him to this, for assistance; but they were too much convulsed with laughter to render him any—not that they would have done so under any circumstances; for the scene between the two principals was far too rich to be spoilt by any interference.

"No double recovers, my boy," said Puffles, winking his eye with intense knowingness, and laughing a little, short, self-satisfied laugh, which implied quite plainly that he rather thought he had had the best of *that*.

The bystanders applauded, and Puffles had apparently attained the summit of human greatness in his own little sphere, when a voice from the crowd urged the advisability of running the race over again as there was a dispute about it.

This was warmly seconded by every one present.

The sudden revulsion that Puffles's feelings underwent paled his usually rubicund cheek, and the victorious air and knowing wink vanished like a flash of lightning. Pop also betrayed an equal amount of emotion, and he hurriedly stated that he had altered his opinion, and that it could not have been a cross.

Puffles, anxious to cede anything rather than have the race run over again, said that he was now equally sure that it must have been, and that he had no doubt about it.

"Now, did you ever see anything like this?" said Tony, appealing to the bystanders, and pretending to work himself up into a rage. "Did you ever see two such provoking old fellows? I'm hanged if they haven't chopped round, and are arguing exactly t'other way now. What's to be done?"

Every one agreed, with mock gravity, that such disputes were highly discreditable, and that there was no alternative except to run the race over again.

"Come on—come on 'ome!" exclaimed Puffles, taking his late adversary by the arm affectionately, as he now recognised in him a fellow-sufferer, and the two, affecting to disregard the general clamour for a second race, were about to proceed off the course; but fate and the crowd willed otherwise, and at last, after a great deal of talking, the two consented to ride the same match over again.

Now there happened to be on the ground, whither his owner, C——, had ridden him, a pony called Dandy, towards whom Puffles entertained the liveliest feelings of aversion and dread, owing to his well-known shying and bolting propensities.

This animal, Tony, prompted by some demon of mischief, determined to substitute for Black Bob in the ensuing race, unknown, of course, to Puffles, who would as soon have ridden a zebra or an ostrich bare-backed.

There was one difficulty, but Tony deemed it not insurmountable—that was, Black Bob, as his name implied, was of a sable hue; Dandy, a bright bay.

Saddles and bridles were transferred from one pony to the other behind the stand; and as Dandy was led forth with orange and black rosettes fluttering in the breeze, he looked quite gay.

"Now, then, Puffles," said Tony, "you'd better get up."

"Woh!" said Captain Puffles, advancing for that purpose.

It was a trying time for Tony and the spectators, who momentarily expected the trick to be discovered, as Puffles, before mounting, narrowly inspected Dandy; but no suspicion flashed across him. His mind was too full of dismal forebodings to grasp such a small fact as difference of colour, and all fears of detection were completely lulled on his patting Dandy's neck, and saying, "Woh! Black Bob! P-o-o-r old fellow! Wo-o-a, then!"

Luckily a difference of opinion, which just then occurred between Bouncer and Pop, afforded a pretext for every one to vent his feelings in roars of laughter, without enlightening Puffles as to the real cause of the merriment. In fact, he innocently joined in the laugh himself, under the impression that Pop and Bouncer had provoked it.

"I say, Tony," said the unsuspecting old party, now on Dandy, who was dancing and fretting in a way which made his rider more purple in the face than usual with the exertion of hanging on; "I say, that gallop 'as freshened up old Black Bob a bit, 'asn't it?"

"Well, I don't know: not very much, I think," returned Tony, as he took a sly glance at the veritable Black Bob, who, at some little distance off, with heaving flanks, drooping head, and distended nostril, looked the very reverse of "freshened up a bit."

"'E's quite beany," again remarked Captain Puffles, in a tone in which he wished to convey to his hearers that he was rather pleased at the fact. "Wo—o—a, Black Bob, wo—o—a!"

Everything was now ready, and as Dandy and Bouncer walked up to the starting-post, or rather, as the former danced and the latter crawled, the excitement was tremendous.

"Are you ready?" said the starter.

"No, no!" replied Puffles, "I'm not. It's puffeckly impossible for the race to go on."

"Why?" inquired every one, crowding round.

"Because," said Puffles——

(To be continued in our next.)

CHAPTER XVII.

GREAT SPORTING EVENT (*Continued*).

"BECAUSE I've split my breeches;" and Puffles stood up in his stirrups with a woe-begone countenance, in order to leave no doubt whatever in the minds of his hearers as to the truth of his statement. We apologise again: this time to our fair readers, if we are fortunate and honoured enough even to have their bright eyes resting on these pages. What a dreadful duty has devolved upon us, this chronicling the sayings and doings of such a dreadful old fellow as this Puffles! He is always leading us into scrapes and apologies.

"That's nothing," said the starter, who was backed up in his opinion by every one. "Come, get into your places!"

"But it's indecent," pleaded Puffles.

However, the starter continued inexorable, and his expostulation was disregarded.

The same means that were adopted to insure a good start in the race before were again resorted to, and the two got away well together without any delays, though not without several faint and unheeded remonstrances, as on the former occasion, from the jockeys.

Dandy's mode of proceeding for the first quarter of a mile was peculiar in the extreme. He danced along sideways, and did not deign to break even into a canter for the whole of that distance. It would be very natural to presume that this conduct would have materially interfered with his chance of success, but not in the least was this the case; for Bouncer was fond of company, and adapted his pace to Dandy's—not as regarded the saltatory movements, for of those he was utterly incapable, but as regarded rate—and the two kept neck and neck. Mr. Pop had not the slightest objection to this—in fact, highly approved of it; for his object in the race was not so much to win as to get through it with the greatest amount of safety to himself, and he rightly conjectured that this was nearer of attainment the slower the pace.

"Now!" said C——, Dandy's owner, looking round him, "I'll give three to one in anything any one likes that Dandy takes Puffles home at the turning. Damme," he continued excitedly, as the turning was nearly reached, "I'll give five to one." Still no one took him up, such a result being looked upon as a certainty; but, to the surprise of every one, Dandy cantered round as composedly and sedately as if he had been a circus horse all his life, and Puffles a young fairy in silken tights and scanty petticoats urging him on with shrill cries of "Hoop-la!"

From the turning to the winning-post there was a strong resemblance to the previous race. They ran together until the finish, when the extra four stone on Dandy completely did for him, and Pop was again adjudged the winner.

"Bravo, Pop!" "Well done, Puffles!" were the shouts that rent the air as Puffles and Pop dismounted, and found themselves once more the centres of attraction.

"Well done, old Puffles!" said C——; "there are not

many fellows who would have steered Dandy round that turn as you did."

Puffles, with evident glee, accounted for the phenomenon by repeating his favourite phrase of "'aving 'im well in 'and."

It was unfortunate that he had chosen this particular expression, as it was so peculiarly calculated to display to the full his little weakness with regard to that letter h.

"Oh, yes; I 'ad 'im well in 'and," he repeated proudly. "But you mean Black Bob, not Dandy;" and Puffles laughed in his superior knowledge of horseflesh.

"No, I don't, old fellow," said C——, bursting into a regular guffaw, and slapping Puffles on the shoulder; "Dandy, and no other, was the pony you rode."

Puffles closed his eyes for a few seconds, and seemed to sicken at the bare thought of the danger passed. He opened them again, and faintly murmured, "You're 'umbugging!"

"No, I'm not, on my word," answered C——. "Tony changed the ponies."

Puffles looked reproachfully at Tony, and was on the point of having a relapse, when he was suddenly stung to the quick and brought to by a derisive shout of laughter from Mr. Pop.

"Ha-ha-ha!" roared that gentleman, as if he had been a party to the joke all through, and was now rejoicing at its success, whereas he had been quite as ignorant of the trick as old Puffles himself. "Ha-ha-ha! Capital!"

Puffles looked at him severely, and then said rather inappositely, "Let 'im laugh 'oo wins."

"Ha-ha!" retorted Pop, taking advantage of Puffles's mistake, "exactly the principle I'm going on; ha-ha-ha!"

But there was a marked abatement in his merriment as Puffles glanced fiercely at him.

The latter seemed conscious of having made a *faux pas*, and was gathering himself together for another and more carefully-delivered home-thrust, which would most likely have led to a stormy altercation between the two, when both were suddenly whipped off their legs in a way that was truly astounding, particularly as regarded Puffles, when one considered that he represented fifteen stone of very solid flesh, and were carried on the shoulders of a dozen stalwart fellows, Tony and B. at their head, while every one cheered lustily.

"Hooray! Bravo! Capital! Go it!" resounded on all sides, as they were borne past the grand stand, Puffles's theatrical boots, as he struggled and kicked to free himself, forming a prominent and conspicuous feature in the procession.

Luckily for Puffles, after having enjoyed the rather dubious delights of this popularity for some moments, his bearers fairly broke down under their frightful burden, and he came to mother earth, burying beneath him about half-a-dozen of his enthusiastic admirers.

On this Pop was set at liberty; and these two heroes shook each other warmly by the hand, and spoke loudly in praise of the way each had behaved on the trying occasion.

"I say!" said Pop, looking round him after these mutual congratulations were over, and affecting an easy and sporting manner, "had any one a stop-watch to take the time of that race?"

A deep groan was heard from one in the crowd.

It proceeded from the Liver Cutter, who exclaimed in

tones of the deepest disgust, "Stop-watch! Oh my G—! Eight-day Dutch clock, you mean. That would be more the style of thing to take *that* race;" and he strode away muttering to himself such broken sentences as "Time of that race! Stop-watch! Oh my goodness! Back a funeral procession to lick their heads off in a canter!" &c., &c.; and in a few minutes he was to be seen venting his feelings in the execution of a series of brilliant finishes on his old screw, in a way which seemed to afford much less satisfaction to that noble animal than it did to the spectators in general.

Pop was decidedly put out of conceit by the candid and open manner in which the Liver Cutter had expressed his disapprobation; and he proposed to Puffles that they should now go home together.

Puffles assented, and requested that Black Bob might be brought to him at once.

"He's been sent home," said Tony, with a shocking disregard for truth; "so you'll have to ride Dandy back."

"I'm 'anged if I do. I'll walk 'ome, then," returned Puffles, with some vehemence.

"Not in those boots, if I know it," put in Rollison, who was our theatrical manager. "You were lent them to ride, and not to walk a mile and a half in."

"Besides," added Tony, "I'm not going to allow you to walk about the country in my colours."

At this Puffles waxed wroth, cursed somewhat, but at last was obliged to give in, and mount Dandy.

The departure of Captain Puffles and Mr. Pop was the signal for every one to leave, and the two were accompanied off the ground by a crowd.

Everything went on very smoothly. Dandy conducted himself like a lamb, and Puffles was radiant and quite happy in the idea that at last his troubles were over.

The ruthless Tony, however, was determined that he should not long be left in this peaceful frame of mind. Armed with a pointed bamboo, carefully selected for its sharpness from a neighbouring hedge, he took every opportunity, when Puffles was not looking, to administer a sharp prod to Dandy's hind quarters.

At the first application of this instrument of torture, Dandy tucked his tail in and gathered in his hind quarters with a start.

"'Ulloa! What's up?" said Captain Puffles, looking round rather suspiciously; but Tony's bamboo was out of sight in a moment, and his face wore an expression of sublime innocence.

Puffles's suspicions were allayed, and he contented himself with anathematising those "cussed 'orse-flies."

At the second application of Tony's bamboo, Dandy flung his heels into the air in a manner which caused his head and Captain Puffles's nose to come into pretty smart contact.

"Stop!" exclaimed Captain Puffles, much in the tone of voice of an old lady addressing a 'bus-conductor, as she sees her destination rapidly receding in the distance. "Stop! I'll get off and walk."

"Nonsense," said Tony. "Why, where's your pluck, old fellow?"

"Pluck! Pluck be damned! What's the use of pluck when it 'urts?" cried Captain Puffles, rubbing his nose. "I tell you I'll get off. 'Ere! 'oo'll 'old my 'orse?"

As no one volunteered this service, Puffles made an attempt to dismount without assistance; that is to say, he got as far as taking his right foot out of the stirrup and clutching the mane with his left hand; but as Dandy, owing to Tony's bamboo, was, to make use of an old simile, like a pea in a frying-pan, he quickly abandoned the attempt, and the right foot nervously sought the assistance of the friendly stirrup.

"What's the matter with him, d'ye think, Tony?" he asked, without looking round, as he was too intently engaged in a little game of "catch me if you can," which was going on between his foot and the stirrup, at which the latter had it all its own way.

"I can't for the life of me make out," replied Tony, delivering a thrust that would have done credit to a lancer in the pursuing exercise.

There is a limit, of course, to equine as well as to human endurance, and this limit Dandy had now been goaded beyond. With a snort and a bound, he started off, and he and his rider were lost to view round a turn in the road before the latter's exclamation of horror had died away.

"By Jove! he has taken the turning to the town instead of to the Camp," said Tony, dropping his bamboo, and putting spurs to his pony in pursuit, followed by most of the party.

* * * * * * *

That evening, at about sunset, as many of the inhabitants of Yokohama, foreign and native, were issuing forth from their houses for their usual stroll after the heat and bustle of the day, they were startled by the astounding spectacle of a somewhat elderly, and decidedly obese gentleman, attired in a silken jacket of orange and black rings, and a pair of huge boots—in short, presenting the appearance of an immense bloated wasp in jack-boots, galloping madly through the streets, mounted on a bright bay pony, who seemed to be possessed with ten thousand devils. As these astonished wayfarers gaped and gazed in amazement at the unusual sight, they were not long in finding out that the rider was a very unwilling actor in this extraordinary performance.

This they gathered from his countenance, and from the fact that as he sped along on his wild career, like a ship in distress firing minute guns, he gasped out at intervals for some one to "stop 'im."

As no one seemed particularly desirous of running the risk of an instantaneous death for the sake of Puffles,— for of course it was no other than our old friend,—these repeated requests were utterly unheeded, and Dandy galloped on unchecked until the rider was fit to drop off with exhaustion.

But nothing in this world can go on for ever: not even a pulling brute with an iron mouth, particularly when he has got fifteen stone on his back, and Dandy's breath came shorter and shorter, and thicker and thicker, until he was nearly as pumped as his rider. His pace got slower and slower, until at last, with a dying effort, Puffles pulled him up.

Then horse and man remained stock still for a few seconds, both too done to stir.

At last Puffles looked round him with a startled gaze, and exclaimed, "By Jove! where the deuce am I?"

He scanned the street he was in up and down,

in hopes of seeing some friendly European who could enlighten him, but none but Japanese were to be seen far or near. Dandy had penetrated into the heart of the Japanese quarter of the town, which, although only about a mile and three-quarters from the Camp, was to Puffles a *terra incognita*, for, as we have said before, he rarely stirred from within the precincts of the Camp.

Here was a dilemma. He knew about as much of Japanese as he did of Hindoostanee; that is to say, he was acquainted with a string of opprobrious epithets, which he was in the habit of using with great effect up in Camp against any coolies, or small native fry of this kind, who happened to incur his displeasure.

That was all very well in his own domains, but now, surrounded as he was by none but Japanese, he felt a delicacy he had seldom before experienced in resorting to such strong language.

There was *one* word in his vocabulary not of this description, coined and used by him in colloquial Japanese: it was "Ikee," which he said meant "Come 'ere!"

It must be admitted that up in Camp it was used with unvarying success; but as it was always there spoken in a tone of authority and accompanied by a beckon, its success may be attributed solely to these two causes.

Selecting a small group of Japanese, mainly for the absence from it of any two-sworded men, he approached them, and invited a parley, with the usual "Ikee!"

Whether it was that the tone of authority was wanting, or that the beckon was nipped in the bud,—for, with the

T

first attempt at it with his whip hand, Dandy began to evince disagreeable symptoms,—we know not, but his invitation was not responded to.

"W-o-o-a!" said Puffles, carefully putting the whip out of Dandy's sight by holding it behind his back, showing about six inches of it over his head, thereby imparting to himself the appearance, as seen from the front, of having a pigtail standing straight on end with terror.

"Ikee!" again said Puffles, still carefully observing the same constrained position as regarded the whip.

The Japanese looked at him, then at each other, and then at him again, but returned no answer.

"Imputtynent brutes! they're sulky. I must 'umbug 'em a bit;" and Puffles approached a little nearer, and addressed them: "Hoio!"—ohio, good day!—in a tone so conciliatory that it verged on the abject.

"Ohio!" burst out the whole group in regular chorus; then followed, as a matter of course, the invariable "Doko' maro maro?"—where are you going?

Puffles understood the question, and wished devoutly he knew himself.

"Tojin Engleesh yakonin, bang, bang, doko?" he inquired, interspersing his speech with imitations of sounds generally heard in a barrack or camp, such as the roll of drums and bugle-calls.

For the benefit of those who have not succeeded in understanding this, we inform them that Puffles intended to intimate that he wished to reach the abode of the British soldiery.

This speech, though of course utterly unintelligible,

met with the greatest enthusiasm; the roll of the drums and bugle-calls being particularly well received, and they roared with laughter.

"Cussed fools!" said Puffles, waxing wroth; "they don't understand their own language."

The group was beginning now to swell to formidable dimensions, and people came running out of their houses in all directions, no doubt attracted by the news that a foreign actor, beautifully dressed, was performing in the streets for nothing.

As Puffles marked the fast-increasing crowd, visions of being cut down by two-sworded men floated before his excited imagination, particularly as he remarked several of these gentry scowling in the crowd. And, as he looked at Dandy, the cause of all his troubles, such a deadly hatred towards that quadruped possessed him, that at last it broke out in the words, "'Ow I'd like to 'it you, you brute!"

As he said this, he involuntarily brought the whip in sight of the excitable animal, who in consequence immediately executed another short dance, which caused Puffles, with a very sudden change in his tone and manner, to pat Dandy, and in a most hypocritical way to call him "Poor old fellow!"

All this the Japanese probably took "for the next thing in the programme," for they laughed and clapped their hands, which made Dandy conduct himself still more eccentrically, in spite of Puffles's caresses and coaxings.

The ill-used old gentleman looked down at his spurs, and what would he not have given to drive those persuaders into Dandy's sides! But he wisely abstained.

and contented himself with grinding his teeth, and calling him a " cow 'ocked beast."

The group soon began to look coldly upon Puffles and his steed, as if they thought the performance was getting rather slow; and spirited imitations of *his* imitations of bugle-calls and drum-rolls proceeded from all parts of the crowd, in polite invitation to give them that part over again.

Forthwith Dandy performed a regular hornpipe, and Puffles, disregarding the *encore*, broke out into curses loud and deep.

Luckily for him, though, in his excitement he mixed up both his accomplishments as a linguist already alluded to, and the jumble of Japanese and Hindoostanee was totally unintelligible to the crowd.

The wretch pinioned on the scaffold, the shipwrecked mariner tossing about on the ocean in a frail open boat—the one, as he sees a horseman galloping madly up, holding a paper fluttering in his hand, and shouting "Reprieve;" the other, as he wakes up from a fevered sleep and sees land close under his bow—experience the same sensations, we should think, that Puffles felt when he heard a cheery and well-known laugh, and, on looking round, saw Tony standing close behind him with his pony.

"I've only just come up," said that individual, perjuring himself in the most deliberate way, as he had been behind the nearest corner narrowly observing the whole scene,—else how could we have given the foregoing succinct and detailed account?—and only now interfered, as he was afraid Puffles might be roughly used by the crowd, if by any chance they happened to catch and understand one of his shockingly-pronounced Japanese maledictions.

"Come on, let's be off out of this!"

Puffles readily assented, and was not long availing himself of Tony's services as guide; and the two rode away, amidst shouts and a regular flourish of bugle-calls from the crowd.

As they proceeded homewards at a walk, Tony suddenly remarked, "What the devil have you got your whip like that for?"

"'Ush!" said Puffles, as if he thought the bare mention of that article of punishment would be sufficient to derange the whole of Dandy's nervous system. "'Ush! That's what set 'im off before, I think. I wasn't careful enough with it."

"By Jove, yes!" said Tony, as if he had been pondering over the cause of Dandy's bolting, and had at last arrived at it. "I dare say that was it."

Oh, Puffles, Puffles, how will your faith in human nature be shaken to its very foundation if you ever read these pages, and learn for the first time the treachery of one you placed so much reliance on!

How you will shudder and sicken as the scales fall from your eyes, and this serpent you have nurtured in your bosom appears in his true light!

And you, too, O Tony! when remorse—for come it will sooner or later—when remorse, we say, gnaws your very vitals, and the iron enters deep into your soul, know that it is only Retribution overtaking you.

That night, after dinner, all Puffles's trials and troubles were drowned in the flowing bowl, and his last words before he sank to rest were, that he would be happy to place his services as jock at the disposal of any one for the approaching meeting.

So ended a day for ever memorable in the annals of our Japanese service; a day that is never recalled without a smile—never spoken of without a merry laugh at its events.

CHAPTER XVIII.

SHOOTING.

We have as yet said little or nothing of the shooting in Japan, beyond giving a list of the different kinds of game that are brought into the Yokohama market during the winter months.

There are considerable quantities of pig and deer in different parts of the country; but it is very seldom that foreigners can get the chance of a shot at either. It was our luck to be present when at Kagosima, in the summer of '66, Prince Satsuma threw open his preserves to Admiral King, Sir Harry Parkes, and their party, for a day's sport. Great preparations were made, beaters and their dogs came in from long distances, and all pains taken to insure a success; but the time of the year was most unfavourable, and the total bag consisted of only *seven deer and five pig.*

Still the whole thing was a novelty, and the manner of conducting it peculiar; so what was wanting in actual sport was in a great measure made up in other ways.

Most of the chief covers were in basins a mile or two in extent, bounded on three sides by steep hills, and on the fourth by the sea. The beaters were ranged round the tops of these hills, while the guns were posted down below, near the water's edge, or in such a position as to guard the passes running from basin to basin between the sea and the hills. The weather, though hot, was fine and clear, and showed out the bold, grand scenery to its fullest advantage. We were told off to our places by a little fellow in high office at the Prince's court, who apparently also held the dignity of Commissioner of the Woods and Forests. He carried a Whitworth carbine, which he knew how to use thoroughly. Two or three other officials—including the Prime Minister—were also present, and went in keenly for the business of the day.

At a given signal the beaters loosed their dogs into the cover, and commenced working their way downwards with loud shouts and continued blowing of conch-shells; the sound of which latter, when reaching us from a distance, being exactly like that of bees humming close to one's ear—so much so that it took us some time to make sure that we were not actually seated on a nest of those much-lauded but unpleasant little insects. The dogs were soon heard giving tongue in different directions; but the cover was so thick, and the heat so great, that they soon tired, and but little game was driven out past the guns.

Some few months after, the Admiral and some of the officers of his flag-ship had a very different day in the preserves of another Daimio. They were invited to beat a small island, which the Prince of Tchikysan kept for his own particular shooting; and so thick was the game, that in a few hours the party knocked over upwards of fifty head of deer.

At Hakodate, again,—the open port of Yesso, the northern island of Japan,—deer and bears may often be

seen brought down from inland, slung on the backs of horses.

These come chiefly from the Eino country, the outskirts of which lie some fifty miles into the interior, and to which there is but scanty access. Moreover, there are no regular means of communication between this isolated port and the rest of Japan, and there are not a dozen English residing in the place; indeed, so remote is it, that they are sometimes as much as six months without receiving any news from the outer world.

The Einos themselves are a most extraordinary race, and but few Europeans have had the opportunity of coming in contact with them.

Quite a distinct people from the rest of the inhabitants of Japan, they are said to be, from some cause or other, gradually dying out, and are even now reduced to one small tribe, who live upon the mountains, and subsist chiefly by hunting and by the sale of skins and furs.

We were most fortunate in being on a visit to Hakodate, in the summer of '67, when the head men came down in state to pay their tribute to the governor of the province,—an event which only takes place once in five years,—and we found them not only civil, but even disposed to make acquaintance with foreigners.

In appearance they are much finer, stouter men than the Japanese, very dark, with bold, manly features hidden up to the eyes in thick black hair, which also covers nearly the whole of their bodies. They have not the slanting, almond-shaped eye peculiar to the Japanese and the Chinese; neither do they wear their hair in any form of a tail, but shaving it off the forehead, part the remainder in the middle, and allow it to fall down long on either side.

The Japanese officials evidently looked down on them as upon some inferior kind of animal, allowing them to retain their submissive posture, without rising, throughout the interview; and in addressing us, referred to them with a kind of pitying smile on their faces.

Seeing the two races together, it struck us that whatever the Einos might be morally, they were certainly not physically inferior to the others. The low estimation, however, in which they are held by the latter is pretty well shown by the origin which they ascribe to them.

They relate how "once upon a time" a favourite daughter of the then reigning Tycoon incurred disgrace in some way at Court. Unable to bear the coldness of her father, and the neglect of his courtiers, she fled to the mountains, where, after a time, she became little better than a wild animal, finally and literally "going to the dogs," and taking as her partner one of the canine race. From this union sprang the Einos.

The chiefs we saw wore handsome robes of scarlet, embroidered with gold; their other garments (of silk) being much after the fashion of the Japanese.

The photograph taken at the time by Mr. Sutton, of H.M.S. *Serpent*, shows their characteristics exactly. The presence of the Japanese in the picture will also enable the reader to compare the two.

The only notice of this curious people that we have ever been able to find is a short description given in the

"British Encyclopædia," which alone is sufficient to show how little is generally known of them:—

"Ainos, or Ainus, the aborigines of Jesso and Saghalin, commonly called *wild Kuriles*, and supposed to be covered with hair in unnatural profusion. They are nearly black, and resemble the Kamtschadales, but have more regular features. The Chinese and Japanese say that they have immense beards. Captain Broughton, who anchored at Endermo harbour, in Jesso, in 1797, remarks that the bodies of the men are covered with long black hair; and Krusenstern, the Russian navigator, mentions that a child of this description was seen in 1805, but that the parents had no such characteristics; and he denies that it is general. Other testimony, *e.g.*, that of the early missionaries at Japan, seems to confirm this peculiarity of the Ainos. The women are very ugly. The Ainos are of a mild, liberal disposition; their manners, however, are very little known. Polygamy is practised among them. Agriculture they know very little of. They fatten bears for winter provision. The Ainos were formerly independent, but are now in subjection to the Japanese."

At Hakodate there is some capital trout and salmon fishing. Two officers of H.M.S. *Scylla* killed upwards of eight dozen fine trout one morning in the course of a few hours. During the short stay we made there we had no opportunity of attempting to follow their example; but we can testify, from remembrance of the way our table was supplied, that fish is plentiful enough.

From Yokohama none of the larger kinds of game are within reach of the foreign sportsman, though both pig and deer are brought into the market from the interior.

It was considered an extraordinary circumstance when a *rara avis* of the latter species strayed down to the woods some few miles from Camp, and afforded Aaron and the Child, who had taken the beagles early one morning in hopes of rattling out a fox, as merry a three-quarters of an hour as is recorded in the annals of that celebrated pack.

It happened on this wise. While crossing a small patch of grass at the foot of a prettily-wooded elevation, —part of a series of hill-covers,—some of the hounds left the horses suddenly, and, without giving tongue, feathered slowly towards the copse.

The dew still lay thick upon the grass; for, dissentient from their drowsy comrades, these two had followed the custom of their ancestors, and exchanged their beds for the saddle some time ere Phœbus— with his footsteps still red above the land of their birth —had thrown his earliest rays o'er the Isles of the Far East.

"Steady, Countess, old woman! Easy there, Bellman!" exclaims Aaron. "That must be the drag of a fox. You get on over the hill, and I will work up towards you."

Accordingly the Child rouses the sluggish nature of the Maneater; and, taking the leeward side of the cover, is soon climbing and scrambling up the hill, and ensconces himself by an open spot on the top, which anything driven forward must cross to gain further shelter.

He is scarcely hidden before Aaron's cheer breaks the stillness of the woods, as he encourages the little ones in their task; and immediately after, a half-doubtful note.

another and another, but still no chorus, float upwards and nearer.

"Hark to Warrior!" as the old hound's voice speaks more determinedly than the others. "Yoi, brush him out!"

As they near the Child in his ambush, he hears a more decided step than ever old Reynard ventured upon; and of a sudden, to his astonished gaze, one of the fine spotted deer of Japan bounds nimbly out of the cover, stops a moment, with ears erect and head half-turned, to listen to his unwelcome followers, then lays his antlers along his back, and seeks refuge in the wood beyond.

No sooner has he disappeared in the thicket than the Child puts his finger in his ear and yells for bare life—making as much noise as if all the foxes in Japan had gone away in a pack, and he was obliged to give a separate view holloa for each one.

"Tally-ho! Gone away!" and the excited pack are soon on the spot, with the noble master immediately in their wake. By this time the Child has dismounted, and, holding the Maneater by the rein at the imminent risk of his life, is trying all he can to get the hounds on to the line.

The three old dwarf fox-hounds—Countess, Warrior, and Bellman, who would hunt anything from an elephant to a mouse—take pretty kindly to the scent, and acknowledge it freely as they dash off in pursuit; but it is only by dint of example, and in obedience to cheers and rates, that the others will condescend to take notice of their unaccustomed quarry.

"Here you are, Aaron! Lay 'em on past that clump

of firs!" shouts the Child. "He's only just gone—a stag as big as a donkey!"

"By Gosh! is he really?" replies Aaron, with a grin of delight. "Put 'em on to me! Here, my little beauties! Huic! Huic!"

"To him! Get to him there, you gaping brutes!" screams the Child in frantic despair, as three or four of the hounds stare wonderingly round, unable to understand the cause of the commotion.

However, the leaders are sticking well to him, and, by degrees, the rest join in, and the whole lot rattle him about from cover to cover. The Child has viewed him again after a second gallop to the front; and at last the little fellows get so close to his heels that he is forced to take to the open—slipping so quietly and quickly away that it is not until Comus is seen a quarter of a mile off, going best pace alone, that anything is known of his departure.

Aaron immediately lifts them forward, and a merry gallop is the result; old Comus still keeping his lead till they mount the hills and enter the woods a mile or two away.

The hunting here becomes slower, though the pace occasionally freshens for a few minutes; but at the end of three-quarters of an hour—by which time the sun has got up, and, in consequence, both the scent and the horses have become pretty well baked—the pack throw up, and, after an ineffectual cast or two, are taken home.

The two lucky individuals who were out on this occasion of course made the most of the unusual bit of sport they had enjoyed; and, though implicit credence was not universally granted to Aaron's glowing account, —given between the mouthfuls of his well-earned and proportionately big breakfast,—many a one repented his own sluggishness, and wished heartily that Morpheus had yielded *place aux dames* to Diana.

B., who was ever most regular at morning exercise, had happened to be on duty, and was ready to tear his hair with vexation. Not even could the gentle influence of "Bell"—arrived that morning—calm the troubled waters of his perturbed spirit; and, throwing the paper aside, he strolled moodily down to the kennels—if not to weep, at least to swear.

He who wishes to shoot in the neighbourhood of Yokohama may find three varieties of the sport with which to amuse himself in turn.

There are pheasants — the ordinary one, like our English bird, except that the plumage of the cock bears a beautiful green gloss in place of the equally lovely purple tinge on the breast of ours; and the more rare kind, the bronze pheasant.

The male of the latter—the Copper Cock, as he is usually termed—is, perhaps, the handsomest of game birds.

As he flashes past you, with the light playing on his glorious plumage, he looks like a gleam of sunshine, and it seems almost sacrilege to destroy anything so beautiful. Still, we have the satisfaction of knowing we are not shooting for the pot; and great is the triumph if a perfect skin—with feathers unblooded, and the long, barred tail unruffled—can be obtained.

A good specimen of the copper cock will measure nearly fifty inches from the tip of the beak to the tip of the tail; and each feather throws out the reflection of the sun like burnished gold.

Very fair snipe-shooting is to be had at times at a distance of twelve or fifteen miles from the Settlement—the highest bags we remember being twenty-one and twenty-two couple between two guns. The walking, or rather wading, is much like that in China, viz., through deep paddy-fields, knee-deep in heavy mud; and many is the time that we have sighed for a breech-loader, as we strove in vain to keep our gun-stock out of the mud while loading.

Lastly, there is—or rather *was*, for the ground has been of late much disturbed by parties of shooters going over from Saturday till Monday; consisting chiefly of cockiolly-bird-slaying Frenchmen, Germans, *et hoc genus omne*, who blaze away at anything and everything—a large quantity and variety of wild-fowl to be met with up the Bay of Yeddo, where the river Logo empties itself into the sea. Geese, duck, and teal were accustomed to assemble there in great numbers; and by staying out a night or two in a covered, flat-bottomed craft, known as a house-boat,—and combining warmth and convenience in a wonderful degree,—good sport could be obtained at certain seasons.

Where the geese have not been attacked by the merciless foreigners, they are still to be seen in immense flocks, as they enjoy a perfect immunity from the natives. For instance, as you ride along the Tokaido—within a certain distance of which it is contrary to law and the terms of treaty to fire a gun—the birds are to be seen feeding sometimes within twenty yards of the road; and often have we cast much the same kind of eyes on them that Reynard is said to have turned on the grapes in the fable, trying to console ourselves with the idea that they were fishy, undesirable game, till, in spiteful anger at their apparent contempt, we have sent a shot from our revolver to disturb them from their peaceful meal.

The two latter kinds of sport require but little description; but as the pheasant-shooting in Japan, and the way of obtaining it, differ essentially from the "warm corner" that ye—our aristocratic and stay-at-home patrons—are probably wont and fortunate enough to enjoy, it may not be out of place to tell how C——, the Captain, Fluffy, and the Child got through what was considered rather more than an average day's sport in that unhallowed country.

The time was but little on one side or the other of Christmas, when the covers were more penetrable than in the earlier part of the season; and the scene fixed upon by Fluffy was at some distance, and a favoured locality which he had kept a rigid secret in his own breast.

Fluffy was not of "ours," but had been left behind by our predecessors to act as guardian over the fairer portion of his regiment, who had remained in Yokohama to escape the fever and ague of China.

We often wondered how the authorities could consistently confide the charge of so much weak beauty— ye who have had experience of camp or barrack life recall the dulcet tones, delicate forms and features, and winning ways of the ordinary run of soldiers' wives!—to one whose flowing, flaxen locks and pendent moustaches would render him dangerous anywhere. But so it was; and we presume that his keen persistence in pursuit of pheasants prevented his flying after other game.

Speaking of those heroic dames whose presence is said to " cheer and elevate the British soldier, and take away half the hardship of his duties in camp or field," we have still before our mind a touching and characteristic scene that took place not so long ago in a certain orderly-room in Yokohama.

Two charming representatives of their class were brought before the Commandant as being the leaders of their respective parties in a slight dispute which had led to a free fight in the women's wash-house the previous evening.

No sooner were they ushered into the august presence than one, who took upon herself the character of complainant,—and whose sparkling orbs were surrounded by a purple tinge that nature could have had nothing to do with,—broke forth into an irresistible flow of eloquence, whose effect was increased doubly by the earnest and emphatic movements of her ruddy fists, that the pretty creature clenched tight and shook in her excitement.

"Ah, now! axing yer honour's pardon, but the baste didn't fight fair. Sure she hot me over the head wi' the lid o' the boiler; or faix, I'd 'a quelted her properly!"

At this point in her narration she was interrupted by the other,—a gaunt Yorkshire woman,—who, stepping across the room, stopped short in front of her, dropped a courtesy, and in the most polite manner,—but breathing the most intense sarcasm in voice and speech,—said :—

"Beg parding, mum! Beg parding, but you're lying!" then, turning to him before whom they were arraigned, added, as she held out her long bony arms,

'It's them two arms as did it, sir; and she knows it! It's them two fisses, and she'll feel 'em agin yet!"

To return to our friend Fluffy. So keen was he with the gun, that had there been left but one pheasant in Japan, he would have pursued that one every day till he got a shot at him—which, by-the-bye, would probably not have been until either Sancho, Dash, Tembar, Drake, or one other of his troop of wild unmanageables, had flushed him half-a-dozen times. Certainly in such a country a few good working dogs are invaluable; but it is trying to the best of tempers—our own, we are bound to admit, can hardly be classed in that category—when birds are scarce, to see one after another get up two hundred yards ahead, in spite of whistling, yells, and execrations.

"What time ought we to start, in order to reach this pet place of yours by a reasonable hour in the morning?" asked C——.

"Well, we ought to be up by three, so as to leave this by four."

"By three? The devil we ought! Why, I am going to a whist-party to-night, and shan't get back before then."

"So much the better," replied Fluffy heartlessly; "then you will be all ready for a start, and can rouse us up."

The Captain and the Child said little, but thought none the less that it would be precious cold at that hour. However, it was arranged that they should leave themselves entirely in Fluffy's hands. The ponies were ordered for 3.30 A.M.; guns and necessary "gear" got ready at once; and the mess waiters directed to lay out a cold breakfast, with a supply of sandwiches, before they went to bed, so that the sportsmen might be able to recruit themselves previous to starting.

Accordingly, C—— went to his whist-party; the Captain and Fluffy turned in early; and the Child intended to do so, but didn't.

At 2 a.m. C—— returned to his hut, and, giving the sentry on the gate orders to call him in an hour's time, lay down for a nap, waking up at the appointed hour apparently the liveliest of the party. The others were roused up, and, taking the darkness and the frosty morning as a sufficient excuse for shirking the cold tub till their return, bundled into their clothes, and hastened down to the stables to see that the ponies were fed and saddled before they adjourned to their own breakfast.

As they sat round some cold pheasants,—the produce of a former day,—Fluffy appeared in the highest spirits, C—— as fresh as paint, the Captain silent and somewhat sulky, wondering how he could have been such a fool as to get up by candlelight, while the Child was too intent on the provender to do more than mutter something about its being "devilish cold"—this witty speech being intended as a kind of semi-apology for a second attack on the beer-jug.

Another half-hour finds them ready for a start, each with a warm pea-jacket on,—which, with the addition of military buttons, is considered uniform in Japan,—gun slung on his back, and cheroot glowing between his lips.

Proceeding to the stables, they receive their ponies from the shivering bettoes; and handing over the horse-rugs to the latter, who wrap them at once round their persons, mount, and follow at a respectful distance from Fluffy and his notorious kicker, to the kennels.

C——'s grand old retriever, Rex, who is a regular regimental pet, is never tied up, and, since the first sign of his master being about to set out shooting, has been with the greatest difficulty prevented from waking up the Camp with his noisy delight; but Fluffy has to unloose some half-dozen wild creatures, one and all of whom appear to be afflicted with the most obstinate deafness.

"Come here, Sancho! Drat you, Tembar! Never mind; come along, C——; they will follow us!" and so saying, Fluffy trots off in the darkness, keeping up a running fire of objurgations on his pack.

It is pretty plain sailing through the Settlement; but as they emerge into the country, the paths become narrow, and the going worse. The ground is frozen and slippery, and the cold intense; while it is so dark that they follow the road with the greatest difficulty.

"Holloa, Fluffy! Pull up a moment; I must get down and walk, or my toes will drop off!" shouts C——; and his example is followed by the others—the whole jogging along in attempts to restore circulation to their feet.

"Hold up, Bob!" yells the Captain with what *might* have been a thanksgiving, but certainly didn't sound like one. "By Jove! the brute was nearly down on the top of me!" Black Bob, as his owner called him, was not the only one that slipped and scrambled during the next mile or so; and our friends themselves found it such bad going that they remounted, and trusted to Providence to provide for their safety.

Fluffy has the advantage of his followers, for he knows the road thoroughly, and rides along quite at his ease.

As he turns into an overhung lane, where the darkness is so intense that the horses' heads are undistinguishable to their riders, he calls out, "Look out for the bridge at the corner!"

It is very kind of him to give the caution; but where is the corner? and where is the bridge?—the said *bridge* being, moreover, a narrow plank over a deep ditch; and by such means, nothing but a Japanese pony would cross even by daylight. It is therefore hardly to be wondered at that the first intimation C—— obtains of its propinquity is the finding himself descending headlong into the gulf.

A few minutes suffice to extricate the unfortunate pair; and, on the principle of its being an ill wind that blows no one any good, the Captain and the Child take warning by the catastrophe, and lead their animals quietly over. At the same time, this little accident threatens to unsettle C——'s nerves much more seriously than the late hours over the whist-table. The well-filled pocket-pistol, though, proves an infallible remedy; and in an incredibly short time they pursue their slippery and uncertain career.

No further accident occurs to hinder their progress; and after another hour's cautious riding, a grey light breaks in the east. By degrees, objects grow more distinct, and before they reach the Tokaido, daylight has become pretty well established.

As they have to follow the Great High Road for some distance, revolvers are loosened in the holsters, and the party close up together. The bettoes have taken a short cut, and will reach Snrima—their destination—before their masters, and in time to see that stabling, forage, &c., are in readiness for their arrival.

Some portions of the Tokaido are remarkably pretty and picturesque; and you are amply rewarded in riding along it, though it is just as well to go in a tolerably strong party, and armed.

As our friends leave the Tokaido and gain the higher ground beyond, the sun is just rising and throwing a warmer tint over the hitherto cold grey sky. The scenery, too, rejoices in its light, and the glad travellers in its grateful heat. Each turn brings out some fresh view, which has its own charms peculiar from its neighbours; and even the Captain is forced to admit that such loveliness of nature almost repays the ordeal of "getting up in the middle of the night."

A cock pheasant is heard crowing close at hand; and immediately after is seen rising above the firs on the ridge of a wooded spur to the left, and skimming down into the corn-field below, followed by half-a-dozen of his kinsfolk. The Child is anxious to "stop and get a bang at them," maintaining that "a bird in the hand is worth two in the bush;" but Fluffy answers that "these birds are still in the bush, and we have no time to lose." The other is obliged to obey orders, but cannot help looking back more than once at the spot where the old cock was last seen.

A little farther on they pull up at a tea-house, which Fluffy says is about two-thirds of the way, and where he is evidently well known, for the proprietor runs out immediately and salutes him with much bowing, and the attendant hissing, which invariably accompanies the Japanese greeting. The buxom landlady and her fair daughters also hasten to offer the ever-ready tea to the travellers; and even Sancho and Co. receive notice and attention. The ponies' mouths are washed out, the tea despatched, and a fresh cheroot lighted previous to remounting.

On renewing their journey, they diverge from the main road they have been following for the last half-dozen miles, and jog along what is hardly worthy of the name of a path, through a rough country, the greater part of which is wooded and uncultivated; fording two or three streams; and then across the rich mulberry plains, whence most of the silken wealth of the district is brought, till, about eight o'clock, they pull up at the village of Surima.

Fluffy is very sanguine of sport, and speaks in the most glowing terms of the abundance of game to be found in this part; and in these statements he is borne out to the full by the good man of the tea-house, who is delighted at the chance of "squeezing" the foreigners.

Wonderful to relate, all Fluffy's dogs are at hand, notwithstanding that they have been engaged in working the whole country contiguous to the line of route, and on two or three occasions have necessitated the return of a mile or so in search of a missing one. Certainly two of them appear as if they have had hunting enough for the day; and it is to be hoped this may have a wholesome effect in keeping them within bounds.

Coats and wrappers are thrown aside, guns flashed off, a coolie hired to carry the tiffin and what birds may be bagged, and all are ready for a start, when a fearful commotion, accompanied by a horrible squealing, is heard from the direction of the place whither the ponies have been led.

All four rush out immediately, and find that the row

is caused by a difference of opinion between two of the steeds. C——'s great, powerful animal has fixed on to the unfortunate little beast that the Child has been riding (and which is no other than the Aide's Muffin Worry), and is shaking him as a terrier would a rat, giving vent, all the time, to a savage neighing, while his victim wriggles helplessly in his jaws.

The combatants are soon parted by dint of impartial punishment; and the same having been dealt out to their respective bettoes for not paying proper attention to their charges, the party proceed to the shooting-ground.

During the first hour or so, but little game is bagged. C—— kills a pheasant and a quail; the Child misses one of the latter, though the shot is all but productive, as a harmless Nippon cutting wood barely escapes receiving the whole of the charge in his head; Fluffy and the Captain get a brace of pheasants and a duck between them.

The cover is very thick and difficult, and more than half the birds get away without a shot being fired; indeed, at times, pheasants may be heard getting up all round, without a glimpse being obtained of them. Fluffy's dogs, too, are apparently determined to save their master as much trouble as possible in beating the ground; for not only do they quarter that immediately on each side, but extend their range usually a couple of hundred yards ahead. Poor Fluffy is, in consequence, kept in a continual state of agitation, and his lungs uninterruptedly exercised throughout the day in attempts to keep them in order.

"Whirr, whirr! bang, bang!" A brace of pheasants

rise near the Child in tolerably open ground, and he makes what he looks upon as rather a neat double shot in knocking them both over; but neglecting to run in and pick them up at once,—a necessary precaution with pheasants in Japan,—proceeds quietly with his loading, after seeing them on the ground.

This operation over, he walks on to recover his birds, but finds, to his astonishment, that one has already made off, while the other is preparing to follow, and, on being chased, gains shelter in the rushes of an adjacent stream.

The Child's shouts soon bring up the dogs in a body; and after much search and scrambling among the reeds, he is so far fortunate as to recover a head from Tembar, and a wing from Sancho. No sign can be discovered of the other bird; so it still remains a mystery whether he escaped to die in peace, or formed a meal for Fluffy's voracious pack. At all events, this was not the first or last occasion that proof was given that the Japanese pheasant can carry off an extraordinary amount of shot; though to all the Child's indignant innuendoes against the dogs and their greedy appetites, the only answer deigned by their infatuated master was, "Well, you should *kill* your birds, instead of tailoring them!"

Towards noon they reach a deep wooded ravine, some miles in extent, where the experienced leader is certain of finding sport; but ere commencing to beat this, they unanimously agree to take advantage of a stream of clear water that bubbles invitingly from the hills, to set aside half an hour for discussion of sandwiches, brandy and water, and a cigar.

The last item is but half finished when the word is given to recommence work. Birds are a little more plentiful than in the early part of the day, and C——, with Rex at his heels, keeps picking them up steadily.

"Hang it! those infernal dogs have put up a copper hen out of that clump of firs!" shouts the Child; and he and C—— rush forward to where they are still at work. Up get a brace of hen pheasants, both of which are bagged; and then a grand old cock, shining dazzling bright in the sun, sweeps across, some seventy yards off. Both blaze a left barrel after him, but at that distance with little effect, though they manage to mark him down a long distance ahead.

Of course everything is sacrificed to the chance of a copper cock, and he is followed up at once. Fluffy goes round him, in case he should run and get up wild; the Captain and the Child come down on either side; and C—— follows him up straight.

Thus surrounded, he has no chance; but, as at length he rises right among the party, and makes a last effort for his life, a volley brings him down through the trees, and the brilliant beauty is rescued just in time from the eager mouths that lust for him.

By three o'clock the ravine has been beaten up; a fair number of birds killed; and the pack have had the delight of devouring another brace among them.

It is then determined to work back towards the tea-house; and for this purpose C—— and Fluffy take one line, and pick up a brace of birds *en route*, while the Captain and the Child take another, and get an odd bird —and a ducking in trying to cross an unfordable stream.

Arrived at the rendezvous, the bag is found to consist of ten brace of pheasants,—exclusive of the copper cock and those considered perquisites by Fluffy's highly-trained pointers,—two couple of quail, and a duck.

Scoff not, we pray you, noble patrons! Such were we wont to consider a fair day's sport in Japan; though you may question whether it was worth the hard work attendant on it, and may say that such a result in the "home covers" would insure a month's wages and an instant dismissal, to him whose province is to provide against the two or three occasions during the season, on which he enters the woods to drive the half-tame pheasants—not as usual to be fed, but to be shot.

Yes, after all, there were some advantages in this style of sport. At least, we had really wild birds; and to men in good condition the hard work was pleasurable rather than otherwise. The delightful climate, too, of a Japan winter—cold frosty nights, with clear, sunny days—braces and strengthens the limbs and gives a tone to the whole system, till fatigue is not felt, and enjoyment found not only in the sport, but in the work itself.

How are we to chronicle the last incident before the return to Camp? or how gloss it over so that the sensitive mind may not start back horrified at its monstrosity?

Notwithstanding the time of the year, the sun was still blazing down with great power when our friends reached the tea-house, warm from their recent exertions.

A bright, clear stream ran foaming close past the house, round which was clustered the crowd of both sexes that invariably assembles whenever foreigners are to be seen in any of the country villages—where, as yet, to the simple peasants, they are scarce human creatures from another sphere. Nor is this to be wondered at. Imagine a Peloo Islander, or even one of the sons of Niphon, in any small town or village in the interior of England! Would he not be stared at by the chawbacons; giggled at by the nursery-maids; ridiculed, and perhaps pelted, by the little boys—those social mosquitoes of our streets?

It is to be feared we highly civilised and favoured people gain but little by the comparison.

"How jolly cool and refreshing that brook looks!" observed the Captain. "If all those villagers weren't here, I should like to have a bathe."

"Oh, bother the villagers! *I*'ll have a dip anyhow. It's their look-out, if they will come staring here; they're not so particular themselves. *They* don't think anything of it; and, besides, I haven't had my tub this morning."

With these words the Child proceeded to divest himself of his clothes. C——, however, with more delicacy than his flippant companion, ordered his betto—who understood English, and was accustomed to do service as interpreter—to explain to the crowd that the "tojin donesan's (foreign masters) were going to wash, and it would perhaps be better if they moved off."

So far from this having the desired effect, the only feeling seemed to be that of pleasurable expectation. The moosmies, among whom were several pretty, brighteyed damsels, seemed particularly delighted at the idea, and skipped about in the highest glee.

Here we must pause for one moment, to beg that you will not allow yourselves to be imbued with the idea that the pardonable enjoyment evinced by these charming creatures at the novelty of the sight, was vilified by any sentiment approaching to immodest curiosity. If blame is due to any concerned, it is to those whose early training should have taught them to behave with a more becoming regard for appearances, but whose sense of modesty was so far blunted by their sojourn in barbarous climes, that they now splashed and gamboled carelessly in water not a foot deep, before an enraptured crowd, who laughed, stared, and chattered in great amusement at the spectacle.

"Kiridonai! See how beautiful and white the foreigners' skins are!"

"They are not like monkeys after all! How tall and big they are! They must be wrestlers."

Such were a few of the remarks passed on the appearance of the quartett as they revelled in the cold stream.

The bath gives a warm glow and fresh strength to their frames, and they start for their ride home thoroughly invigorated.

The game is to be brought over to the Camp on the morrow. Two of the bettoes lead the dogs on slowly, while the others will run their sixteen miles back as easily as they came.

Making the most of what is left of daylight, our friends reach their quarters just in time to dress for dinner; the only incident, or rather *a*ccident, of the road, being that the Child's pony, becoming a little leg-weary, turns a complete somersault, and chucks his rider, gun

and all, into a deep paddy-field on the side of the path—completely annulling any good effects that may have resulted from his recent bathe, and necessitating a lavish use of hot water and soap before he is fit to re-enter society.

CHAPTER XIX.

TRAINING FOR THE RACES.

How much more difficult is it to begin a chapter than to go on with one! Having once made a start, the thoughts seem to travel, and the pen to run, of their own accord; and though the track they follow may be in itself feeble and uninteresting, one is compelled unconsciously to adopt it.

We were reading the other day—*where* we cannot just at the moment remember; nor is it of sufficient interest to our readers, or worth the trouble to ourselves, to look out—how some of the most celebrated writers of late days were at times racked and tortured for ideas; how Thackeray would draw and scribble over two-thirds of his paper as he wrote; how another would rave up and down the room, tearing his hair; and how a third would lie and roll on the floor in his literary agony.

If these giants were sometimes at a loss, how much more must we pigmies suffer!

However, as we ourselves are not—thank Heaven!—writing for a livelihood, but merely with the view of passing away some of the dull, idle days of a long sea voyage, and in humble hopes of providing an occasional half-hour's amusement for *you*, we do not allow ourselves to be much vexed with such difficulties as these; but striking off at a tangent, follow wherever the thought of the moment may lead us.

Some two or three months after what we wrote of in the last chapter, the committee of the Yokohama Race Club issued their programme for the Spring Meeting; and, as the military provided by far the greater proportion of jockeys, and their full share of contending animals, the publishing of the card caused considerable excitement in the Camp. Every race was discussed, and the most varied opinions freely given as to the weights, conditions, &c.

There were still six weeks before the meeting was to take place, and those who had ponies to enter commenced strict training forthwith.

Meanwhile, two of the characters who have hitherto figured prominently in these pages have disappeared from the scene.

Jolly has gone to the depôt, whence he occasionally writes letters teeming with his hair-breadth escapes from matrimonial nets; while poor Aaron had at last to succumb to his liver, and has been invalided home "for the preservation of his life." It would seem, though, that his native hills did for him what even the air of Japan could not; for, not many months after, "Bell" records him steering his own horse a good last in a garrison steeple-chase, and immediately afterwards erasing the blot, and, at the same time, wiping the eyes of his comrades, at the "five traps, twenty-five yards rise," &c. It is rather unfair of us to mention this; for should he ever try his hand at Hurlingham—which is by no means unlikely—it might possibly be the means of preventing

x

Mr. Frank Heathcote from placing him among the short-distance novices.

It might appear but a piece of presumption on our part to suppose that the "great handicapper" will even read this; but in our own mind we are certain that he who, with presentation-Purdey in hand—we mean the one that *did* suit him!—has given us many a useful hint among the Lincolnshire stubbles, will not now withhold his favour, nor scruple to tell us of our shortcomings as of yore.

Tom Brown, at Aaron's departure, went into Bones' hands, with a view to running him at the ensuing meeting, when the latter expects his jumping powers and turn of speed will serve him in a hurdle-race.

As the training, or at all events the galloping part of it, has to be conducted on the race-course itself,—which, being of ample dimensions, can afford to be divided into two widths for the purpose; the inner ring being preserved for the actual contests,—every morning sees the interested and the knowing, carefully taking stock of the work done by the favourites.

It may not therefore be amiss, and may give you a better acquaintance with those likely to perform at the coming festival, if you will for once adopt the early-rising movement, and accompany us to the Course some morning about a fortnight before the races.

We promise that you shall do it with as little discomfort as possible. A cup of hot coffee shall be ready for you when you are called, and an easy hack shall be at your door waiting for you.

You will probably have to get into your breeches and boots by candlelight; but you must not mind that, though Abdul may perhaps try to dissuade you by telling you that " *le jeu ne vaut pas la chandelle.*"

Receive his advice as being worth about as much as his joke, and wrap yourself well up against the cold morning air.

You have agreed—got up—not kept us waiting more than half an hour—and mounted your horse, with but one eye open, and an expression of countenance more rueful than that of a criminal riding to his doom.

It is still starlight, and we ought to be able to get to the scene of action before the earliest have been round; so take a light from our cheroot, and we will canter on.

Two or three fellows are already bustling about the stables, hurrying their bettoes, and slanging them for their dilatoriness; and, as we proceed on our way, we pass more than one " lot " being led up to the course, which is nearly two miles away from the Settlement.

Who can those be who are *leaving* the ground at this hour?

Had we been but a few minutes sooner, we might have picked up a wrinkle worth knowing. Those two —the one on a well-known galloper, the other on a raw-looking but finely-shaped chestnut—are no others but Alexander and his jockey, Cope, both of whom you have already met. They have evidently been giving the griffin a spin; and, to judge from the satisfied look on the former's face, the trial has been a favourable one.

" Morning, Alexander! Got something good for the Griffin's Plate as usual?"

Asking this question is merely a matter of form; for we do not in the least expect to obtain any information by so doing; consequently the answer does not disappoint us.

"No; I'm afraid the beggar's no good for racing, though I dare say he will make a useful hack some day."

Notwithstanding this speech, we are at liberty to draw our own conclusions; and taking into consideration what is already known to us, viz., that Alexander got a griffin down from Nambu (the province where all the best ponies are bred) a short time ago, at the price of a thousand ichiboos; and that, if trouble or money can procure it, he always *will* have a real good one; we put two and two together, and, influenced by the expression we noticed on the owner's countenance, advise you solemnly to "mark that griffin as *dangerous!*"

"But," you ask, "how can it repay a man to give such a price for an untried animal on the chance of winning a thirty or forty pound stake? Even if he is lucky enough to get hold of a veritable 'out-and-outer,' you have no betting-ring where he may back his horse, and no amateurs are likely to give him anything like the current odds!"

"Ah," we answer, "you don't understand the Selling Lotteries—and *selling* they are, too, in more senses than one—which supply the place of the Ring all over the East! If you do *not* know about them, let us explain as concisely and clearly as we can.

"The entries having been published, the lotteries are held shortly before the races. Say there are ten horses entered for a certain race, and a hundred individuals take tickets for the lottery at five dollars each—making in all five hundred dollars. The names of the horses having been

TRAINING FOR THE RACES. 309

drawn, each is put up to auction in turn, and sold to the highest bidder. The favourite would sell for—say one hundred dollars; *i.e.*, that sum has to be paid by the buyer to the man who drew the horse, and the same amount BESIDES to the fund of the lottery itself. Thus, when all the horses have been sold, the lottery is sometimes worth double its original value; the whole amount going to the purchaser of the winning horse. So you see, if a man wishes to back his horse, he must buy him in the lotteries, when he will, in all probability, get quite as long odds against him as if we had a regular betting arena."

"Would, though," we go on, waxing almost eloquent as we warm to the subject, "would that we had the Ring in these countries instead of the system of lotteries, which—though a necessary evil—are in truth the curse of racing in the East! Artifices are employed, and stratagems resorted to, that would never be tolerated at home, even in these days of laxest morality on the turf; and every inducement is held out to owners of horses to put such means into practice. For instance, what is easier for a man to do, who owns the most likely horse in a race—but finds that others are running the price up against him—than to buy in what he considers the next best, and scratch his own? And thus he in turn has the opportunity of crippling his neighbour's chance of gain by out-bidding him, and—as it were—taking the bread out of his mouth. Such things are constantly done; and hence racing, instead of being a fair and honourable amusement, is very apt to degenerate into a mere gambling speculation, wherein the great object is to "do in the eye" all others engaged. However, as we said before, lotteries are a necessary evil, and we will not declaim against them any more. Besides, have not we ourselves occasionally picked up a few honest little crumbs at the same?"

You saw the pains those two fellows we met just now had taken to keep their secret—whatever it may be—quiet? That was, of course, with a view of buying their griffin in cheaper, should he have turned out satisfactorily.

It was only last week that we tried one by *moonlight;* and as *you* are not likely to "split," we may add that he beat old Nameless, who is one of the fastest half-milers here, by four lengths. So, though he only cost about a sixth part of what the chestnut did, we have great hopes of his upsetting *their* pot, and building up a great one for ourselves.

Our best plan is to ride quietly round, keeping close to the railings, so as not to interfere with the gallops.

It is not a bad course for this part of the world, is it, though the hill *is* rather a stiff one? But you must bear in mind that this high embankment had to be carried some two or three hundred yards across the deep valley, and every pound of earth was conveyed on the shoulders of coolies.

We don't know how many thousand dollars it took to build it; but this we do know to our cost—that the Japanese Government make us pay a yearly rental of sixteen hundred, which falls rather heavy on such a small community as ours; for, in addition to that, we have had to build the Grand Stand, fence out the paddock, and keep the course in order. But here comes

Mr. Rudolph, whose acquaintance you made the other day at the Drag Hunt. He is the Honorary Secretary and working man of the Committee, and can tell you anything more you may wish to know.

"Good morning, Rudolph! You are here in good time; nothing has been round yet."

"Good morning! Delighted to see your friend out, too. Good morning, sir!" as the "polite foreigner" raises his hat. "I expected to meet Bones and B., who have kindly undertaken to ride my ponies for me; they said they should be here by daylight to give them their work. Ah, here they come! I will go and meet them, so 'Chin-chin' for the present. You will come to tiffin on Sunday? and I shall feel honoured if your friend will accompany you. Mind you are in time for the champagne cock-tail!"

Of course you think of what we have already told you about Rudolph's table, and accept; and if Duckworth does not give us too long a sermon, we shall manage to be in time for the cock-tail.

B. and Bones, who have got more than a dozen ponies —some their own, the rest the property of different owners—are soon hard at work, taking each in turn; and as they pass us, while giving a sharp spin to two of the lot, they have barely time to hail us.

They have begun on two old acquaintances of ours— to wit, Tom Brown and Pericles. B., who looks perfectly happy while at this sort of work, is going smoothly along at a good round gallop on Tom Brown, who appears in as good form as we ever saw him; while Bones, who stands very much over his saddle, is pegging away continually at Pericles. The old horse, though free as

Lottery across country, hates this preparatory part on the flat heartily, and shirks it all he can.

Who is this now coming on to the course? Were it not for the shabby breeches and gaiters, we should take him to be some wealthy owner of horses, as he rides in with his stud-groom, followed by a string of five. No, this is none other than the Child; and the abused continuations are what he calls his "working rig for the mornings," and which he regards with the reverence due to old age.

Leaving the remainder to be walked round under the charge of his subordinate, he commences by giving the animal he is riding, what in his sage opinion is sufficient for the morning. That done, the pony is clothed and led home, while the next in order supplies its place.

As he comes swinging past, all intent on his work, standing up in his stirrups, with hands low on the withers, you remark, "That fellow looks hardly the measure for a light-weight jock! What weights do you ride here?"

"Not feather weights," we answer; "but certainly it is no easy job to put up a six-foot man, with saddle, even at 10 stone 7lbs. However, the Child will manage it before the day. In addition to the work attendant on galloping those five or six before breakfast, he will, directly after parade, be running or walking for a couple of hours with extra coats and waistcoats on; and if this is one of his "sweating" days, he will turn in afterwards under a feather bed and half-a-dozen blankets. At half-past one he will eat beef-steak enough for three —but nothing else; and this, with the exception of tea and dry toast, will last him till the same hour to-morrow.

All the afternoon he and B. will take their ponies out for walking exercise.

This regimen will bring him out as fine as a bowstring by the races; and, though looking rather lean about the chops, all the better and stronger for it.

Here comes Bobby, cantering along, his eye-glass in his eye, looking as self-satisfied and innocent of all guile as if he had not been "keeping it up" nearly the whole night.

Bob goes in for everything, whether it be sport, science, literature, painting, botany, geology, languages, or dissipation. Each and all of these he dabbles in, and on the most abstruse branches of which he is ready at a moment's notice to converse with the utmost ease and self-possession, when thrown in company with those who, from interest or profession, are likely to be skilled in any one of them.

The only subject we have never heard him discuss is astrology, though we doubt not it is but for lack of opportunity, and that should he chance to come across Professor Airy, he would maintain his own ideas on the Newtonian theory of gravitation, against all the arguments of that profound astronomer.

We would not give twopence for a man who has not a fair amount of self-confidence; and, measured by this law, Bobby is certainly worthy of the highest esteem.

On one occasion, in a crowd, he chanced by accident to tread on the toe of a big, burly individual standing next to him. Bobby naturally turned round to apologise, but the proffered reparation was received in the most ungracious manner; whereupon our hero, who stands fully five feet nothing in his shoes, carefully placing his glass in his eye, and speaking with even more than his customary deliberation, addressed his huge neighbour as follows: "Ah-wah; my good fellar, you know I've apologised; and I couldn't do more if I punched your head!"

His universal talents are now employed in training three or four ponies, the chief of whom are the chestnut China pony, Sweet William, whom you may remember his riding in the drag, and whom he is going to pilot in the steeple-chase—and a rare good little animal called Tommy, with whom he hopes to win a hurdle-race.

"Why, surely this is a dromedary going round the course alone!" you exclaim suddenly.

No, worthy friend (forgive the familiarity!); far from it! That is the distinguished Dr. Quock, alike skilled in the science of medicine and the art of equitation. Curled up over the neck of his steed, he will chirrup and cluck confidentially into Pluck's ear at least four times more round the circle, in a canter little faster than a walk; then go home to breakfast, and dilate rapturously and incoherently upon the "thplendid wind my horth Pluck hath got! God bleth my thoul, thir! after a four-mile gallop he wathn't blown a bit!"

There is the Aide, riding side by side and talking earnestly with his friend, Sœpius Tight. Both the ponies —and likely animals they are—are under the charge of the former; and the present conversation of course forms part of one of the many consultations held over their present state of condition, and their future chance of success.

The Aide is of opinion that Antelope should have a good brushing gallop this morning; Tight thinks that a short canter will be better for him, with the gallop reserved for to-morrow.

"Velocipede ought to have his sweat in clothing;" Tight "fancies he is almost fine enough, and that the clothing might be dispensed with."

In the end, it generally happens that the Aide gets his own way; the other yielding to his more confirmed experience, and the sound reputation as a trainer that the Aide has established for himself ever since he brought Sea-gull to the post.

One point, however, they are both agreed upon; and that is, that the great surprise of the meeting will be the performances of Antelope and Velocipede, who are to carry all before them—the only question now remaining being, what races each is to be allowed to win.

He on the grey China pony is the Liver Cutter; and, as he finishes with a sharp burst for the last quarter of a mile of his gallop, the long spurs go in deep and often.

Coming round again, he is riding another of the same hue; and with these two greys the Public—knowing ones, prying ones, and verdant ones alike—are fated to be as completely gulled as were ever that greedy crowd of injured innocents,—gambling preachers of self-sacrificing frankness,—gluttonous outsiders, who would fain make money out of other men's horses, of other men's expenditure, of other men's anxiety, toil, and labour—as thoroughly deceived by their own avaricious curiosity as ever the spirit of revenge, gain, or ambition could desire.

Hayn is a man who, having received his education on the English Turf,—with the ins and outs of which he is intimately acquainted,—now frequently reaps the fruits of his experience among his less gifted brother-sportsmen of the colonies.

Importing from China, at a cost of many dollars, one of the fastest ponies in training, he purchased at the same time another *indifferent* animal much resembling him; and the two arrived just in time to be prepared for the Yokohama Spring Meeting.

Mog was the flyer, Mag was the slow one; but in the stable their owner, in speaking of them to his grooms, took the precaution to interchange their names; and as he was of a known taciturn disposition,—particularly with regard to racing matters,—his friends seldom put any questions to him about his stud.

The news spread like wild-fire that Hayn had landed two new China ponies, and that one was a crack.

When they began to take their work, every one was on the *qui vive* to watch them; and, as they often went round together, it was soon seen which could gallop and which could not; but an impression—chiefly conveyed by grooms from stable to stable—existed that the fast one was *Mag;* and by degrees, though some few had heard of Mog's performances in Shanghae, even these came to the conclusion that *Mag* was the better of the two.

Both were entered in the great race for China ponies:

The one as Mr. Hayn's grey China pony, Mog;

The other as Mr. Hayn's grey China pony, Mag.

And the public were hot upon *Mag.* The knowing owner had two or three friends about at work snapping them up on all sides, in addition to buying *Mog* in at every lottery; and great must have been his inward chuckling as he saw the would-be clever ones playing into his hands.

When the race was run, one grey pony bearing the Tartar colours had it all to himself at the distance; while the other was seen tailing far behind.

The backers of Mag cheered lustily at their supposed victory; but dire indeed was their consternation when the number was hoisted, and *Mog* proclaimed the winner.

Mog's identity was proved beyond dispute; and the unfortunate losers found out too late that they had been backing the *right* horse under the *wrong* name.

So close had the secret been kept, that even the Liver Cutter, who was to ride the crack—but whose discretion could not be relied upon to the same extent as his horsemanship—had fallen unconsciously into the same trap as the others; and it was only on the night before the race that Hayn undeceived him—transferring whatever bad bets he might have made on the subject to his own book.

We have been anticipating somewhat with this anecdote—in fact, robbing what belongs properly to another chapter; so, to avoid further digressions, we must return to the course.

After watching the different ponies taking their exercise, we turn into the enclosure, where we meet a number of acquaintances on the same errand as ourselves; and, dismounting, enter the Stand itself, and ascend to the top.

Now tell us if you have been on any Grand Stand in the world that can boast of such a view!

In front—and beyond the bright green ring of turf,

still dotted with men and horses—Mississippi Bay, studded with little islets, sparkles in the sun, which is just rising above the wooded hills of the opposite coast, and lighting up the snow cap of Fusiyama, boldly prominent on your right.

The great Holy Mountain itself stands out more beautiful than ever through the clear morning air; and as it looks proudly down on its comparatively insignificant neighbours, seems to claim for itself the reverence and worship accorded to it by the Japanese.

Behind and below, you get a bird's-eye view of the Settlement, and the harbour full of ships; and, as we look, the flags of various nations rise simultaneously on the different vessels, proclaiming it eight o'clock.

Beyond the Settlement, hill and valley follow each other as far as the eye can reach—the woods on the hills just bursting into new life, while the valleys are radiant in their fresh spring crops.

On the left is the Bay of Yeddo, stretching away to the capital of the Tycoon—the grim brown fort of Kanagawa bristling threateningly on one shore, and soft blue mountains marking its extreme boundaries on the other.

Come along! we mustn't stop any longer if we are going home by a different way. We will take you by some choice bits of scenery, which ought to enchant you with Japan.

Why, here's Tony just entering the course, as everybody else is leaving it.

He protests, with the most amiable and idle of smiles, that he "should have been up long ago, but that his servant was on guard and couldn't call him."

As he seems in no hurry to begin his morning's work, we stop to chat with him for a few minutes, when he goes on to relate of the aforesaid servant, how, when at last he turned up to assist his master, he had asked him in his broad Yorkshire dialect: "Now, sir, whoy don't yer 'ave a try at them woild geese? Last night, when oi wur on sentry, a 'ole drove on 'em comed over me, not twenty yards off. *If oi'd been a loaded sentry, I could a knocked over two or three on 'em*"—thus throwing a new and startling light on the duties of a loaded sentry.

What could have induced Tony, who is himself a bit of a dandy, to take such an extraordinary chawbacon as his valet? The fact is that Ugly—as he is called by his comrades—was promoted from the office of dog-keeper to his present status, in spite of the frightfully hideous indian-rubber-looking physiognomy he possesses; and though Tony himself confesses that he would rather pay fifty pounds than drive a cab through the Park, with Ugly perched behind *en tigre*, he is honest as he is stupid, and looks upon his master, not only as immaculate, but as a kind of Admirable Crichton.

That such is his idea was proved beyond doubt, when, not long ago, he was twitted by some of his fellow-servants about his personal appearance, and at the same time taunted with his nickname of "Ugly." "Oogly!" he repeated, with bitter irony, " Oogly! Now, coom, me and my master 'll show agin you and yourn for a quart!"

Would you like to see how a Japanese pony can go down a drop? Yours can jump like a bird, so let's drive down these two or three banks! Catch tight hold of his head, send him at it, and sit well back! That's the style! It's odd if a Leicestershire man wants much tutoring at any kind of jumping. Pull up now, and we can give 'em their wind.

Holloa! Here are two fellows coming over the hill like madmen. There's a grand line of drops between them and us, so stand still and watch.

Surely, it's the Child on Iona? Yes; and that's the Aide on the Maneater.

Iona is in for the steeple-chase, and his stable companion is probably giving him a lead for a spin across country.

By Jove, though, the Maneater seems beat already! and the Child is yelling to the Aide to shove him along to keep pace.

Iona is safe down the first, and so is the Maneater, though he labours heavily through the deep ground. Still, like most vicious ones, he carries a stout heart, and doesn't shirk his work.

That next drop is a puzzler for a blown horse—eight feet sheer, with a nasty little trench running along the top. The Child, who narrowly escapes a cropper at it, shouts to him, "Look out!" and his chum, warned of some unknown danger, gathers his pony as well as he can, and rouses him with whip and spur.

In vain! He only hurries to his doom. The Maneater knuckles helplessly over the trench—pitches on to his head on the top—poises for one moment on the brink—then crashes down with a double somersault into the field below.

The advantage of the good old principle of "always taking a line of your own," has, perhaps, never been better illustrated than on this occasion; for instead of waiting to be rolled upon, no sooner does the Aide feel that his time is come, than he skims like a swallow—or rather, like a spread-eagle—legs and arms outstretched, far into the next field, alighting at last to burrow deep into the bowels of the earth, scattering the soft ground with his face as with a shell.

Luckless youth! Had thy doting parent beheld thee descending through mid-air like an avalanche, grovelling helplessly in the mire, and arising, at last, with bewildered senses and face plastered with mire, think you she would have given vent to the heartless bursts of merriment that shook and convulsed us as we gazed on thee?

Nay, rather would she have been prompted to annihilate utterly that graceless Child, who—although it is in his own cause and interest this calamity has befallen his friend—now stands by screaming, choking, and gasping with laughter.

We mustn't wait any longer if you wish to be back in Camp in time to get through your dressing, and breakfast comfortably.

We will just have a lark over the artificial jumps on the Rifle Range. Mind the bog, where the Liver Cutter so distinguished himself. You see a Japanese pony can fly a water-jump, and manage a double on and off, as it ought to be done, besides being able to go down a bank.

Up here, through this bamboo grove, is the shortest and prettiest way, and it will give you an opportunity of seeing Smith's Farm—the only specimen of English agriculture in Japan. He says it only just pays its way, but that makes us all the more inclined to believe that it answers well. At all events, he succeeds in one thing, *i.e.*, in growing cauliflowers that you can stand underneath. Probably that will be a new sight to you? There he is himself, as usual, hard at work. Nobody ever yet saw "Public-spirited Smith" idle; and as he generally has about a dozen irons in the fire, it is hard if some of them do not get hot. Somehow, though, he always finds time to talk to you, has ever the latest news about everything and everybody, and is invariably ready and anxious to assist any one.

"How are you, Smith?"

"Holloa! How are you?" returns that cheery individual. "Come in and look at my new calf. Can't stop? Oh, but you must. I know your weakness for new milk."

There is no doubt about it, we *are* fond of warm new milk; and so are you, though you have perhaps been longer weaned than we have.

We knew you would be pleased with our jovial host. That five minutes wasn't wasted? This is your way. Turn in through the gate on your right. Here we are back at the stables. Give your horse over to one of those two tattooed and naked savages running to meet us.

"Now, you young rascal, how often have we told you to loosen the horse's girths before leading into the stable?"—that's about the translation of the dog-Japanese we are obliged to pick up for stable use. "Why, what is Bobby doing?"

The individual spoken of is employed in the middle of the parade-ground, with a long rope attached to a raw griffin, to whom he expects to give a mouth by lungeing him round for about an hour in the same direction. As we approach him, he stops to talk to us; but the poor animal he is tutoring has by this time become so giddy with his circumgyrations (Good word, that! you will say), that he is unable to pull up, but goes on staggering and rolling all over the place.

"What's the matter with him?" cries Bobby. "Is he going to have a fit?" And he runs up quickly to find out the cause of the unusual proceeding—attempting to afford relief by rubbing vigorously at the ears and head of his pony. At this moment, however, the poor beast seems to recover his consciousness; and as if aware that all his disagreeable sensations are owing to him who is close beside him, and who may even now be planning some fresh persecution, he turns suddenly round, and seizes him fiercely by the shoulder.

In vain does Bobby yell and curse as he feels himself lifted bodily from the ground. In vain does he kick with his legs and wave frantically with his arms. Sweet is revenge; and for long to come will Bobby think ruefully of that power of jaw and keenness of teeth.

CHAPTER XX.

A FIRE AT YOKOHAMA.

The thirst for knowledge amongst the Japanese was as strong as Captain Puffles's thirst for sodas and B.'s. Not a machine, nor a rifle, nor an engine of any description, could they see that they did not burn to possess it, and then even to improve upon it.

Their enthusiasm for the novel was of the most red-hot description, and occasionally led them into dilemmas which were productive of much amusement.

On one occasion, some years ago, they bought one of our small gun-boats.

It was the first steamer they had ever owned, and great was the excitement consequent thereon. Officers from Yeddo were sent to our naval authorities, to be instructed in navigation and engineering; but, like children with a new toy, they could not wait for them to be properly taught, and shipped them on board the gun-boat, when they had acquired only a very rudimentary knowledge of their duties.

The day arrived for the trial trip. High officials came down from Yeddo, proceeded on board the gun-boat, and all felt that Japan was on the eve of becoming one of the first maritime powers of the world.

Gaily the little ship steamed out of harbour, spluttering, and fussing, and fizzing, as only a little 60-horse-power gun-boat can.

Reader, have you ever been on board one of these little craft? If you have not, rest contented, and don't go if you can help it.

But should hard fate ever oblige you to, be advised, and don't be taken in by them.

Their puffing, fussing, shivering, and trembling are apt to impress the un-nautical mind with the idea that a great deal is being accomplished by them.

Oh, how bitterly is the individual who indulges in this idea, awakened to a sense of his mistake—as he finds that after the lapse of perhaps two hours, she has made about five knots!

Yes, gaily the little ship steamed out of harbour, with the flag of the rising sun of Japan fluttering from every available stick, her decks crowded with Japanese officers of high degree, and her progress watched with intense interest by excited groups ashore.

On she went, spluttering and fussing, out to sea, until the swells on board had had enough of their namesakes, and her head was turned homewards, the trip being pronounced so far a decided success.

Back she came to her moorings; but, instead of taking them up, she swept past them with undiminished speed, to the surprise of all who were watching her movements.

After this inexplicable conduct, she proceeded to describe a series of circles round the harbour, while from her deck frantic gesticulations and waving of hands were observed.

At last, after having performed numerous intricate manœuvres through the shipping in harbour, she passed close astern of one of our men-of-war, which her commanding officer hailed, begging some one to be sent on board, for *the engineers had forgotten how to stop the engines.*

Of course the required assistance was promptly rendered. Two engineers were sent on board, and in a few minutes she had taken up her moorings.

This is only one of very many instances of how the Japanese are apt to try to run before they can walk.

They have by this time, though, or they ought to have, received several lessons to look before they leap, for assuredly the tojins of all nations have made them pay dearly for their experience in all their transactions with them.

As we glance up our page, and again read through the few lines descriptive of the first Japanese practical essay on steam, we are reminded forcibly of two circumstances which occurred during our stay in the Far East; and in a spirit of fairness, to prevent the laugh being entirely against our Japanese friends, we give an account of them.

A certain steam ship-of-war, a few years ago, on the China and Japan station, was commanded by one of the old school of naval officers—one of that sort who get red in the face, and snort at you that "Damme, sir, the service is going to the dogs!" After which, they look at you fixedly and fiercely for a few moments with a don't-contradict-me-for-I-know-better sort of look.

Fine old fellows in their way! and, as a rule, in every other person's as well.

This was the first steamer this old gentleman had ever

commanded, or had ever even served in, and as he was fidgety in the extreme, he always insisted on taking her into harbour and giving all the words of command himself, instead of leaving it in a great measure to the master.

On these occasions he brooked no interference, any attempt at it being met with instant reproof, and the favourite quotation already given.

On going into one of the chief harbours of China, he followed his usual plan.

Solely by his own orders, sail was gradually taken in, as the ship neared the crowded roadstead. Topsails were backed, and all the words of command requisite for stopping her course, as far as the sails were concerned, were given, but on she still glided majestically.

A few seconds, and then there was a crash and a grating, as she ran into a large tea-clipper.

Too late! too late! the old gentleman found out his mistake; and, as he threw up his hands, he exclaimed, in accents of despair, "O Lor'! O Lor'! I forgot I was a steamer! What will the Admiral say?"

A fit of apoplexy, induced by rage and mortification, would probably have resulted; but, luckily for him, a small midshipman happened to be standing near, with just the shadow of a smile on his countenance, and a few moments of bullying this juvenile afforded him immediate relief, and proved quite as beneficial as a little judicious bleeding could have done.

Now for the other case in point.

Two friends of ours at Yokohama, of an ingenious and mechanical turn of mind, had constructed a small **steamer**, which was to them a source of the greatest pride and happiness. A numerous party of friends were invited to proceed in her on her first trip, which was fixed for a certain Sunday.

If we have an old lady reader, she, of course, *now* predicts that they naturally came to grief.

All necessary arrangements being satisfactorily concluded—not forgetting sundry cases of champagne, *pâtés de foie gras*, and all kinds of delicacies,—away the party started, all in high spirits; the two owners, more particularly, in great feather, receiving the congratulations of their friends on the splendid success which had crowned their undertaking—she was going at the terrific speed of about a knot and a half an hour.

A large black combined in himself the offices of chief engineer, assistant ditto, and stoker.

As far as we could afterwards learn, he had been selected for these duties principally on the grounds of his being "such a fine nigger!" and "*such* a capital hand at training a horse for a race!"—qualifications, however likely to lead to distinction on shore, hardly calculated to be of much practical use afloat.

Scarcely had they got well among the shipping in the bay, when the merry laugh and the ready jest were suddenly hushed by a most awful and appalling rumbling sound proceeding from the engine-room.

The dismay produced by this was heightened tenfold by the sudden appearance from below of the engineer, now of a muddy, leaden colour from terror.

As he rushed past them to the stern of the little ship, he shrieked out, "The biler's a-goin' to bust!" and immediately disappeared beneath the waves, on the sur-

A FIRE AT YOKOHAMA.

face of which, in a few seconds, his black head was seen bobbing, while a grin suffused his countenance, as he felt himself in comparative safety.

Not a moment was lost by the whole party on board in following an example so nobly set.

They were soon picked up by a man-of-war's boat, and their feelings were rather those of disappointment at not seeing the little vessel blown up into ten thousand atoms.

Wet, miserable, and crest-fallen, they were all landed; but they made the most of the only satisfaction they could avail themselves of, which was to vent their wrath on the unfortunate black, who was first rated by all the guests, and then disrated as engineer by his employers.

In the meantime the little steamer proceeded calmly, though somewhat eccentrically, on her course; and after attempting to bore a passage for herself through one or two ships, she finally deposited herself peacefully on a mud-bank, whence she was brought the next day by her broken-spirited owners; their return forming a painful contrast to the merriment and joy of their departure from the ditch the day before!

The then enthusiastic and admiring friends were now sarcastic and sneering unbelievers, indulging in unkind and cutting remarks.

* * * * * *

One of the greatest bugbears of our service in Japan was the constant occurrence of fires in the Japanese town.

During the winter months a week seldom passed without one or two of these little excitements.

Frequent as these fires were, we often wondered they were not more so.

All the Japanese dwelling-houses in a town are made of little else but thin dry wood and paper: the consequence is, a spark kindles wherever it falls, and in a very short space of time whole streets are enveloped in sheets of flame.

What astonished us was that the Japanese seemed to profit nothing by experience, and to go on with the same foolish disregard of the most ordinary precautions against this awful element.—We speak of the general public, not of the Government; for it has organised fire-brigades, which are most efficient and well conducted.

The people sit in these frail and highly combustible tenements round their charcoal fire, which is placed, with the driest of matting all round it, in the centre of the room, and as occasion demands, pass red-hot cinders to each other, to light their pipes with, in the most careless manner. This, of course, is a most fruitful source of conflagrations.

Again, their lanterns are of the most dangerous description, made of oiled paper and bamboo cane. When the candle burns down to the socket, unless some one is near to extinguish it, a blaze is the invariable result; and as they are often, in fact generally, hung up against the paper partition of the room, every chance and opportunity is given to the devouring element.

It is scarcely surprising, then, that we were so often awakened out of our sleep, with a lurid glare lighting up our huts, and with the horrible clang of the fire-bell, mingled with the screams and shouts of excited men and women, whose voices were half drowned in the dreadful roar and crackling of the consuming flame, ringing in our ears.

Every well-to-do merchant or tradesman has on his premises a fire-proof godown, or store, which is built of clay, with a coating of white cement smoothed and polished until it looks like marble, and in which are stored his most valuable articles.

Besides the private godowns, there are also public ones, of which there are two or three in every street, where the poorer tradesmen and small shopkeepers can deposit their goods, on some small periodical payment.

Sometimes, however, these godowns, although not destroyed themselves by the fire, become almost red-hot, and their contents burnt or utterly spoilt.

This seldom happens, though; for, as a rule, the fire is so very rapid in its progress, owing to the tinder-like substance on which it feeds, that they are exposed for a few minutes only to very great heat.

In the event of a private godown coming to grief, the matter simply lies with the owner, who either blames himself for not having made it of better material, or else curses his ill-luck.

In the case of a public one, we do not know how the affair is settled between the proprietor and the depositors, whether the former is bound to give any compensation for loss or damage, or whether the latter in storing their goods accept all risks.

The way in which the Japanese run up new houses on the sites of the old ones which have been burnt down is astounding.

While the remains of the latter are still smouldering, the former are seen to rise Phœnix-like from their ashes; and in a few hours after the fire has passed, a whole street will be very nearly rebuilt.

At the great fire at Yokohama, in November, 1866, nearly an entire street had been rebuilt in this manner, when the wind suddenly shifting, the fire retraced its course, and utterly consumed the newly-built dwellings.

A fire in a Japanese town, when seen for the first time, is novel and exciting.

We will suppose you to be one of the first on the scene in a fire in the Japanese quarter of Yokohama.

It has first broken out in some house, and the inmates are seen madly endeavouring to save a few articles; but the fire is too quick for them: what was only a spark a few minutes ago, is now a raging flame, bursting forth from every window.

The whole street is soon alarmed, and out of every house the inhabitants pour forth, staggering under as much of their household goods as they can carry; and to increase the confusion and din, each one is screeching at the top of his or her voice; and the fire-bells are "going it like mad."

Now, mind your eye! or you will be probably cursed by a Japanese for bringing it into collision with the corner of his box; for the whole street is soon filled with a densely-packed mass of human beings, heavily laden with every conceivable description of goods and chattels, all struggling and pouring forth in the same direction, each one intent on his own property.

No attempt is yet made to arrest the progress of the fire.

All that is thought of is to get the most valuable portion of their property to some place of safety. Now is the time for the public godown keepers to reap a good harvest; they can command their own conditions.

As it is only a few minutes since the fire broke out, the fire-brigade have not yet arrived—here they are, though, they have not been long turning out.

That regular shout you hear rising and falling in the distance is made by them in time to their steps.

More and more distinct you hear it as they approach nearer and nearer, until at last they enter the street you are in; then you hear a jingling, ringing noise, and you are at a loss to know what it is, until you see the excited crowd opening and surging before two or three men, who, as they run, are striking on the ground with long iron staves with rings of the same metal attached to them.

These men are clearing the way for the fire-brigade. They are the night police of Japan.

Now take care of yourself more than ever, or you will be half squeezed to death against the houses, for the crowd is driven to the sides from the centre of the street, which is filled as far as you can see down it by the fire-brigade.

On they come at a good swinging trot, keeping regular time to their shouting chorus, the officers' silver helmets gleaming in the glare, and the white fire-standards,—we can think of no other name for the articles used as signals for the firemen to rally and collect round any particular point where the fire is hottest, or where their services are most required,—looking weird-like and ghostly in the unnatural glare, as they sway and wave backwards and forwards far above the heads of the approaching body of men.

Arrived opposite that part of the fire where they mean to commence operations, they halt; and, after a few directions from the principal officer, the small fire-engines, looking like square boxes, are unslung from the men's shoulders, and at once set to work; the bamboo ladders are placed against the houses, the tops of which are in a few moments covered with firemen, each one doing his own work thoroughly, while the officers direct from below, or from some exalted and very often perilous positions.

There is a certain amount of dash among the officers. They are, as a rule, beautifully dressed—rather a queer occasion to choose for donning one's fine clothes; but there is a strong spice of the swell in them, and as this is a time when they appear to advantage before the public, they like to look their best. Most of them have highly-polished silver helmets, and with their smart little lacquered canes in their hands, and a tolerable degree of swagger on, they excite no little admiration amongst the surrounding crowd.

Inch by inch the fire is combated with; no point being abandoned until it is absolutely impossible to hold it any longer.

That man standing with one of the white fire-standards in his hand on the roof of a house, far in advance of every one else, close up to the flames, which leap and dart fiercely at him, is the person who will give the

signal to retire to the next point; and, until he gives it, no one will budge.

A cry from the crowd, who excitedly point to this solitary figure, draws your attention to him. You look up, and see that he is on fire. He has not retreated a step, though. A slight motion of his hand, to the firemen below is the only movement he makes, and instantly three or four engines are playing on him, and his burning clothes are extinguished.

An officer now comes up and tells off these engines, solely for the purpose of playing on and about this standard-bearer.

More and more angrily the flames beset him, and in a few minutes he is on fire again. This time, the firemen below are much longer in subduing it. At last they succeed; but the fastening of his vizor has been burned away, and it drops down uselessly on his breast.

The crowd cry out, and urge him to retire; but he motions them to be quiet.

He is a little pale; but he looks determined. His time for retiring has not yet arrived, he thinks; and until the last chance is gone, he will stay at his post of honour.

Who knows? There may be some Japanese maiden, with bursting heart, watching him fondly and proudly, and clenching her little hands in her efforts to restrain the cry which is almost on her lips.

Who knows? we asked. Well, perhaps *he* does; and perhaps that may have something to do with the pluck which he is showing.

Who is not brave when he knows he is watched by bright eyes, in whose glances he has learned a secret?

We recollect, when we were of a very tender age, we were on the point of shirking a fight with a bigger boy, towards whom we possessed feelings of unmistakeable funk. We don't mind confessing it now, after the lapse of nearly twenty years. He had insulted us grossly. He said we fudged at marbles, and that he would knock our head off for "tuppence."

We were pocketing this affront, and retiring ignominiously, when we turned and saw the blue eyes of our little sweetheart fixed on us half sorrowfully, half scornfully.

What a change our feelings underwent! Come on! Anything! Anybody!! Our little jacket was off in a jiffy,—that is how we spoke in those days,—and in a few minutes the big boy was vanquished.

Triumph! Glory! The victory was complete. He was at our feet, blubbering, and on our smeared and bloody face we received the reward of our gallantry from our dear little lady-love. God bless her!

She is married now,—not to us, more is the pity!— and has little boys and girls of her own, who, I dare say, may have had their claret tapped and faces smeared as we and she had.

We are certain, though, if they have, that the recollection of the little boy with his bloody little nose, nearly twenty years ago, must have made her deal leniently with them.

During this digression we have left the standard-bearer exposed to the scorching heat of the flames. There he is where we left him. He now appears enveloped in the fire, and as he shields his face with his arm, the crowd again call upon him to retire;

but he takes no notice of them, and remains unmoved.

There has always been to us a strong spice of the romantic investing this solitary figure, as we have seen it standing immovable on the summit of a roof, with its outline defined sharply against the lurid sky or background of vivid flame.

Sometimes it happens there is a crash, a smothered cry; and the volume of smoke, which rolls up as the roof falls in, envelops the intrepid standard-bearer as in a black pall, and nothing more is seen or heard of him until the fire has passed over the spot which has been his tomb, and he is dragged out a charred and blackened corpse.

It is not often, though, that he meets this tragic end; for his experience generally teaches him the exact moment when to retreat, and he makes his escape a few seconds before the rafters give way, to take up his position at another point a little more remote from the flames, probably the next house to the one he has just left, and the same thing is again gone through.

Thus, as we have said, the cruel element is fought and battled with almost inch by inch.

You are watching these men with some admiration, when you hear the sound of horses' feet and the clanking of a steel scabbard. This is an officer from the English Camp come down to observe and report whether the presence of the military will be of any use.

He looks about him, and at last remarks, in an injured tone, to some of the bystanders, civilian acquaintances of his, "Confound these Nippons and their fires! They're always at it. It seems to agree with them well enough. Why we ever bother our heads to help to put 'em out, I don't know! I'm hanged if I don't think they must be half salamanders! Just look at that fellow on the roof!" pointing to our friend, the standard-bearer; "he doesn't seem to mind it much."

"Well, to give the devil his due," continues this talkative young officer, "he's got lots of pluck. The whole of Japan might be burned before I'd risk my precious body like that, I can tell you!"

"Why, you don't seem to be in a very good temper, old fellow!" remarks one of the civilians.

"Good temper!" rejoins the hard-worked warrior; "well, I don't feel particularly angelic at being turned out of bed after a hard day's snipe-shooting at Kanasawa marshes; but I mustn't stop talking here all night, or I shall have the chief walking down my throat, spurs and all."

"Any of the military coming down?" inquires some one in the crowd.

"Oh yes!" answers his gallant friend, "I suppose so. We've only had two fires and three night alarms this week, and it will never do for us to draw our magnificent pay for nothing," with which burst of sarcasm the "galloper" rams the spurs in, and his horse's hoofs are heard clattering on the hard road back to Camp.

Despite the exertions of the Japanese fire-brigade, the flames get the better of them, and house after house is given up to their fury.

Nothing seems able to check them, and you are perhaps beginning to get rather tired of looking on at a game where one side has it all its own way, when a little additional interest is imparted to the scene by the arrival of a company from the Camp.

The unmistakable, measured, solid tramp of the British infantry is heard, until it is suddenly brought to a stop by a voice which, in an unmelodious bellow, cries "'Alt!"

Do you recognise Captain Puffles, and his little weakness, in this word of command, wherewith the progress of the men is arrested?

Yes—much to that distinguished veteran's disgust, his company is for fire duty this week, and here he is, red and out of breath, after his double down from Camp; and with him is his lieutenant, Tony, whom you also know, and who is certain to lead Puffles into some scrape or difficulty before they get back to quarters.

Another sound of the tramp of men, but this time lighter and quicker, and the "Matelots Fusiliers," as the letters on the ribbons round their hats proclaim them to be, appear on the ground.

They are fine smart fellows, and always do good service at these fires.

Between them and the men of the English Garrison the *entente cordiale* exists in undisturbed harmony; the medium of communication being a kind of dog Japanese, which, scanty though it may be as a vehicle of one's thoughts as a rule, is still found fully to answer all their purposes, as the intercourse seldom consists of more than invitations to drink and replies in the affirmative thereto.

Captain Puffles is very fussy and arbitrary, as he is on all occasions where he finds himself invested with power. He is, in fact, what an old woman would call a "Jack in office."

He is now busy posting a chain of sentries, and blusters and fusses to that extent that he soon finds himself the centre of attraction to the crowd, and the fire becomes to them of quite secondary importance.

"Don't let any of those infernal niggers pass!" says Captain Puffles, in an angry tone of authority to his sentries, as a string of Nippons, carrying their goods away from the fire, endeavour to pass through.

With Captain Puffles all nations other than European are niggers.

"My dear Puffles," expostulates Tony, "the poor creatures are only trying to save their property."

"Pray," asks Puffles, with a sudden assumption of extreme dignity, "may I ask 'oo's commanding this company—me, or you?"

"Oh, you are, of course!" says Tony, shrugging his shoulders, and inwardly making up his mind to take the change out of his captain in a practical joke before many hours.

"Oh! because," says Captain Puffles, changing from the dignified to the sarcastic, "I thought per'aps you were;" then turning from Tony, as if he had quite disposed of *him*, to an acquaintance he recognises in the crowd, he profanely remarks: "This place is a puffeck 'ell with its everlasting fire;" and then he glares fiercely at the conflagration.

"Ah, but," replies his friend to whom he makes this remark,—turning away Puffles's wrath with infinite tact, —"nothing like a fire, you know, with its heat and smoke, to make one enjoy a soda and B. afterwards."

Puffles answers not, but an angelic smile steals over his features—a smile such as one may see playing on the face of a sleeping infant, and which the fond young mother ascribes to the whisperings of angels.

"A beautiful sight, ain't it?" he murmurs, now contemplating the fire with a look of affection.

"I say, let those poor people pass with their traps. Ah-bong swor, mossoo; bong swor!"

This is in return to the salutation of the French officer commanding "les Matelots Fusiliers," who comes up, cap in hand, bowing gracefully. "Pardon—est-ce que monsieur parle Français?" he asks.

"Ong poo, soolmong ong poo!" replies Puffles, in a way which rather implies that he says "ong poo" solely out of modesty. "May mong looternong," waving his hand towards Tony, "parley com ong—ong—woyso."

This last simile he evidently looks upon as a hit; for he chuckles, and repeats, "Wee com ong woyso, mossoo."

The Frenchman looks puzzled; but he inclines his head as he says, "Oh, oui, je sais bien que Monsieur Tonie parle comme un Français, et *vous* aussi, monsieur. Oh, oui," insists the polite Frenchman, as Puffles shakes his head. "Oui, certainement oui!"

Even Puffles cannot swallow this, and he tries hard to think of the French for his favourite expression, "No double recovers!" but not succeeding, he says, jocosely pointing to his left eye, "Ah, say too dong mays yoo."

The Frenchman looks even more puzzled than when he was told that Tony spoke French like "ong woyso;" but seeing that Captain Puffles is under the impression that he has said "a real good thing" in French, he laughs, as if he understood and enjoyed it; but turning to Tony, whom he knows well, he asks him for an explanation, which is given.

"Voulez-vous une cigarette?" he asks, offering one of those mild little articles.

"Nong, mairsee bocoo. Je foom ong peep tooshore," replies Captain Puffles, diving into his trousers pocket, and fishing out therefrom, with some difficulty, a black, pestilential-looking pipe, shorn of half its honours; that is to say, the greater part of the bowl has been broken away at one time or another in the different encounters its owner is perpetually engaged in.

"Ah!" says Puffles, with a sigh of relief, and rather red in the face with the exertion of getting it out, as this process of extrication is not half such an easy matter as may be supposed.

Of course, getting the hand into the pocket is all plain sailing, but the difficulty is to get it out when clutched affectionately round the pipe.

As far as the region of the waistband of the trousers the extrication is proceeded with smoothly, but when it has got so far there are violent throes and a struggle of some moments' duration, until at last it bursts into the light with a jerk.

But when once got out, there is no time wasted over such matters as loading; for there are always the remains of the last pipeful, which are lighted at once, and smoked with great zest.

"Voolay voo?" asks Puffles, handing a scrap of newspaper, dingy from a long sojourn in his pocket, in which is wrapped some villainously strong tobacco.

The Frenchman, barely able to repress a shudder as he glances at the proffered delicacy, thanks him, and says he prefers a cigarette of his own.

"Sharkung ar song goo," remarks Captain Puffles, pocketing the dingy little roll of paper, and blowing a cloud which veils for some moments his fat old face, and sets every one, within a radius of five yards, coughing and spluttering.

"Que diable!" exclaims the Frenchman, after a very pronounced sneeze, quite forgetting his polished manners in the intensity of his feelings. "Que diable! quel vilain tabac!"

"What does 'e say, Tony?" asks Puffles, from behind his dense cloud.

"Oh, he says," replies Tony, "that he hopes you'll step into his quarters, and have a soda and brandy on your way up to Camp."

"Oh, suttonly, surtongmong wee, mossoo, arvek playsere;" and Puffles beams through his smoke affectionately on the Frenchman, and wonders if his brandy is good, and whether his soda-water is Schweppe's.

"Good fellow, that," he murmurs: "no 'umbug about 'im. Just what I like."

"Comment?" asks the Frenchman, turning to Tony for a translation, as, during these remarks, Puffles's eyes are fixed upon him, and he thinks he is being addressed by him.

"Oh," says Tony, "il parle seulement de l'incendie."

"Ah, oui, c'est terrible, n'est-ce pas?" responds the Frenchman. "Mais," he adds, smiling, as he gets the full benefit of another whiff of Puffles's pipe, "ce n'est pas aussi terrible que la fumée de Monsieur le Capitaine !"

" What does 'e say, Tony ?" again demands Puffles, thinking that perhaps the subject of the soda and B. is still under discussion; and as he feels that this is a topic on which he is peculiarly fitted to give an opinion, is anxious not to lose a word of it.

" He says" replies Tony, " that you're to mind and not forget to drop in, and have a liquor up, after the fire."

Puffles looks hurt. Has he ever been known to forget an appointment of this nature? Why then should he now be doubted? So there is some dignity in his manner as he says, " Nong, mossoo, surtongmong nong. Jer nur forgetteray par."

After this the Frenchman wishes them good night, and superintends his men working at their engine.

Puffles takes a few more whiffs, and then, according to his invariable custom, puts his pipe lighted as it is into his trousers pocket, where it smoulders like a slumbering volcano, until it eventually goes out, owing, we suppose, to an absence of oxygen.

But the most extraordinary part of the proceeding is, that it never seems to occasion the slightest inconvenience to Puffles, who, in fact, appears rather to enjoy the genial warmth.

This same pocket is the receptacle for his small change, which, when occasion requires, has to be dug out of a bed of ashes, like ruins of Pompeii on a small scale.

This excavatory process is not always attended with success; very often the only result being the dreadful traces it leaves in the finger-nails.

Another point in common with Pompeiian relics that this small change possesses is its scarcity.

Here is another arrival on the scene — no less a personage than His Excellency the Governor of Kanagawa, who ambles up on his pony, amidst a general uncovering and bowing of heads.

He is surrounded by a group of richly-dressed yakonins, and followed by a host of retainers carrying the insignia of his office and rank.

He moves about visiting different points, occasionally here and there personally directing the movements of the fire-brigade, or consulting with some of the foreign officers.

"What's he doing here?" asks some individual.

"Oh," replies a foreign gentleman who is well known and esteemed throughout the Far East, "I think he been to keep up his position."

After thus keeping up his position and satisfying, as he thinks, all claims upon him as a public servant, His Excellency and his followers trot off home.

One peculiar feature in a Yokohama fire is the presence of numerous fire-engines belonging to different nationalities.

There is one in particular which ought to catch your eye. It is a most gorgeous article: the body of it is plated with silver, while on each side are views, in medallions, of different places in New York; the whole being surmounted by silver bells, which chime merrily while the engine is being worked.

Of course it is American; and the owners of it assure you that it throws so tarnation high, that, on one occasion, when it was pushed to its utmost, the country-people some hours afterwards took the spray, which then descended, for a shower of rain.

We are afraid to say how many thousand dollars this cost.

There are also numerous English and French engines; and a Dutch one, famed for the promptitude with which its owner brings it on the spot a few minutes after the outbreak of a fire.

Compared with these, the wooden Japanese contrivances, like small square boxes, and worked by one or two men, are rather feeble, but they do some good from their numbers, and also from being so small and handy that they can be got into position on tops of houses, or at any point where they can be of the slightest service.

The old barrack engine once appeared at a fire in the town, but it disgraced itself so thoroughly that it at once received from the Colonel a sentence of confinement to barracks for the remainder of its existence.

The behaviour that brought upon it this severe sentence was a rather too lavish and general distribution of its favours on the bystanders, who seemed to occupy the whole of its attention. The few drops of water that traversed the whole of the hose in the direction of the fire, simply ended in a feeble dribble, which, as a rule, found its way into the pocket of the devoted man who held the nozzle.

We possess a thorough knowledge of its character, for it was taken out to be exercised in Camp every month; and we had always to be present at these farces, from which we invariably returned with angry countenance and bespattered uniform.

It bore, we believe, a mark of a IV., with a G. R. above it, so that we may ascribe all its little peculiarities, not to the giddiness of youth, but to the foolishness of extreme old age.

To return to the particular fire at which you are supposed to be present.

Two or three whole streets have been already consumed, and there seems every chance of its spreading still more; but, luckily, just before daybreak, the wind falls, and there is a dead calm.

It is wonderful how quickly the flames are now got under; and in about an hour a smouldering black tract is to be seen, where all a short time before was flame, bustle, and confusion.

In place of Captain Puffles's company, the French "Matelots Fusiliers," the fire-engines, and the crowd of all nations, are now to be seen the late owners of the houses which have been burned, prowling about amongst the charred ruins looking for their landmarks, on finding which, they will at once commence to rebuild.

"I say, Tony," says Captain Puffles, as his company approaches the French barracks on its way home, "you march 'ome the company, for I promised that mossoo so faithfully that I'd drop in and have a liquor with him."

"All right, good night, or rather good morning," says Tony; and he marches away at the head of the company, bursting with suppressed laughter.

* * * * * *

An hour or so has elapsed.

Tony has been fast asleep in bed for some time, when he is awakened by some one pulling him by the shoulder.

"What's the matter?—who's that?" he naturally asks.

"I say, Tony," says a voice which belongs to Puffles, but which is so pitiful that it is hardly recognisable, "'ave you any brandy in your room?"

"No," answers Tony; "why, haven't you had a liquor down at the French barracks?"

"No," groans poor Puffles. "I've 'ad something that makes me puffeckly sick."

"What was it?" asks Tony.

"O sacray, he called it, I think," said Puffles.

"No, no; *eau sucré* it must have been," says Tony, hardly able to restrain his laughter.

"Well, O soocray then, if you're so cussed pertickler," returns Puffles, whose temper has evidently been ruffled. "But what's the English for O sacray?"

"Well," replies Tony, "holy water, I suppose."

"Then it *was* O sacray," says Puffles determinedly. "It was wholly water, and no mistake; for devil a drop of anything else was there in it, bar, pr'aps, a lump or two of sugar. Ugh!"

"Excuse me, Puffles," says Tony; "how can a drop be a lump of sugar?"

"Yes, it can," replies Puffles, "if it's an acid drop. 'Ad you there, old boy!"

Puffles was so pleased at his own sharpness that he nearly recovered his usual good-temper, notwithstanding the frightful trial it had been put to; but a vivid recollection of what he had undergone, coming upon him suddenly, made him shudder as if he had just had a dose of castor-oil.

At this, Tony's head suddenly dives under the bedclothes, and the most extraordinary choking sounds are heard to proceed from him.

"Well, I'm 'anged!" says Puffles, "if he's not asleep already, and snoring like a 'ouse a-fire;" and Puffles walks off in high dudgeon.

CHAPTER XXI.

THE RACES.

WHAT are you going to the races for? Is it to see and talk to the ladies? If so, you cannot do better than go with Belleville; who, with an extra touch of scent and pomatum, will be there in all his glory, and delighted to introduce you to all the fashion and beauty of Yokohama.

Is it to watch the racing, and more particularly the part taken in it by your friends of the Holy Boys?

Then C—— and the Captain, who are two of the stewards, shall chaperone you, and give you all the information you may require.

After all, we fancy your best plan is to take the same hack you had the other morning, and honour *us* with your company. We think we know nearly everybody who will be there; and if we succeed in getting ourselves up as nicely as we hope to do, we can almost promise that you shall make the acquaintance of each lovely face that may adorn the Stand.

Besides, we have received an invitation—in common with all others of the Camp interested in the races—to the same hospitable board where you tiffined the other Sunday; for Rudolph always gives a big breakfast on each morning of the meeting.

No, you won't want a tall hat or a frock coat. Such things are unknown in Japan.

We shall have to go in uniform—breeches and boots being part and parcel thereof—but as far as you are concerned, that blue bird's-eye tie, black hunting coat, and billycock hat will be just the thing.

By-the-bye, whom are we to go to for clothes when we get home? For more than three years we have worn nothing but what the native artists have made for us; and for the last two have never been out of our warpaint. Verily, it is a subject requiring deep consideration.

"The tailor makes the man," and in our case the tailor will have it all his own way; for what know we of ye fashions of ye dress — or even, perhaps, of ye manners, after serving our term of transportation?

'Twould require a man self-confident and strong of mind to walk down by the Ladies' Mile in the high-buttoned coat and baggy unmentionables of '64! and from what we can gather, the ruder sex, in curtailing the proportions of their garments, have but followed the example of those who, in many more serious matters, lead us with their silken threads.

Ah! will it not be a sight to craze the minds of us poor exiles, when we first behold again a group of Old England's fair maids, with their twinkling little feet no longer glancing surreptitiously from under hateful voluminous curtains, but facing boldly the light of day in all the pride of natural beauty and graceful symmetry?

Alas, how weak is the heart of man! To their shame be it written, some of "ours"—the few old bachelors alone, 'tis true—have actually been heard to canvass the possibility of there being some truth in the horrible pictures—nay, scurrilous caricatures—of the "Girl of the Period," that certain sneering, sceptical, but clever writers have of late been drawing in the great fountainhead of criticism.

Worse than unbelievers must they be who can stoop to receive such unworthy libels as unprejudiced truths. As well might we be expected to believe that heaven is peopled with fallen angels; or that civilisation is rotten at the root, and that the present tone of society—as said by these calumniators to be thus represented in the persons of its fairest ornaments—is but the sign of a first step towards the resumption of our aboriginal state of savage simplicity!

What a prospect should we indeed have before us, if one tithe of these unrestrained tirades were true!

But one course would be left open to us! but one refuge would offer itself to our crushed and bleeding hearts! Straightway would we hurry back whence we came, cast hope and happiness away for ever, and linger out a blighted and joyless existence in the isles of Niphon.

The last words recall our wandering thoughts to the point from which they started.

The eventful morning of the races has at length arrived. B., Bones, and the Child have despatched their ponies to the Course in all the panoply of ribbons, plaited manes, &c., and now adjourn to dress, preparatory to riding down to join the same breakfast at which we are about to assist.

The Liver Cutter is already got up to the nines, and the Aide will not lose sight of Antelope and Velocipede, e'en at the cost of his breakfast; while Bobby will probably begin to think of arraying himself by the time the others have started.

It has been an anxious night for them all; and none but Bobby can boast that he really slept soundly through it. Two or three visits to the stables, where wakeful grooms kept watch and ward over their charges,—for the Japanese bettoes, who will stake to their uttermost "cash" on the event of a race, are as ready to poison or otherwise nobble a horse as the lowest blackleg at Newmarket,—two or three examinations into the prospect of the weather, and two or three cheroots, have served, with an occasional nap, to pass away the hours till daylight, when they superintended the feeding, cleaning, and final adorning of their favourites.

Each one muses silently over his chances of success —perhaps sanguinely conjuring up a masterly win; perhaps doubtfully picturing an unlucky defeat by a head.

Pericles is indulged with a double feed of corn, as if to make up for past shortcomings; Iona is decked out with ribbons, like a prize pig; while Tom Brown's tail has to be cut another couple of inches shorter. Bobby sticks a big rosette on each side of Tommy's head, and another on the hat of his groom. Antelope and Velocipede can hardly see for the head-band smothered in chocolate-and-white ribbons.

Amid all this splendour, "my horth Pluck" stands conspicuous for the unpretending plainness of his caparison. The empty vanities of braid and ribbon, gay harness and holiday trappings, what have they in common with the workmanlike simplicity of his own appearance, and that of his talented rider, Dr. Quock?

A A

A rusty snaffle without side-bars, on a venerable single-reined bridle, mended with string, and an enormous saddle of some past era, unite to show off to advantage a many-cornered carcass, and a head which, though it might not have been ungainly on a Clydesdale cart-horse, is—to say the least—scarcely in proportion to the frame of a China pony under fourteen hands in height.

Quock himself is equipped in a pair of the thickest and yellowest of hunting cords, below which two very new white tops are supported by two very old Wellingtons, destitute alike of fit and polish, but set off by a heavy hunting spur on the right foot and a bent racing ditto on the left.

At 10.30 A.M. to the minute, we sit down to such a *déjeuner* as we have seen nowhere else; except at some favoured and hospitable seat, when the Pytchley have allowed an extra five minutes' grace for those who are inclined, or may feel it *necessary*, to take a little jumping powder on board: and on such occasions as these, we have ever found that *inclination* led us to make the best use of our time, though we devoutly pray it may be many years before *necessity* bids us brace up our failing nerves with the valour-giving cherry-brandy, that figures so prominently at the hunting breakfast.

Being thus early, we have a better opportunity of taking stock of others as they enter. The Captain, C——, and the other stewards are already here; and as Rudolph knows their presence will be required early, he has set them to work at once. A dozen or so more, the leaders of sport and good-fellowship in Yokohama, are also seated round.

Each one, of course, thinks he can spot the winner of any particular race; and every now and then a bet is booked, while many more are offered.

Rudolph himself is ready to back his own animals for anything; and he is generally as lucky as his spirit and keenness deserve.

Sitting—the one on his right, the other on his left—are two members of the Royal House of Bourbon, who happen to be taking Japan in their travels; and as they are here during our Carnival, we may fairly expect that the blood of the Duc d'Aumale will find some interest in the sport they are about to witness.

Here come Bones and his companions, all in proper racing costume.

The colours of the former, which we get just a peep of at the throat, are apparently of about the same date as the once mahogany tops that flood and field have now died almost to an ebony hue.

B. is quite the correct card, and does no discredit to the county where every man you meet can tell you the latest odds against each horse in the "Sellinger."

The Child enters with his friend Lothario—the two looking like men who know a good thing, and mean to make use of it. May they not overreach themselves in their efforts!

The latter looks more killing than ever, with the white-and-black colours round his hat, and with a favour of the same, stitched by fair fingers, conspicuous in his button-hole.

The Child, for the nonce in mufti,—the cut and style of which may, he thinks, complete an eminently racing appearance,—has contrived to squeeze his attenuated lower limbs into a pair of white kerseymeres, the tightness of whose fit it makes one almost nervous to contemplate.

Why does he not take warning from the remembrance of the awful accident that befell him when, on the stage of the Amateur Theatre at Hong-Kong, he displayed his charming proportions in satin tights, to the fairest audience the histrionic talent of the Holy Boys ever succeeded in drawing?

Theatrical garments are not always made of the best materials, as was proved on this occasion; for as Lorenzo assisted the fair Jessica to escape by a ladder from the house of her father Shylock, the poor page's wooing was interrupted by a loud crack, and he awoke from his love-dream to the painful consciousness that he was pursuing his courtship with an utter disregard of outward appearance.

By a certain portion of the spectators, though, this unpremeditated piece of by-play was received as a decided hit, and cheers, yells, and applause thundered as the unhappy Child—— But here let us draw the curtain—not ineffectually behind him, as the despairing manager contrived to do, thus for the moment totally barring his escape—but over the most trying scene of his young life.

B. and Bones set to work vigorously on the good things before them; and on the arrival of Dr. Quock an extra supply of woffles is called for, and he proceeds with great steadiness to indulge his insatiable appetite for those delicacies.

The Child, meanwhile, looks wistfully on, as he sips a glass of sherry and draws his belt to a narrowed limit, that would be more becoming to a ballet-dancer—his only consolation being the thought of what a *blow out* (to use his own expression) he will have to-night; though when he finds afterwards, in the scales, that he has a pound to spare, he will look back regretfully to the game pie that now stands so invitingly before him.

Boot and saddle! we must be off! No; no more champagne, thanks! We shall find it anything but easy to avoid taking it very frequently up at the Course.

This is not like the road to a race-course at home, is it? though it is our Derby, and crowds are moving on to see it. No four-in-hands, cabs, or donkey-carts; but an occasional carriage, and any number of men on horseback.

Japanese by hundreds, Europeans by scores, and Chinese by tens, wend their dusty way in the same direction.

Yonder is the Governor of Kanagawa with his suite; and his train is on the present occasion swelled by a number of yakonins, who are about to contend in a race specially got up for them.

The costume of these jockeys, in their loose silk trousers and enormous lacquer hats, with their feet resting on huge wooden stirrups—though certainly adding variety to the scene—would scarcely be accepted as orthodox at Croxton Park. By way of according with the customs of the foreigners, each aspirant for honours wears his distinguishing colour in a sash over his "chimono," or upper robe, and carries a steel-tipped riding-rod of whalebone in his hand.

Here is the Stand; and as we are in good time, we

will suppose you to have been introduced to the ladies, —whose bright eyes are here, as usual, to encourage us, —and will now go down to the paddock and see the griffins saddled for the first race.

Alexander's crack is looking fit and well, though he rears up and comes backwards with the Liver Cutter the first time he attempts to mount him.

B. is riding a quiet, rough-looking beast for Rudolph, who only purchased him a fortnight ago, in hopes of his being able to go the half mile without training.

Bones is on a wild, unbroken creature, that takes the first opportunity of rushing up against the paddock palings; and though the shock throws him right back on to his haunches, his rider does not appear much disconcerted.

The Child is about to steer a well-shaped little pony, whom we told you had performed so satisfactorily in his moonlight trial, but who is now terrified out of his wits at the crowd and noise, making the faces of both his rider and Lothario appear anxious and troubled.

Altogether sixteen go to the post for the Griffins' Plate, most of them being raw, half-trained, half-broken animals that are scarcely yet reconciled to the saddle.

One after another they go past the Stand on their way to the post—the greater number objecting strenuously; and it is very certain that, though at last all have been got by, some will never face the crowd on their return.

We need not dwell over the race. On the word at length being given, after several ineffectual attempts and much confused mobbing,—during which one pony is lamed, another goes over the railings and bolts clean away, while one of the riders gets his stirrup-iron bent on his foot by a kick,—about half the field start in the right direction. Of the others, some swerve right across the course, some refuse to move at all, and two or three wheel round, and set off in exactly the opposite direction.

The Liver Cutter sets to work from the post, the astonished griffin springing frantically to the unaccustomed torture; B. waits close on him; the Child on Tom Thumb alongside of the pair, till they reach the distance, where the first shout of the mob sends the latter across to the opposite rails. Bones then becomes third, some three or four lengths ahead of the swerving, cannoning crowd.

Alexander's griffin is now forging ahead, amid the delighted yells of his party, who have put a small fortune on, even at the short price they could get; but he cannot take the sustained punishment accorded to him, and of a sudden bolts out of his line.

He is set going again almost without loss of ground; but his spirit is broken, and Rudolph's sober, straight-going outsider wins by a head, to the surprise of every one, not even excepting his owner.

Bones is third; while the others come in for ten minutes afterwards.

Between the races you can either visit the refreshment-room, listen to the band of the Holy Boys, or make yourself agreeable to the ladies.

Ah! you didn't think we had such forms and faces in Yokohama, did you? And are they not indeed worthy of our worship, who brighten with their presence a place so far from that garden of beauty where they were reared?

How much more real good would be done if the philanthropic societies at home, who send out missionaries to lose themselves among the countless millions of barbarians,—failing to change them, as a few scattered grains of lime would fail to whiten the sea-shore,—would, instead, engage the same number of these fair beings,—approaching in their own natures, as they do, so nearly to divinity,—with a view to soften the rugged minds of their benighted countrymen by their soothing presence and gentle refinement! Then might we return home, not as unpolished reprobates, bearish in our uncouthness, with the stable, the kennel, or the billiard-room cropping up in every sentence, but as fit and becoming members of society.

Passing over the next two or three events, we come to the steeple-chase, which possesses the chief interest of the day to our several friends, and apparently also to the assembled spectators, for at the first sound of the saddling bell, they rush to different points, from which they expect to get the best view of the course or some of its principal features.

We will stand down here till just before they start, when we will go to the top of the Stand, where you can get a view of almost every fence.

Dr. Quock, who has ridden Pluck up to the course, and has been waiting on him ever since, is the first to show, and canters proudly past the stand twice before he proceeds to the post.

The Aide appears next on Ugly; but as he is imprudently riding him in a plain, single-reined snaffle without a martingale, the odds are—from what we know of the old pony—decidedly against his being able to hold him straight.

Holloa! Mr. Jorrocks? Why, this is not a fifteen-stone welter! Nevertheless, here, in most solid flesh and blood, is our old acquaintance; and it is to be hoped that the extra four stone will prove effectual in steadying the strong, well-built, but unmanageable chestnut that he is riding, and which *might* be a clipper across country, if he only would.

Though on such an animal he is almost certain to get a smash, his ruddy face bears as happy, confident a smile as ever; and he looks round patronisingly as a prince in answer to the cheers that salute his appearance—straightening his burly legs in the stirrups; thrusting out his portly stern, looking more portly still in snowy kerseymere, over the crupper; and bending his Falstaff-like form gracefully over the withers.

After him Pericles emerges from the paddock, yawing viciously with his head; followed by Iona, whose legs look almost too short for the deep ground—a fault of formation that cannot be applied with the same justice to his owner, whose lower limbs look lengthier than ever in the four-pound saddle he is sitting in.

Mulvey is seen next on a black, clever animal, called Lucifer; and fully five minutes after everybody else, Bobby comes dawdling out on Sweet William.

Not much fault can be found in the *form* of most of the competitors. Their course of training has been gone through as carefully and systematically as if they were about to run for the Grand National; though naturally the preparation considered necessary at home has to be much adapted and modified to suit their inferior breeding, pluck, and constitution. Six weeks' actual training, supposing him to be in thorough good *condition* at the commencement of that time, is quite sufficient to bring out any Japanese horse or pony in as fit a state as he can be expected to attain. The great secret is to bring them to the post fresh and full of spirits—not fine-drawn or stale; and we should imagine this rule must be applicable to all inferior breeds of horses. Walk them as much, and gallop them as little, as possible; for once let them get sick of their work, they lose heart and pluck immediately. We found the plan that succeeded best was to give them two or three long slow gallops per week, and *always in company*—the last three *only* being fast, with a spurt of something less than a quarter of a mile at the end; and those prepared on this principle ever ran stouter, better, and even faster, than others who had done more quick work.

C—— goes down to start them in a field just within the railings; and after they have taken their preliminary, and all are mustered, he is faced by ten. It does not take long to despatch them; all are keen and anxious to be off. There is no drawing for places, but each one settles into the line at once.

"Now, gentlemen, you all understand? Keep the red flag on your right and the white on your left. Walk up, please, walk up!—Easy a little, Mr. Jorrocks!—Come up, Mr. Mulvey!—Steady! *Steady* a moment on the left! Are you ready?——Go!!" and off they start as level as a wall, with their heads pointed parallel to the rails, and in the direction of the Stand.

Bones, the Child, and Bobby make running over the

first field, and down the easy drop into the one below, the others lying close up.

At the top of the next drop some stakes and bushes have been driven in, while below a ditch has been cut.

Sweet William jumps a little short at this, and Bobby is shot on to his neck, but scrambles back without a fall. Quock takes his place, and races with the leaders for the awkward dug-out ditch at the corner of the last field before the road: Pluck, however, doesn't like the look of it, and shutting up at every stride, only gets over with a scramble.

Pericles, with his head still in the air, and apparently hardly looking at what he is jumping, takes it all sideways—nearly upsetting Iona and the Child, who land beside him.

Old Ugly rushes at it, his ears and his one eye cocked viciously; but, following Pericles' example, he swerves off, and cannons against Mulvey, whose pony is just about to rise. A headlong descent is the natural result, as far as Mulvey and Lucifer are concerned, while the Aide and Ugly go on their way victorious—if not rejoicing.

Deep and dirty is the gulf into which it is his hard fate to be plunged in all the splendour of gayest silk and whitest leather. Originally a boggy drain, its dimensions have been enlarged, till a waggon might almost be buried in it.

Jorrocks, who seems to be only just getting under weigh, skims over the pair, as poor Mulvey emerges, gasping and spluttering, from under his horse; but the frightful apparition so startles the last of the field, who has almost succeeded in screwing up the courage of an unwilling brute to the jumping point, that he appears to lose all presence of mind and power of action. His slackened reins encouraging his already doubtful horse to refuse, he himself glides helplessly over to join the pair below; and alighting on the head of the other unfortunate, the two—clasped lovingly in each other's arms—dive down to wallow in the slush. This aggravation to his catastrophe is nearly the death of Mulvey, and it is some time ere, half drowned and thoroughly bruised, he finds himself again on *terra firma;* when Abdul, after ministering to his wants, advises him to "give up steeple-chases and those dangerous Lucifers, and take to Safety Matches on the flat."

Meanwhile, the others have mounted from the low ground up on to what was, before the race-course was formed, a broad carriage road—or, to speak more accurately, part of the one road made by the Japanese Government for the recreation of the foreign residents of Yokohama.

It is level and stoneless; and down the half mile of its length, contained within the race-course railings, fair hunting jumps have been built, quite big enough to make a horse stretch himself to get over them. Down this they rattle, forty miles an hour, with but little to choose between them.

All safe over the first fence—Quock chirping and spluttering with all his might, in order to keep Pluck up to the mark; and Bobby turning on all steam to get a lead at the double fence just in front.

This is the sensation jump, and round it an excited crowd is assembled—praying, probably, in their hearts, if not for an accident, at least for a fall or two. Soldiers and civilians, mixed up together, are crowding and stretching their necks for a view, shouting encouragement, and even advice, to their favourites.

A nine-foot ditch on each side, with only five feet of room between, on which to put the spare leg down, at least fulfils the definition of a 'fair hunting jump' for the style of horse we are at present dealing with.

At it they come, the three leaders racing neck and neck—Bones managing to pull Pericles' head down a bit to steady him, and relieving his own feelings by a mild anathema on the obstinate perverseness of his horse; the Child, looking as pleased as Punch, hustling Iona—who is going rather sluggishly—along, then settling himself in his saddle for a pull as they approach the jump; Jorrocks, who has joined them with a rush as soon as they get out of the deep ground, standing up in his stirrups with a merry smile on his jovial face,—now redder and fuller than ever,—and shouting out: "Come along, you fellows: it's plain sailing now!"

"Hold up, you clumsy brute!" yells Bones, as Pericles blunders on to his nose and knees, but saves an absolute fall cleverly; while "That's the style, Cap'n!" "You are all there yet!" "Send the old hoss along!" and many other such pieces of encouragement, ring out from the Sappers. Many a quart of porter, many a gill of rum, depend on Bones' repeating his former successes on Pericles, who is to them what Blink Bonny or Blair Athol was to the Yorkshiremen; and when the usual prompt settling comes off at the canteen to-night, whether they receive or pay, they will still be as ready as ever to back their champion through thick and thin.

Jorrocks and the Child get well over, as does Bobby on Sweet William; but the second ditch is more than old Ugly, with his one eye, can understand, and the Aide gets farther over it than his horse. A dozen ready pairs of hands push him into his seat, the rein is shoved into his hand, Ugly's head turned in the right direction, and he is set going again some time before he quite knows where he is. This one idea, however, remains uppermost in his confused mind, sufficiently prominent to have some influence on his course of action—namely, that he is riding a steeple-chase—his maiden one, too— and that the great object is to get over the ground as quickly as possible. With this view,—the sole guiding star of the chaos into which excitement, praiseworthy anxiety to shine, and the effects of his fall have worked his usually clear and enlightened brain,—he wires desperately into old Ugly, urging him to exert every effort in pursuit.

"Served you right for going hard at timber!" the 'Governor' once said to us, as he saw his offspring rising all abroad from under a four-year-old, whom in our youthful ignorance we had pushed too quickly at four unbreakable bars; and well would it have been for the Aide, if ever the maxim thus implied had been impressed upon his mind.

The post and rails, which all the others in front have negotiated in safety, are tall and stiff. At the pace he is going, poor Ugly does not get a chance to collect himself; but with a broken-hearted groan breasts the obstacle, and rolls over with a loud crash. Fortunately the Aide has fallen clear, and the only things that suffer are the girths, both of which fly like packthread at the shock.

Ugly now naturally comes to the conclusion that he has had enough of this kind of thing; and thinking he could perhaps do better by himself, leaves his rider to look after the saddle, and sets off at full speed after his antagonists.

The Aide is soon on his feet again, and as eager for the fray as ever; but he is too late to stop his faithless steed.

In an agony of mind he snatches up the saddle, and rushes frantically after him, shouting out an entreaty to the bystanders to stop him.

It is of no avail. Old birds are not to be caught with chaff; and Ugly pursues his career till he becomes blown, and stops of his own accord—his luckless rider at length returning crest-fallen to the Stand, and appearing but little disposed to relish the unfeeling jokes of his comrades.

All this woeful misfortune—or, at all events, the climax of it—might he have avoided, had he remembered Asheton Smith's sound advice, "never to let go of your bridle under *any* circumstances," together with the undeniably true remark with which he enforced it, that "a man never looks such a fool as when running and shout-out, 'Catch my horse!'"

Jorrocks takes the water with a clear lead; but when they leave the road and breast the hill, where heavy going and stiff up-jumps try both strength and stamina, weight begins to tell; and as he drops back and then behind, his jolly face loses the bright, happy expression it wore when he was leading, and his sobbing steed staggers painfully as he scrambles up each bank.

Across the race-course and over the hill, Jorrocks's

broad back is the last we see of them for some little time.

When again they reappear in sight Pericles and Iona are leading, and charge the bullfinch together. Not more than fifteen yards beyond is the ten-foot drop, which Pericles spins down in his usual style, gaining two or three lengths on the other, who takes a good deal of recovering after landing.

The little doctor is close behind—Pluck refusing to be hurried, but, pulling up short on the top, drops carefully down.

Bobby and Jorrocks come through the bullfinch together, the latter carrying a goodly portion of the fence with him; and in honourable rivalry they thrust full split at the big drop.

Trying as the pace is to Sweet William,—who for the second time buries his nose in the earth, but scrambles up again,—what must it be to the poor animal who is expected to carry fifteen stone down in safety? As he approaches with tail cocked and neck stiffened, Jorrocks tries in vain to rouse him with whip and spur.

As well might *we* apply the same goads to the sides of the good ship that is even now labouring wearily against a foul wind and heavy dragging sea, and hope thereby to hasten our arrival at the loving homes we trust ere long to see again.

The poor beast answers only by a jerk of his head and a sad protesting switch with his tail. Too exhausted to spring, he can merely roll helplessly down, carrying Jorrocks to what would seem to be nothing short of utter destruction.

Ah! Jorrocks! Jorrocks! Bold of heart and fond of

sport though you are, the great god Daiboots has as much chance of winning a steeple-chase as yourself! and till you can afford to keep a stud of thoroughly-trained elephants, take the advice of those who, while they offer it, do not forget that they have always looked out for your cheery presence as a *sine-quâ-non* attribute to every meet of the Beagles, and give up cross-country work— at all events among the ploughs and banks of Japan.

We must not linger over Jorrocks; but merely stopping long enough to pick him up out of the pit, that his own weight, added to the impetus of his fall, has made for him,—and having satisfied ourselves that the goodly covering of solid beef has prevented any actual breakage of bones,—leave him to rub his bruised and stiffened joints, and with rueful countenance to beseech his still prostrate horse to "Come Hup!" while we get on with all speed to witness the finish of the chase.

After the drop at which our lusty friend came to grief, Pericles, whose length of stride gives him a great advantage, draws ahead of Iona. The latter seems rather out of his element in the heavy ground, and is already showing signs of being nearly pumped out, his "pretty tail" working laboriously.

Seeing this, Dr. Quock redoubles his efforts, chirruping and spluttering as hard as his little remaining wind will allow him; and with Bobby some distance behind, they struggle on in hot pursuit of Pericles over the last half-dozen jumps.

Approaching the final one—a steep-cut bank some five feet high—before entering the course for the straight run-in, the last named is about a couple of lengths ahead; and the crowd assembled near the jump are

B B

already shouting excitedly the names of their favourites. Bones, who has been screwing all he can out of his horse for some time, nerves himself for one last effort; and with voice, whip, and spur at work together, heads the jaded animal for what appears the easiest part.

Better, Bones, far better had it been for thee never to have fostered the fatally false principle of "keeping 'em low between the races!"

To rise a sheer five feet, up hill, out of plough, and after a prolonged struggle, is a heart-breaking test for a half-prepared one. Poor Pericles, sinking from fatigue and want of condition, has done all that nature will allow him; and not even the determined hand he knows so well, nor the heavy punishment dealt out to him, avails to bring him to the scratch; but whipping round, he stands with glassy eye, extended legs, and heaving flanks, a living remonstrance against the fallacy of throwing horses out of work and food, with the idea that at a few weeks' notice they can be called upon to exercise their full powers.

The excitement, if great before, is now tremendous.

"Pluck! Pluck!!" "Come on, Quock!" yell the adherents of the medical party.

"Iona! Iona!!" from the admirers of the chestnut.

Both animals are as nearly dead beat as possible; and so is the little doctor, who can no longer chirp or chick, but splutters, froths, and flogs, till wild excitement and exhaustion combined threaten to bring on a fit.

The Child's training stands him in some little stead, and he does not show as much distress as his opponent; but as he feels that he may yet win, sits down in his seat, grasps the saddle more firmly with his knees, catches tight hold of his horse's head, and with almost desperate energy attempts to gather him for the effort.

Who is that dancing, yelling figure, mad with excitement, who stands above the most feasible spot in the jump, waving his hat and screaming, as all notions of difference between master and man are lost in his wild delirium, "Here it is, darling! Lay into him now! Holy Virgin! *Here*, I tell ye!! God and St. Patrick, but I'll have a drink if ye win!"

His groom's entreaties reach the ear of the Child, and with renewed hope he steers for the point where the faithful Irishman is standing. Even Iona appears to catch up a portion of his excitement, cocks his ears, and strives hard to collect his failing powers. Gallantly he rises at the leap, and for a moment it seems that he will gain a footing on the top.

Alas! the relaxed muscles cannot complete their task. He just reaches the summit, but in vain does he try to plant his hind-legs for a hold. Twice, thrice he struggles with all his might, then with a despairing moan sinks backwards to the ground; nor can all the exertions of the Child, or the shillelah and tearful prayers of his groom, induce him to rise.

Meanwhile, as Pluck approaches the jump, his fiddle-head droops lower and his tail rises higher at every stride; and to the doctor's disgust, he sticks his nose into the bank and refuses even to try.

"Bobby!" "Now, Bobby!" is the cry; and while some are pulling Iona on to his legs, others turning Pluck round for another trial, Sweet William's strong hind-quarters and good condition just suffice to lift him high enough, and to his astonishment, almost as much as his satisfaction, Bobby canters in alone—and thus is produced a sporting edition of the old fable of the hare and the tortoise.

* * * * * *

You may now go in for luncheon, if you feel equal to any after Rudolph's solid repast of the morning; for a full half-hour is allowed after the steeple-chase, to give the several jockeys time to recruit their strength, as most of them are riding in the following race.

However, as we do not intend to weary you by a detailed account of each event during the day, we need only add that, as before told, Hayn gammoned the public with his two grey China ponies; Bobby on Tommy was beaten by Bones on Tom Brown in the light-weight hurdle-race; but when Clog steered Tommy in the Welter, the positions were reversed, and the little pony won in gallant style—despite the crusher of twelve stone seven, and the hurdles three feet six in height. The Child took one race, which repaid him for his former defeats, consequent mortification, and pecuniary losses; but we regret to say that the Aide did *not*—nay, more, so disgusted was he with the performance of Antelope and Velocipede, that, after the steeple-chase, he wrapped up his spurs and colours together, sent them with his compliments to Sæpius Tight, and took an unfrequented path back to Camp; leaving his ill-treated friend to "ride his ponies himself, should he think it worth his while to start them in their other engagements."

CHAPTER XXII.

JAPANESE JOTTINGS.

WHILE going well within ourselves in the middle of a totally different chapter—feeling almost "in the vein"—a sudden thought struck us, and has caused a horrid doubt to take possession of our mind ever since.

'Tis possible to have too much even of a good thing—and this occurred to us with unpleasant vividness, as we glanced back through past pages, and found so little that can interest the non-horsey portion of the public, but, rather, sufficient to afford a surfeit even for those who, like ourselves, willingly offer up a moiety of their heart to their Equine Deity.

Accordingly, kicking our half-finished chapter into a corner, we have armed ourselves with a new quill and a fresh quire of foolscap,—thus to avoid all chance of contagion,—and have sat down with a steady determination to turn over a new leaf, and string together a chapter in which, if possible, there shall be no mention of a horse, no horsey expressions, and which, in fact, shall be totally free from the odour of the stable. Would to heaven, though, that bouquet could now be greeting our nostrils, in place of the sickly sea breeze that sailors call bracing, but we poor land-lubbers call bilious!

Believe us; and allow us this one word for ourselves!

We do not as a rule affect the horsey (we are again compelled to repeat the word, for we can think of no other). We do not wear extremely tight trousers. We do not at all times carry a whip or a short ash-plant, when an ordinary walking-stick would be much more convenient. We do not—though evil men do sometimes call us noisy—salute every friend, with whom we happen to be on good terms, with a view holloa; nor do we speak of a young lady, whose juvenility we wish delicately to call into question, as being "rather long in the tooth."

Nay,—though here we are perhaps running to extremes,—very much should we prefer to be deemed wanting in the outward observances, than be classed as a certain gallant gentleman before us, who was described by an observant groom as being "the 'ossiest man on fut, and the futtiest man on a 'oss, as ever he seed."

This pithy judgment we rather fancy to have seen honoured with a place among Mr. Punch's weekly witticisms; but as we happen to remember its earliest birth, the place thereof, the attendants thereon, the chaff thereat, and the aptness contained therein, we offer no apology for its reproduction here.

What makes it more awkward for me at the present moment is the knowledge that I am trespassing on my partner's peculiar province.

This is the first time that the personal pronoun I has appeared in these pages: but what matters it? You cannot say whether *I* am R.M.J. or E.P.E. who am now speaking! We are but two: take your choice, worshipful readers!

This much will I tell you—R.M.J. and E.P.E. agreed

to write conjointly; I (E.P.E. or R.M.J.) to treat of sporting matters, He (R.M.J. or E.P.E.) of matters Japanese proper and miscellaneous.

With such a fair division of labour, each sets to work with good and diligent resolutions to commence his share. But, alas! as we near our destination, and consequently our time for writing becomes shorter—for we have great doubts as to our being able to muster up sufficient application for such work on shore—*I* (E.P.E. or R.M.J.) become painfully conscious that *He* (R.M.J. or E.P.E.) is growing—how can I express myself without wounding his feelings?—is not quite so keen and industrious as he was. I dare not reproach him with it, or perhaps he might turn round and throw up the whole thing in disgust—indeed, I must, at all risks, prevent his suspecting that such an idea has even occurred to me.

However, something must be done; and in a fever of mind I hover about him, trying by all sorts of artifices to bring his inclinations to point whither I would have them; scarcely daring, at the same time, to name the subject, for very fear lest I might defeat my own object by over-anxiety.

At one moment I beg his advice or opinion on some part of my own labours; at another I ask him to "oblige me by reading the last few pages of that uncommonly amusing chapter he finished the other day,"—*the other day* being a week ago, since which he has contented himself with resting on his oars, and has cleverly avoided overtasking himself by striking work altogether.

Sometimes I congratulate myself that, having, after much ingenious strategy, wheedled him into settling down with pen and paper before him, the Mighty Brain (as he terms it) will at last have a chance; when, entering his cabin shortly after, in all probability he is stretched on his bed, snoring loudly as if to mock me in my agony.

At another time he volunteers the information, that he is "just going on deck for a breath of fresh air, after which he means to come down and work like a demon." After allowing sufficient time for the most capacious pair of lungs to inhale many "breaths of fresh air," I put on my cap, and a *dégagé* sort of manner, as if I, too, considered such a respiratory process necessary for my health, and sally forth in search of him. The first sight that meets my eyes on emerging up the saloon staircase is my misguided friend, deep in the second chapter of a three-volume novel, with his legs on the poop railings and his body on the easiest of lounging-chairs. Sorrow-stricken I sigh,—sometimes I almost swear,—and again descend to the lower regions to labour alone.

Such are some of the trials of joint authorship, and such are the reasons that I (E.P.E. or R.M.J.) have been driven to touch on subjects that were to have been left to my fellow-workman. I am bound, however, to do him justice on one point. He will listen patiently and attentively whenever I inflict my own productions upon him, maintaining an expression of interest on his face, that many a learned judge would give half his income to be able to affect; laughing rapturously at the proper moment (though occasionally, I regret to say, also at the wrong), and, figuratively speaking, clapping one on the back at every opportunity. All this is very encouraging, and induces one to think that a man who can be so appreciative of merit, must undoubtedly be a clever, sensible fellow, and that it would be but presumption to call his little failings into account.

So much for ourselves; now for the Japanese; and though rather late in the day, the fact that so little is known of them by most people at home, is a sufficient excuse for a few words of description even now.

Arriving among them, as we did, from China,—the land of pug-noses and yellow-skins,—we were at once struck with their fresh ruddy complexions, and, in many instances, well-cut features.

Besides the difference in their personal appearance, too, they offer a marked contrast to the Chinese in manner and bearing. In place of the abject, cringing demeanour of the latter, they—the yakonins, of course, in a greater, the lower classes in a lesser degree—carry themselves as becomes men, fearlessly and uprightly, look you straight in the face, and consider themselves inferior to none.

The yakonins are a fine, bold set of men. Like our knights of old, they are ever ready to avenge, or even to provoke, a quarrel, and, with their terrible two-handed swords, would be anything but contemptible antagonists in hand-to-hand fighting.

The men shave the crowns of their heads, bringing the remainder of the hair, trimmed and plastered into a thin cord, forward over the bare part of the scalp; while the women tie up their long black locks in the most tasty fashion, with gold, silver, and scarlet cord. The illustrations given will go farther than any description of ours to render an idea of their personal appearance.

Their dress, though of course most peculiar, according

to our stereotyped notions, is both convenient and elegant. The loose trousers and "chimonos" (an outer garment, like the mantle of the Jews) of the men, and the robes of the women, are made of silken fabric, varying from the gauze for summer wear, to the wadded quilt that can withstand the cutting blasts of winter. The women's dress is confined to their waists by a coloured wrapper, also of silk, and long enough to wind in perhaps a dozen folds round their bodies. This "obi" is also worn by the men, but underneath the "chimono."

Instead of the Japanese being the uncivilised barbarians that Englishmen are apt to imagine them, no people in the world are more polished in their manner, not only towards strangers, but each other. Even among the lower classes, two friends meeting in the street never approach until after bowing low two or three times in succession, while making that peculiar hissing noise that they use to convey a greeting. On parting, the same process is repeated, with the addition of compliments, good wishes, &c. Indeed, when two officials come into each other's presence on a visit of ceremony, the interchange of mutual homage is almost ludicrous to watch. Advancing but a few paces at a time, at almost every step they bow their heads to the ground; their hands, with palms touching, following the movements of the body. In the same way, inferiors bend reverentially when coming into the presence of superiors, awaiting their permission to rise.

This sense of courtesy is carried into their speech, not only in its expressions, but its words,—so much so, that what they term "the polite language" differs most essentially from the equally grammatical and much more

concise "common language." The latter is much shorter, rougher, and to the point, and is used in giving orders to inferiors, by the lower classes in their ordinary conversation, and a great deal in quick writing; while the polite language, requiring longer forms of words, more profuse verbiage, endless particles, terminations, and additions, is universally employed by the higher classes in their intercourse.

Of the language itself we dare say but little, for fear of getting out of our depth; but a certain amount of it we were obliged to learn for our own convenience. Some satisfied themselves by picking up what they could as they went along; others saved themselves much trouble by engaging a teacher for a short time on first arrival. It is not difficult to acquire sufficient for conversational purposes, or, at all events, for communicating one's wants; and though it is doubtful whether we learnt the purest dialect, it served our ends equally well.

So far from Japanese in any way resembling the guttural gibberish of Chinese,—a language that always reminded us of the noise made by a dog when gnawing a bone,—it is not at all unlike Italian; and when heard gliding musically from the cherry lips of a pretty moosmi, had ever a soft and pleasant sound—at least to our young ears.

Now a word or two as to their dwellings. It is extraordinary how little these vary, from the prince's palace (we do not refer to their stone castles) to the peasant's cottage. They are all equally and scrupulously clean; and even about those of the highest in the land, there are little or no signs of ornament—a handsome screen or two, and perhaps some carved panels, being the only attempts at decoration ever observable. It has always puzzled us to imagine where all the beautiful bronze-work, porcelain, &c., exposed for sale in every town, can go to; for they do not appear in any of the houses we have visited.

The edifices themselves are the most flimsy affairs possible; and it might seem that we intended to put your credulity to the test when we tell you two curious facts about them—viz., that they are made in a great measure of paper, and that the Japanese, in erecting a house, build the roof first.

The skeleton of the roof is always put together on the ground, as the first step towards the completion of the future house; each beam is fitted and dovetailed into the others; and when the whole framework is finished, it is raised bodily and placed on its supports. Two of the sides are then boarded in, and the other two are closed by means of sliding screens of *paper;* those answering for windows being made of paper thin and transparent enough to admit the light. The floors are raised about a foot above the ground, and covered with fine matting, which is always clean in the extreme—so particular are they on this point, that you have to take off your shoes before stepping on to it; and on this account, however low an ebb we unwittingly allowed our kit to reach, as the years of exile passed, very shame prevented us from bringing ridicule on ourselves and our country by inattention to the state of our socks.

As may be imagined, such buildings scarcely answer the purpose of keeping out the cold; and in winter you may see whole families, swaddled up in quilts, crowding closely round the big "shibatchi,"* placed in the middle of the room.

The Japanese put paper to many other curious uses besides making window-panes. It is a much more woolly and less tearable fabric than any made in England. Their pocket-handkerchiefs are of paper, and so are their tobacco pouches—the material prepared to look exactly like leather. In its oiled state, they make of it, besides the windows we have referred to, *umbrellas and waterproof coats*; and these two, as being very cheap, and better suited to the climate, we used constantly, in preference to any obtained from England.

Extreme cleanliness characterises not only their dwellings, but their food, manner of cooking, serving it, &c. As an instance to show how well assured we became of this, we may mention that on more than one occasion, when returning home late at night, we have partaken of the delicate seaweed soup that is hawked about in the streets of every town, and *that* without any fear of either the materials of the soup itself, or the cups we drank out of, being less clean than at our own table. When you come to consider that the price of the soup rendered it accessible to the meanest coolie, and ask yourself if you dare venture on the same article, or the hot pies, vended in our own streets, you will agree with us that it is saying no little in favour of the Japanese.

They consume little or no meat, except in the form of soups; and though, at a dinner of any pretensions, many great delicacies are served up, there is but little to tempt the appetite of an Englishman. It takes, too, some time

* A wooden box containing an earthenware charcoal-burner.

to learn to use the chopsticks properly, and everything has to be eaten with them; but when once the art is acquired, they are very much more easily managed than would be imagined. For instance, any one accustomed to them will pick up a single grain of rice with ease.

The first Japanese dinner we ever went to, caused us more wonderment at the time, and appeared to possess more novelty, than anything we had seen before. This was an entertainment given at Nagasaki by some of the chief officers of Prince Satsuma to the British Admiral and his friends.

The guests, about ten in number, were met at the entrance of the banquet-house by their hosts, who, with a profusion of bows and compliments, invited them to enter. After taking off our shoes,—a proceeding which caused considerable merriment amongst one or two of the party, to whom it was totally unexpected, and who consequently had not looked out their latest relay of merinos,—we were shown into a large apartment, the greater portion of the *walls* (?) of which were, as usual, made of paper, and tastefully painted. There was no furniture of any description in the room, which was brilliantly lighted with paper lanterns; but carpets were spread, on which to sit *à la Turc*, and the rest of the floor was covered with fine matting.

As a commencement to the evening's entertainment, tea was brought, in cups about the size of an ordinary liqueur glass, and drunk, of course, according to the Eastern fashion, without milk or sugar. This was handed to each guest by a pretty little maiden, who was told off to wait upon him during the evening, and whose bright eyes and merry smile were enough to make a man eat a scorpion, had she handed it to him. After partaking of the tea, some ten minutes were devoted to smoking; and, not unnaturally, we preferred our own tobacco to that provided by our hosts, whose little metal pipes—with bowls holding only sufficient for two or three whiffs—and light, insipid tobacco, were hardly suited to the taste of foreigners.

A box of *confiture*, consisting of barley-sugar, sugar fish, tortoises, &c.—all very good in their way for those who have not yet lost their "sweet tooth," though not exactly the thing to begin dinner on—was next placed before each. Then came a little cup of soup, made of the delicate *bêche du mer*, followed by dish after dish, or rather, covered cup after covered cup, of various Japanese delicacies, by no means the least of which was *raw fish*.

Everything was served on the most beautiful lacquer ware, no one set appearing twice throughout the evening. The drink, in addition to some English champagne specially obtained for the occasion, was a spirit called *săki*, which is extracted from rice; it is not at all unlike whiskey in flavour, and is taken "hot without."

One was expected to taste a little of everything that was placed before one; and as there is, unfortunately, a limit to man's powers in that line, after eighteen courses had been gone through we were forced to cry, Enough. They then brought in fruit, and we thought, of course, the dinner was over, for it had already lasted more than three hours; but, to our astonishment, in a few minutes' time there appeared, in special compliment to the foreigners, a series of solids—enormous fish, haunches of beef, fowls, &c. All these, not unnaturally, were removed untouched; when they began again, and kept on for another couple of hours, putting before one soups and eatables till some forty courses must have been sent up, about fifteen of which were different kinds of soups.

The little handmaids did their work delightfully, and everything was served with the greatest regard to taste and neatness.

At the same time with what might be called the second, or solid period, dancing-girls entered the room, with another band, who accompanied their movements on guitars—not striking the chords with their fingers, but with a small, flat piece of wood triangular in shape. The dancing was remarkably graceful and pretty; and the guitar-girls, if they did not give exactly what *we* should call music, kept up a lively accompaniment.

After a time the dancers retired, and were replaced by singers,—including a man or two as bass,—who treated us to the most extraordinary and excruciating succession of noises.

Our hosts were most civil, agreeable fellows, and did all in their power to make us feel at home at our strange repast. Two of them had just returned from England, whither they had gone with the first party of Japanese who ever visited Europe; and they amused us much with their account of all they had seen and done during their stay.

A month or two afterwards we made one of a party entertained by Prince Satsuma, in his Summer Palace at Kagosima.

On landing from the ships, the English Minister and Admiral were conducted, with their followers, into the gardens of the Prince's palace by his officers, and there refreshed with fruit and ice-cold water—a luxury by no means to be despised, as, notwithstanding it was the middle of summer, they were tight-bound in all the splendid misery of full dress; though, by permission of their host, cooler garments had been sent on by each individual with a view to dining in comfort.

In about half an hour the Prince appeared; and, after he had engaged in a short conference with the English representatives, dinner was announced. This was at half-past twelve, and they did not get up until five; during which time forty courses were brought on in succession, each being served to every guest at the same moment, in lacquer cups and platters, on stands and trays of the same work.

We had the curiosity to note down the details of the feast, and, fortunately, have the list still by us. It may be depended upon as being correct, inasmuch as what we ourselves did not recognise, we inquired about through one of the interpreters.

BILL OF FARE.
DINNER GIVEN BY PRINCE SATSUMA, KAGOSIMA, JULY 28, 1866.

1. Bitter Green Tea (whipped).
2. Sweetmeats.

Band arrives, and tobacco is brought on to fill up time between the courses

3. Fish, Soup, and Raw Fish, with hot Saki.
4. Soup of Mushroom, Green Vegetable, and Fish.
    Exit Band, to the great relief of guests.
5. Dish of Prawns and Seaweed, and miscellaneous.
6. Soup of Seaweed, Vegetable, &c.
7. Hard-boiled Eggs, and Sliced Pears.
8. Soup of Lobster and Mushrooms, with very diminutive Lobsters.
9. Cold Fried Lampreys.
10. Soup of Loochoo Pork Fat, and various Vegetables.
11. Fish, with Salted Plums and Vegetables. (N.B. Plums not unlike tobacco.)

12. Soup of Wild Boar and Young Bamboo.
13. Cold Fowl and Pickled Shoots of Bamboo.
14. Soup of Fish and Seaweed.
15. Cake of Fish, Eggs, and Rice, with Green Beans and Fungus.
16. Soup of White Berries, and Sprats.
17. Small Fried Trout.
18. Soup with Acorns, &c.
19. Raw Cuttle-fish.
20. Soup of Fowl and Fruit.
21. Green Ginger, Fish in Batter, Cucumber, and Bamboo.
22. Bêche du Mer in batter.
23. Small Bones of Chicken, and *Unlaid Eggs*.
24. Soup of Fish and Roe, with Ginger Leaves.
25. Soup of Cockles (with their shells).
26. Raw Bonita, Rice, Apple and Chili Leaves.
27. Soup of Vermicelli, with " Soy " and Red Berries.
28. Sweatmeats.
29. Seaweed Jelly, Preserved Beans, Bonbons.
30. A Tray with Rice, thick Soup, and Pickles.
31. Another Tray containing " Daimio Fish" and various Soupçons.
32. A third Tray with Fish " Conglomerate; followed by Saki."
33. Hot Water in the Rice Bowl (as an appetiser).
34. Gelatine Sweetmeat (like stewed india-rubber), a Chestnut, and Pickled Tripe.
35. Bitter Green Tea.
36. Large dish of Elaborate Sweetmeats.
37. Bitter Green Tea again.
38. Imitation Peaches made of Sugar, Sweet Jelly.
39. Red Berry Syrup, Slices of Turnip, Salt, &c.
40. Dried Fish (very small) with thick Soup, and hot strong Saki.

At the conclusion of the banquet, or rather, we ought to say, at this period of it,—for it was only at the entreaty of the Minister that we were allowed to rise when this much had been gone through,—we again donned our martial attire, and were taken out to see a body of the Prince's soldiers exercised.

A marquee had been erected by the side of their parade-ground, and under the shade of this we sat, while about a hundred of his men—looking like monkeys, in the semi-European costume they had adopted—went through what was intended to represent the English system of drill, which they were now learning. They were armed with short Enfields; and though they appeared considerably bewildered at times, and evidently found the change from their own long swords to their present weapons most awkward and inconvenient, we felt bound to express unqualified approbation at their movements and high state of discipline.

Another body then fired shot and shell from field-pieces, at a target placed some distance off in the bay, and made some really capital practice.

This finished the proceedings; and bidding adieu to "His Highness," his father (the Prince inherits his title by marriage with his cousin, the daughter of the late Daimio), and his brothers, all of whom had treated us with the greatest courtesy and politeness, we returned on board.

The next morning a boat came off to the ship, bringing presents to those who had dined with the Prince. To each one of the party he sent his "visiting-card," and, as a token of friendship, *a dried fish*, pressed flat and thin as a wafer, and tied up with gold and silver cord; also the tray of sweetmeats that had composed the first item of the dinner on the evening before. In addition to these were sent rolls of silk, embroidery, porcelain, &c., &c.; while the Minister and the Admiral received magnificent gifts—such as handsome screens, exquisitely-finished swords, and suits of armour.

Before leaving the subject of Prince Satsuma's Summer Palace, we certainly ought not to omit mention of the lovely gardens and grounds that surround it.

The palace itself is rather an ordinary-looking building, not much superior to other Japanese houses of the better class. A picture of it appeared in the *Illustrated London News* shortly after the visit we refer to—and which was the first introduction of Europeans to the presence of a Prince, whose only previous acquaintance with us was derived from the occasion on which our China squadron, after an absurd attempt to reduce strong and well-defended forts during the raging violence of a typhoon, obtained no more satisfaction for the cruel murder of an English merchant, than the very doubtful glory of carrying off their own brave dead, *and with the town still firing on them.*

Subjoined is a copy from a photograph of the "Summer Residence," taken by Captain Lord Walter Kerr, which will, we think, give a better idea of it than the print that has already appeared.

Besides this seat, the Prince has, like all other powerful Daimios, a strong stone castle, with stout parapets and a broad moat, that it would take a regular siege to subdue.

But it is not of the building, but of the beautiful landscape gardens, that we were about to speak—such gardens as you read of in the "Arabian Nights," or see in the fairy scenes at the opera; but never, at any rate in England, come across in real life.

They are two or three miles in extent, a perfect labyrinth of taste and beauty; and who could look on these glimpses of fairy-land, and deny for a moment that the best of our miniature landscape gardeners are generations behind the great masters of the art in so-called barbarous Japan?

An almost perpendicular hill, along the base of which they lie, affords a strikingly beautiful background, with its thick bright mantle of dwarf trees and flowering shrubs—through which many a silvery stream glances out at times, till it finally leaps forth in a sparkling jet to the gold fish in the pools below, and thence is led in a number of miniature torrents and cascades—to form its share of a scene that might give the roughest nature an excuse for a feeling of poetry.

During our short stay at Kagosima, we spent some hours every day in wandering about this lovely spot— at each turn finding some fresh beauty to admire, some new imitation of nature to wonder at.

The town of Kagosima itself is, perhaps, the most favourable specimen of its kind in Japan.

On landing, the first day after arrival, we were conducted through the greater part of it, along streets, many of which are as broad and well-kept as Regent Street itself, and over fine stone bridges crossing the various canals and streams. On either side of most of the streets are trees growing, and rows of them are also planted along the edges of all the water-courses. Each house stands out separate from its neighbour; and almost every one of them has its own little garden, with the invariable miniature pond for gold fish, model bridge, and tiny representation of natural scenery.

It was very curious to watch the intense deference paid by the Prince's subjects to their sovereign; for such, in their notions of feudal rights, was he to them, and they recognised no other—being willing to uphold him even against the Supreme Majesty of the Tycoon; a test that their fidelity has actually undergone during the last few months. As he passed through the crowds assembled to gaze on the foreigners,—or, indeed, as soon as he was caught sight of by the multitude,—every forehead was bent reverently to the ground, and the sea of heads rose and fell, marking his presence by a great wave that moved along with him.

Such homage, however, is not alone the effect of courtesy, for compulsion takes its part in the feeling. So tenacious are the great nobles of the land of their dignity, and so exacting of the respect due to it, that when a Daimio is travelling with his train, no person is allowed to meet or pass, but must draw up on one side till the procession has gone by; no one may remain on horseback, but must dismount; and should any persons cross the road immediately in front, or in any way obstruct the path, they may be cut down at once, without regard to sex or age. An example of this occurred at Nagasaki very shortly previous to the period of which we have just been speaking; when a little girl, running across the road before the train of a prince who chanced to be passing, was mercilessly hewn down by the leading swordsman.

Fearful weapons are those two-handed swords! Very long and heavy, keen and finely-tempered as a razor, no wonder that a single blow will almost cut a man in two. Most expert, too, are the Japanese in using them, the result of long practice at sword-play with the thick bamboo staves they use for the purpose. The swords themselves they never unsheathe except in private; and it is looked upon as a dishonourable act to return a sword, once drawn, without blooding it.

Their favourite and most telling cut is delivered in

the very act of drawing; and thus, immediately you see a man lay his hand on his sword, you had best bring out your revolver at once—or, in certain cases, are even justified in shooting him.

Pushing the long handle forward, and seizing the wooden scabbard with the left hand, the blade is shot forth with wondrous rapidity, outwards and upwards; the weight and velocity alone being sufficient to lay open an antagonist from belt to shoulder.

Here let us remark, in passing, that for preserving a sword—whether from wear, weather, or climate—and maintaining its original edge and temper, the only scabbard that avails is undoubtedly a wooden one. They are light and convenient, and sufficiently strong to stand any work to which they are liable to be exposed—though true, with reference to those the far-seeing authorities enforce upon *us*, they are neither so well calculated to invite damp and rust as the old leather ones, nor have they such a martial clatter, or aptitude for rounding off point and edges, as our present steel rattletraps.

The small sword, too, which is worn by all above a certain rank, might prove very useful—or disagreeable, as the case might be—at close quarters. But it is not so much as a fighting sword that our ideas are connected with it, but rather as the instrument for carrying out the act of *Harakiri*.

This extraordinary custom—if *custom* it can be called—is confined exclusively to the Japanese; and, revolting as it may appear in itself, there is much that is heroic, or even romantic, about it.

Every writer on Japan has described it; but as some

people may possibly glance over this, who, from lack of time or inclination, trouble themselves but little about " manners and customs " of foreign lands, we, too, will follow suit, and say a word or two on the subject.

First, to explain the name—*Harakiri* (*hara*, the belly, and *kiri*, to cut) means simply and literally *cutting open the belly;* life being extinguished by the second self-operation of plunging the short sword into the throat.

There are many circumstances under which *harakiri* may be committed, though it must not for a moment be placed in the same scale as *suicide* among other nations. Causes that would bring about the former a dozen times over, would scarcely be sufficient to drive a native of any other country to self-destruction; inasmuch as *harakiri*, instead of carrying with it the disgrace to memory and kindred consequent on suicide, is looked upon rather as the brave act of a devoted man.

Disappointment, pecuniary loss, dishonour, or even an insult, have all frequently brought it about; and in the last-named case, he who cast the insult is bound, by the laws of honour, to follow the example, and immolate himself in the same manner.

We might quote numberless instances that occurred during our service in Japan; *e.g.*: But the other day, immediately on the declaration by the Tycoon of his determination to abdicate, rather than attempt to maintain his position, in defiance of the Mikado and his confederacy of the Daimios of the South, his prime minister, considering the resolution disgraceful both to the sovereign and his adherents, preferred death to dishonour, and at once committed *harakiri*.

Again, we remember a case at Nagasaki of quite a

different character. A yakonin, in some money transaction with a European merchant at that place, was detected in substituting bricks for the square shapes in which ichiboos are done up, a hundred in a block. When discovered, he attempted to cut down the Englishman; but failing in that, rushed out and disembowelled himself.

Fac-simile of an Ichiboo.

At times *harakiri* is a privilege, and, as such, only accorded to men of rank. Thus, a high official who has incurred disgrace is usually commanded to perform the *harakiri*, in place of suffering capital punishment. The advantage of the alternative is, that instead of the unfortunate man's family being degraded, and his goods forfeited, as in the case of death at the hands of the executioner, his relatives rather gain caste by his fate.

The act of *harakiri* is wonderfully represented on the stage. It is quite a part of their juggling performances; for even when very close in front of the actor, you could almost swear that it was really gone through. The smooth flesh surface severed by the keen blade, the burst of blood, and the gushing, quivering bowels,— nothing is wanted to make up the lifelike scene,—and you turn from it with a shudder, unable to persuade yourself that it is not real.

The Japanese are great actors, and a visit to one of their theatres is well worth the trouble. They excel in imitating the various passions; though they occasionally carry their representations of nature into such minute details, and leave so little to the imagination, that even Madame Schneider, could she witness them, would have to confess herself fairly outdone.

CHAPTER XXIII.

ALL AT SEA.

We have more than once alluded to the difficulties of writing on board a crowded ship; but we really cannot help harping on the subject.

It is a relief to pour out our griefs through our pen, and we *will* do so, at the risk of being thought tedious by many, in the hopes of being condoled with by a few.

Bear with us, kind reader; we know that we ourselves possess not an over-patient spirit, yet we have listened sometimes for hours to a friend droning into our ear trifles which he magnifies into troubles, and even as we have listened to him, have in our hearts bewailed the morbid delight he takes in recounting and dwelling on them; but we have, notwithstanding, kept up an outward semblance of sympathy, preserved a concerned countenance, and have borne with him.

Let us at once plunge into our grief; but first let us tell you that this chapter was to have been on quite a different and more interesting subject than the one we feel ourselves driven into, by circumstances which beset us and distract our attention from everything but themselves.

We ask you, have you not, when writing a particular letter, or perhaps attempting a scrap of poetry,—doing anything, in fact, which demands your entire attention,

—in the bosom of your family, have you not glared fiercely at the brother who whistled a note, or the sister who hummed a snatch of an air, or the innocent who prattled? and have you not positively hated, for the moment, the individual who sneezed—as you thought unnecessarily loudly—and then gave a yawn of relief afterwards?

Have you not cursed that most uninteresting campaign, as given with all its particulars by your great uncle? and have not your feelings been so worked upon by this last interruption, that you have for a moment almost wished that the venerable warrior had been included in the list of killed?

Has not some old maiden aunt, on these occasions, awoke your indignation by some trick or habit,—harmless in itself,—such as a click with the jaw, or a clearing of the throat at intervals? and have you not allowed this indignation to get so far the better of you that you have muttered something which, had she heard, might have seriously affected your after welfare?

And has not there been an odd kind of fascination, too, about this same click, or whatever other guileless trick it may have been?

Have you not timed it, and waited for it, and counted upon its falling due, to the exclusion of all other thoughts? And if it has been a few seconds late—oh, dear!—has it not fidgeted you? And even when it does come—click, or ahem!—there has been no relief; for the next is watched and waited for in the same way.

Aha! we feel we are working you up into a proper frame of mind to make you appreciate fully our sufferings. And what—what, we ask, are these little annoyances of yours compared with ours?

You have the remedy in your own hands. *You* can snatch up the manuscript or the letter, rush to your own room, and bolt yourself in.

We cannot—we know of no place where we could retire to for quiet, except one of the empty coal-bunks, and we could not see there.

With us, the whistling boy, the humming girl, the veteran and his campaign, are multiplied tenfold. The prattling innocent is also fully represented.

The maiden aunt,—well, we will let you have her,—we will throw *her* in; but then we have a piano at the end of the saloon, and we boast of several very talented and persevering performers with one finger, who find time hang heavily on their hands. This last is, or ought to be, in itself enough to awaken the compassion of the most unfeeling.

But this is not all—no, nor a half, nor a quarter. Aha! we are beginning now—such is the state of mind we are reduced to—to glory in our misery, and we repeat that what we have enumerated is not half nor a quarter of our miseries.

Is there not the incessant rattle of the dice at backgammon, and the uproarious mirth of the individual who says, "Deuce quatre will just suit him," and then throws it?

Oh, how his laugh distracts us!

But to give you a better idea of what we have to endure, we will recount this morning's bitter experiences.

At half-past ten we sit down to our work at the quietest end of one of the saloon tables.

Sprawling about in all attitudes, some attempting to read, some to write, others to paint, are ten or twelve officers, naval and military.

At the far end of the table at which we are sitting are five or six ladies crocheting, tatting, and engaged in such feminine occupations.

Poor things! even in the midst of our own misery, we have a corner of our heart which aches for them.

Cut off from all true enjoyment! No tea and scandal! No new bonnets on Sundays! They have been long enough at sea to know each other's wardrobes thoroughly! No milliners' shops at which to run up bills! Enough! Let us draw the veil! we will not harrow the feelings of our fair readers by further contemplation of such real misery.

At the end of the other table there is a group of five or six heroes, of either service, chatting, laughing, and making jokes of so purely local a character that an outsider would pronounce their conversation mere jargon—though, alas! *we* understand it but too well.

However, we brace ourselves up, and start with our work. Just as we are getting into the swing, we feel ourselves gradually but irresistibly becoming interested in a discussion which is going on amongst the group, as to whether the sun is over the yard-arm or not. At last it is agreed *nem. con.* that it is, and they proceed immediately to "cut" for bitter beer all round.

A popular naval officer, known nearly throughout the service as "The Cheerful One," presides at this matutinal meeting; and during the process of "cutting," any member making a remark irrelevant to the business on hand is severely called to order by him, and is informed that "business is business:" should the offender make any rejoinder, the Cheerful One gets out of all further discussion by saying decisively, "*That's* not the question!" and then at once proceeds to carry on his duties.

We may be writing in an unknown tongue to some, when we use the technical terms, "Sun over the yardarm" and "cutting." The former is an expression which means simply, that the sun has arrived at that particular point in his course when the nautical, or temporarily nautical, individual can with propriety commence to imbibe intoxicating liquors.

Should one begin before this, he is looked upon as lost to all sense of decency.

There is no objection, though, in this code, to his making up for lost time in season, which is usually done.

There is never any "tossing"—except in that sense of the word which leads to the utter misery of sea-sickness (how we wish we could with truth have omitted this reservation!)—on board ship, owing perhaps to a general absence of coin.

You always "cut." There are two at it now. A. holds a book in his hand, and says, "Two, two right,"—that is, the second letter of the second line on the right-hand page. B. says, "Two, two left." The book is opened at random, and they looked anxiously at the open page. A.'s letter is a c, B.'s an n; A. is consequently the winner, and gives a roar of laughter because he is glad. B. does the same because he is sorry, and does not want to show it.

Oh, their combined roar, how it grates on our ears!

Now this cutting is in itself a source of great annoyance; it goes on nearly all day long. There are some men who have been at sea nearly all their lives, who look upon a book solely as an article for "cutting" with. Even the services of this manuscript —bitter desecration!—have been solicited for cutting; and when we have explained that it is not adapted for that purpose, we have been asked in an injured tone, "Then what the devil's the good of it?"

That last roar of laughter from A. and B. has completely broken our train of thought; and as we look up from our task for inspiration, our gaze is met immediately by numerous imitations of the conventional literary bore. Even the ladies conspire against us, and, assuming an attitude of deep thought, some of them place their crochet-needles to their foreheads as though they were pens, and look musingly up at the skylight. The male perpetrators of this joke we treat with scornful indifference; but the ladies we smile upon, somewhat in the manner, though, that we smile when we are bidden by the photographer to look pleasantly at the handle of a door or a chalk-mark upon the wall.

This little joke never seems to lose its point. It is always going on; they never get tired of it.

Well, we "buckle to" once more, and have just finished what we consider a rather well-rounded sentence. We read it over to ourselves, and we suppose that in so doing must have unconsciously allowed an appreciative smile to light up our intellectual features, for, all of a sudden, we are startled out of our senses by a yell of "Holloa! what's the joke?"

A chorus of "Yes; don't keep it all to yourself!"

"Let's have it!" "Out with it!" &c., &c., is taken up by about half-a-dozen.

On the first author of this new infliction—a young midshipman with a sextant under his arm—we bestow a withering glance; but it does not seem to blight his young existence; in fact, he becomes emboldened, and continues: "Sorry I can't wait, old fellow, to correct your spelling, or stick in the stops for you, as I've got to go and shoot the sun." That is his easy way of saying he is going to take an observation.

Horrid boy! We fervently hope his angles will be all wrong, and that he will catch it from the master, or rather, navigating lieutenant, as he is now called.

Then there are a class of men who come up perpetually and ask—" I say, old fella, what's it all about? Is there anything in it about *me*?"

As a rule we can answer this question with a decided negative, as it is generally asked by individuals who are *not* honoured by mention in these pages.

The above class have been very persistent in their inquiries this morning.

We are a little cooler now, and hope we have not made enemies of any of them.

Another objectionable creature we have to contend against is the funny man, who winks all round to attract attention, and then commences a series of feeble remarks. Under ordinary circumstances, we think we could beat this adversary off very easily; but now it is quite different: the audience will see the points of his remarks, and not of ours; for every man's hand is against us, and they make common cause to harass us as much as possible. At last they leave us; but there is still a worse trial in store.

All these annoyances have we endured this morning, which is only a sample of every other.

With our eyes fixed on a skylight above us, we are ransacking our brain for a bright thought, and are just on the point of grasping something good, when a little girl, aged four, suddenly makes her appearance on the scene, armed with a squirt, which she points menacingly at each in turn. We are all in white; there are no laundresses on board; and the charge for her dreaded weapon has probably been obtained from the dirtiest bucket on deck.

The little creature feels herself mistress of the occasion, and a confident smile lights up the tiny face, as she stands defiantly, ready to play upon the first person who attempts to interfere with her.

Numerous bribes, in the shape of sweetmeats, are offered on all sides; but a shake of the head is her only response. Cunning little atom, she knows that we are about two thousand miles away from the nearest pastry-cook's shop.

At last, her gaze rests upon us, and we fancy we read in the roguish twinkle of her eye a determination to make us the victim. Hastily we gather up our precious manuscript, clasp it fondly to our bosom, and confusedly pledge ourselves to a fabulous supply of sugar-plums. She is not to be conciliated. Now she advances a step or two, with the horrid squirt presented point blank at us; but, like a cat playing with a mouse, she keeps us in suspense. Any attempt at retreat on our part would at once, we know, be the signal for the disgusting engine to be discharged, and we remain spellbound.

Deliverance is at hand, though! Her nurse is quietly and dexterously executing a flank manœuvre. With breathless interest we watch the movement, and all assist to rivet the little imp's attention while she is being taken in rear.

Saved! Like an eagle pouncing upon its prey, the nurse swoops down upon her, snatches her off the floor, and hurries away with her.

A shriek; two little red legs kicking in the air; the squirt goes off harmlessly; and we sink faintly into our seat.

In a second she is a prisoner in one of the cabins, to which all the ladies at once flock; and the sounds of yells and sobs, mingled with "Did 'umses" and "poo itty sings," which proceed from it for the next half-hour, reduce us to such a state of utter imbecility, that for the whole of that time not one word is added to this great work, but we sit glaring vacantly at nothing, until we find ourselves gently joining in the idiotic chorus of "Did 'ums," &c.

We awake from the infatuation with a start, and tremble for the state of our intellect.

After a time, the mighty brain reasserts itself, we set to work again, and nothing of any consequence occurs for the rest of the morning, except a *matinée musicale* held by the one-fingered performers, a perpetual laying of cloths—a ceremony necessitating a sweeping away of all our materials—and the upsetting of a bottle of Bass's pale ale down our back.

The evening brings with it no change except for the

worse. The funny men are more obtrusive, general conversation louder, the backgammon players more demonstrative over their throws, and, in short, everything partakes of a slightly postprandial nature.

There! we have done. We shall inflict you no longer with our grievances; but thanking you for your sympathy,—for you must feel some,—we dismiss the painful subject, which would never have found its way into this book had we felt able to repress our feelings.

We feel much better now, thank you!

CHAPTER XXIV.

THE QUEEN'S BIRTHDAY.

WHAT a fascinating pleasure there is in talking over "Old Times!"—a pleasure not peculiar to any disposition, tastes, or temperament, but shared alike by every particle of that varied miscellany which forms the composite mass called Society.

At the same time, there is a great deal of selfishness and egotism in the feeling; for, fond as one ever is of indulging in it oneself, one does not always care about being an excluded listener to recollections in which one has no share; and the wittily-pointed allusion or mirth-provoking reference often falls insipidly on one's heretical and unheeding ears. For instance, what can be a greater bore than to be compelled to feign a polite attention to a couple of prosy old Indians, vying with each other in recalling stupid things that are supposed to have happened at "Kafooslabad in the hot season of '28? Let me see, was it '28? Yes, I think it was. No, it was '27! You know when I mean? I'm almost sure it was '27. However, never mind, I shall remember by-and-by!"

Nor does the supposed truism of *in vino veritas* apply here; for it is an invariable rule that the marvellous improbability of these memories increases in direct ratio with the number of times the bottle has been round.

On the other hand, have we not often gained both amusement and instruction, as, silently sipping our wine, we have leant back in rapt attention to two or three of our elders—such men as we have ever borne in mind as models for our humble imitation,—and from each story deduced its moral for our own use?

As they speak of the days of Osbaldeston and Meynell Ingram, or of the time when Sir Richard first took the Quorn, or Tom Smith the Pytchley, before the country was cut up by railways, and "when men rode to hunt, not hunted to ride;"—as they grow eloquent over the respective merits of the Beaufort Justice and the Yarborough Ranter, or the performances of some of the leading favourites of the pack they saw most of in the field (for in *those* days it would appear that others besides the master, the huntsman, and his whips, took an interest in the working of the hounds);—as they tell of *the* Waterloo Run, or recall the well-known match between Clinker and Clasher;—as they boast of the gentlemen of *their* day being superior to the players;—as they call up a thousand reminiscences of the "good old days,"—we are unconsciously carried away, and feel almost inclined to envy them the quiet delight of looking back on the companionship of such men, and the enjoyment of such scenes as these, in preference to *our* privilege of looking forward to what will, in all probability, be found to possess its interest in anticipation rather than reality. And while under the influence of this feeling, we forget to resent—*mentally*, of course, for may we never be so irreverent as by *word* or *sign* to hold up the smallest protestation against the judgment of these Nestors—the unmerciful way in which our own shortcomings are dealt with.

Very prone are they to inveigh against the failings of the present and the rising generation. One introduction of modern days they are particularly fond of condemning in the strongest terms; to wit, the practice of battue-shooting. "Call it sport, to stand (or perhaps *sit on a camp-stool*) at the end of a wood, one breech-loader in your hands, a servant holding another close beside you ready for use, and a lot of tame barn-door fowls flopping out by scores?

"*A brace of breech-loaders, too!!* Why, I remember the time when it was thought unsportsmanlike to use a double-barrel; and when percussion caps first appeared, they were objected to on the same score! Indeed, my father kept to his single-barrelled flint-lock to his death; and he shot a good many birds after he was seventy! There were some first-rate bags made in these days, too, but by dint of hard work and straight shooting! Birds were wild, but dogs were good; no walking up and potting a lot of late squeakers just released from a hen-coop! We were particular about how our dogs were bred; and when we got them, we trained 'em carefully. Instead of the incessant piping, screeching, and flogging that goes on nowadays, whenever they condescend to make use of dogs at all, we used to think a single whistle and a wave of the hand quite sufficient to express, and obtain obedience to, all our wishes. Ah, things were very different forty years ago" (this last being a very favourite expression), "when you and I were young fellows! Weren't they, John? To one man who carried a gun then, there are at least a score now. Every shopkeeper shoots; and if your birds show their beaks outside your boundary fence, they are nobbled at once. Nay, not content with remaining outside your preserves, these fellows are continually sneaking in; if caught, on the pretence of picking up a wounded bird!

"As I was saying, they can't do anything without noise. Why, they scream and yell as much now, when a fox is to be killed, as we used to do at rat-hunting! Instead of letting the hounds work, and giving them time to find things out for themselves, they are all for getting forward to holloas, and casting ahead at the slightest difficulty. I wonder they don't do away with fox-covers altogether, and keep a few couple of draghounds! They could then have the scent as strong, and the line as straight, as they chose. We used to enjoy *hunting* a fox, not *mobbing* him!

"Moreover, what is the country like now? Yes, go on a little longer! Plough your grass, put up your wire fences, and very soon Ackerman's prints will be all that is left of fox-hunting!

"The bottle lies with you, John; help yourself, and pass it on. Hold that up to the light, and look at its colour! That wine is five-and-thirty years old! I should like to know where you can get anything like it now! Thank goodness, I have got another pipe of it in my cellar! Now, *there*, again, things are not as they used to be! You don't see men take their bottle of good old port before leaving the table; but when some bad, washy claret has been sent round a couple of times, they adjourn to loll about the drawing-room, where they expect the ladies to admire and amuse *them*, instead of *their* paying the sex all the attention we were taught to—and it is a bad sign when it comes to that! I think we can manage one more bottle of the '34, eh? Bring your chair nearer the fire, and I will tell you how we at last accounted for that old customer who gave us the slip four different times from Winnick Warren. It will do that youngster good, too, to hear how we managed things in those days" (the presence of the said youngster having, throughout the whole of the rest of the harangue, been completely ignored). . . . .

Such a song as this you have all, no doubt, ofttimes heard sung; and though these *laudatores temporis acti* are anything but complimentary in their reflections on the degeneracy of the age,—and unpleasant truths are apt to hit hard,—we are willing to submit to what is disagreeable in the taste of the medicine, in the knowledge that it is good for us.

Drawing out and dwelling upon incidents and associations that have long lain fallow in one's mind, is almost like living the time over again. Indeed, when old friends and boon companions meet together after a long separation, and unconsciously, but of necessity, fly at once to the subject of old times—as one mutual remembrance succeeds, is excited by, and in turn excites another—as reference to events, in which they engaged in common, follows reference—as each assists the memory, and adds some forgotten item to the allusions of the other—as insensibly they grow eloquent and excited in their praises of bygone scenes, past enjoyments, and former comrades,—it would seem that there

THE QUEEN'S BIRTHDAY.

is as much, if not more, real pleasure in thus discussing the days that are past, than in the actual experience of them at the time. And there is the more reason in this supposition, inasmuch as, while in those days themselves sweets and sours had to be taken alike, as they happened to come, the only recollections that, as a rule, we evoke, are pleasing ones.

One of the pleasantest memories of our life at Yokohama, and which has often since been the subject of conversation and laughter among us, is the occasion of the forty-eighth anniversary of Her Majesty's birthday, and the way in which we celebrated it.

Eleven o'clock in the forenoon—and a very hot forenoon it was—of the 24th May, saw the Holy Boys—as we suppose it also saw every other corps in the British service—assembled on parade in all the glory and discomfort of tightly-buttoned tunics and marvellously snowy pipeclay.

In all humility—and certainly without a hope of your being able to solve a problem which has ever presented insurmountable difficulties, not only to *our* feeble comprehension, but to the minds of many more gifted and experienced individuals—we venture to ask what possible object can be answered by, or even what end can be aimed at in, enclosing the unhappy soldier on this one particular day—and in climates in which, at that season of the year, white linen clothing is allowed to be the only suitable dress—in a garment eminently calculated to keep out the cold of an Iceland winter?

Surely our gracious Queen would be just as well pleased, and our loyalty would not be thereby materially diminished, if her humble servants were permitted to do honour to the date of her nativity in comparative coolness and comfort! It cannot be doubted that such an innovation, striking though it does at the root of military discipline and sacred routine, would at all events have the effect of making the anniversary a more agreeable one to many a faithful vassal, and allow more room for the free development of feelings at present compressed within too narrow limits. It is true that we in Japan had not as much to suffer in this respect as many thousands of unfortunates who have yearly to undergo this ceremonial rite; but the remembrance of the same ordeal in the tropics is still fresh in our memory.

Most of our friends were there "in full fig;" and in addition to the Holy Boys, there were a demi-battery of artillery and a detachment of another regiment.

Bones on Pericles, Mr. Pop on Bouncer, and Podgy on Rubbles, were attached to the personal staff of the Commandant as "gallopers."

Bones, as you know, could ride "above a bit," although his seat was, to say the least of it, more fitted for cross-country work than the pomp of the parade-ground; and as his loose trousers gradually worked up to his knees, showing how much more suited they were to breeches and boots, and he kept banging old Pericles down the shoulder with his sword, he looked altogether a little out of his element.

Neither did the other two appear to fall naturally into the character of "the dashing A.D.C." Mr. Pop looked, as he felt, extremely nervous as to how Bouncer was likely to behave; and at the last moment decided not to allow pride to render him indiscreet, but removed the military spurs that he had donned for the occasion.

Podgy, on the contrary, though also much disturbed as to the probable conduct of his horse, feared not that "Wubbles" would be unpleasantly restive, but that he might take it into his head, as he often did, to suspend work altogether. On an occasion like this, such a *contretemps* would have been a fearful blow to his feelings; for was he not got up totally regardless of expense, and looking forward to appearing in the most favourable light before the eyes of many a fair lady? Blessed with the advantages of great, not to say peculiar, powers of elocution, and a figure that grows more portly and magnificent every day, is it to be wondered at that Podgy should be a confirmed lady-killer?—so much so, as on one occasion to have drawn forth from an old and experienced man of the world the following judgment, delivered in a loud tone before a crowded assembly: "In my opinion, Podgy, you are a DEVIL of a fellow!"

Captain Puffles was also there in gorgeous array; but as he had grown somewhat "larger round the chest" than when he left home, he found, after immense exertion, that it was an utter impossibility to fasten the two lower buttons of his tunic, and, in consequence, a becoming frill of white shirt showed under his sword-belt. Notwithstanding the relief thus afforded, the poor old gentleman's face looked sadly woe-begone. The usual fresh colour of his cheeks was now deepened into an ominous purple, his little eyes twinkled prominently, his neck looked pinched, the big drops rolled off his forehead, and his whole appearance was dangerously apoplectic. As he knocked the ashes out of his beloved pipe, and took a last soda and B. to fortify himself against all he had to go through, he was heard to murmur sorrowfully,

"Oh, 'ow I 'ate this 'umbug!"—and if the stout heart that had fought in Burmah and Central India could thus break down, how well might we youngsters be allowed a growl against our fate!

At 11.45 A.M. the army was drawn up in battle array on a large level piece of ground in the Settlement, hitherto unoccupied, and going by the name of "the Swamp."

Field-pieces and rifles were loaded with blank cartridge, and with open ranks the troops only awaited the moment when twelve o'clock should strike, to give Her Majesty the honours customary to the day.

"The brigade will fire a *feu de joie!*"

As this dread warning issued from the lips of the Commandant, Mr. Pop perceptibly trembled, and was seen to clutch the pommel of his saddle, while his pallid face worked in terror-stricken agitation.

"Ready! Present!!"

Almost simultaneously with the boom from the first gun, and the crack from the first rifle, a piteous cry was heard to escape from Mr. Pop, as, dropping his reins and casting away his sword, he twined his legs under the girths and his arms round the neck of Bouncer, who, with startled eye and tail erect, set off at full speed, and carried his rider along the whole length of the line. Each report gave a fresh impetus to their flight, wrung a fresh kick from Bouncer, and another cry of anguish from Mr. Pop, till at length, overcome by terror and exhaustion, the unfortunate aspirant to staff honours must inevitably have fallen to the earth, had not some welcome volunteers from the crowd arrested his mad career, and reinstated him in his saddle.

Nor was this the only unforeseen addition to the initiation of the ceremonies; for at the same moment as Bouncer commenced his vagaries, a like disposition appeared to seize upon Pericles, and, taking the bit between his teeth, he stiffened his neck, threw his head into the air, and dashed off. The more Bones pulled, the higher went Pericles' head, till, as he neared the line, he presented much the appearance, and produced much of the effect, of an elephant charging with uplifted trunk.

Scattering confusion on all sides, they burst through the ranks, upsetting all who came in their way, and driving Captain Puffles, whose company they had thus ruthlessly broken up, to the verge of despair. The effect of this feeling—added to the intense personal fear that possessed him, as he saw Bones bearing directly down upon him at a railway pace—so disorganised him, that, perfectly unable to reform his men, or even find words strong enough to express his indignation against the intruder, he could only flourish his sword and dance up and down in front of his company, his fat little legs moving with unwonted activity, and his tongue vituperating in English, Welsh, Hindustani, Burmese, Chinese, Japanese, and a dozen other dialects—for singularly inapt as is Captain Puffles at learning a strange language, he can pick out, and with wonderful readiness confide to memory, its *discursive* parts. (Forgive the horrible but *bonâ fide* unpremeditated *jeu de mot*.)

Pericles carried his rider half-way back to Camp before he could be stopped; when, after Bones had forcibly impressed on him the error of his ways, he returned slowly and unwillingly to the group around the Commandant, which had just been joined by Mr. Pop. The latter had lost all the freshness of appearance and grandeur of carriage which had characterised him when he first left barracks; and, in place, a settled melancholy had laid hold on him. He had recovered his sword and regained his seat; but nought but Time could give him back his equanimity.

Misfortunes never come singly, and poor Mr. Pop was destined yet again to figure too prominently on the scene.

The firing was by this time over; Bouncer had quieted down to his normal state of sloth; and Mr. Pop, congratulating himself that his troubles were over, gradually grew more composed and reassured, when he was suddenly awakened from his false security by the voice of authority, saying, "Mr. Pop, be good enough to ride with all despatch, and bid the officer commanding the artillery to take ground to his right. And you, Mr. Podgy, take an order to the left battalion to throw out the flank companies in skirmishing order!"

The two gallant officers addressed, saluted and immediately set about making a start on their separate missions—Mr. Pop determined, by increased alacrity and efficiency, to wipe out the disgrace he still smarted under; the other, in the justifiable pride and consciousness of superiority, prepared to maintain, or perhaps strengthen, his position by his readiness and soldier-like activity.

To get Bouncer under weigh was always a task requiring a vast amount of anxious persuasion—never coercion —on the part of Mr. Pop, necessitating much shrugging of shoulders, working of knees and elbows, many coaxing "Come, Bouncers," and an occasional timid touch of hand or heel. Now, however, he had neither whip nor spur to assist his entreaties, nor, if he had, is it at all probable he would have dared to use them, after the signal way in which Bouncer had that day asserted his superiority; and as the latter considered that he had already done enough for honour or inclination, he steadily refused to move. 'Twas of no avail that Mr. Pop jerked at the bridle, wriggled in his saddle, and implored his treacherous Rosinante to "Get up." The only answer Bouncer gave was by gathering up his back ominously, and stepping backwards towards the rest of the Staff.

This movement brought him in contact with Rubbles —whom Podgy had at last, after much exertion, succeeded in inducing to leave the company—and excited that worthy animal's ire to such an extent, that, laying his long lop ears back viciously, he gave vent to a savage scream, and commenced letting out with all his might at the impertinent aggressor.

Bouncer defended himself gallantly, and a determined fight ensued—the two ponies, stern to stern, squealing, kicking, and pushing furiously, while their riders strove desperately to keep their legs out of the way, and at the same time to maintain their seats. Worse than all, in their twisting and turning, the combatants gradually approached the Commander-in-Chief; and Flying Isaac, scenting the battle from afar, naturally obeyed the first impulse of a generous charger, and rushed in to join it.

Assuredly such a triangular duel has not been witnessed since the one described by Captain Marryat; and if another point of resemblance were wanted, it would be found in the position of the only wound received; for Flying Isaac, dashing in, with commendable impartiality seized upon the nearest object that presented itself—which happened to be Mr. Pop's overalls—and, fortunately, just missing the skinny frame within, tore the part bodily away from the rest of the garment.

With the assistance of orderlies, buglers, &c., the combatants were at length parted; and the Chief wisely dismissed his aides to take the route to Camp.

Meantime, the moment had passed for the contemplated manœuvre, and the brigade had been halted to await the termination of the trying scene before them. It happened that the disgraced gallopers had to pass along the face of the whole line; and as Mr. Pop wended his way mournfully past, sitting, contrary to his custom, right back in the saddle, the tails of his tunic carefully tucked under him, nothing could suppress the general titter that, like the *feu de joie* just before, ran from one end of the line to the other. But when Bouncer gave one of his periodical stumbles, and Mr. Pop was pitched from his leaning-back position to cower on his horse's neck, a guffaw broke out that not even the force of discipline could restrain.

These disturbers of the peace having been got rid of, the parade proceeded.

Several high officers—members of Girojio, or Grand Council of Japan—were present, and eagerly watching the movements gone through; and, as the newspapers (for even Yokohama has its three daily papers!) kindly informed the public, "expressed themselves much struck by the imposing aspect of the English troops;" or we might quote the complimentary speech of an American officer, delivered the same evening: "Well, I guess you Britishers astonished those Nippons a few!"

Oh, wasn't that a delicious glass of beer which we poured down our parched and dusty throats, when, after pitching down our swords and throwing open our coats, we rushed in a body to the anteroom to obtain it?

We doubt if the fainting Arab—whom all authors quote when they wish to give an idea of extreme thirst —after struggling painfully across the burning desert, hoping against hope, still pushing on, though no prospect of relief is present to cheer him—we question if even he feels a more all-absorbing delight, as at length he reaches a stream of crystal water, than did we as that cool, amber draught almost hissed in meeting our heated palates.

It did not take very long to get into a more seasonable dress; and by that time the lawn was sprinkled with guests, for it had been decided to celebrate the day with a " big tiffin " and a ball in the evening.

Everybody had been asked to one or both, and nearly everybody had been good enough to accept. In order to get the mess-room ready for the dance, the furniture had been cleared out of it for two days; the billiard-room had been seized upon for the supper; and the Holy Boys had to 'pig it' as best they could—loafing about, like dogs without a home.

Thus, the only place available for the tiffin in question was the anteroom; and for a quarter of an hour previous to its being announced, the guests basked on the lawn in the sun—a sun whose rays were genial and pleasant, when not experienced through the thick shell of a full-dress tunic. "Come, we've had enough about the tunics," you will say. A thousand pardons! The thought farthest of all from our minds is to treat you to anything savouring of "shop."

Ah, but what a *faux pas* have we made! What an opening have we given to ill-natured critics in this apology—to criticism, above all, from that mass of detractors, whose knowledge of such matters is derived only from superficial signs!

"Exactly," they will say; "is not that what we have always said? The last thing the young military man of the present day cares to speak of, or discuss, is his profession! Is it not a subject tabooed from ordinary conversation, and avoided as men avoid talking of their own sins?"

True, most worthy reprovers! Thank heaven, a good part of this *is* true!

"Shop"—and no other word is so expressive—is *not* dragged in, in preference to all other subjects, wherever military men may be congregated; as, to our cost, we have known *their* especial "shop" to be brought forward, at all hours, by members of some other professions (we do not intend to particularise). Wearisome and disagreeable indeed is it, when thus pushed down one's throat, and still more so to the unlucky auditor having no personal interest in the subject; but, nevertheless, it is not truth to say that military matters are the last care of military men.

At fit times and proper places, such things are very well; but may we never live to associate with the officer of the outside, or, at all events, the democratic world— the officer of the radical M.P.'s, who rave against the present state of the army, and bellow for reform; merely because "Reform" is their cant word, expressing their desire to upset everything that is unfortunate enough to have had its origin from any other source than their own evil machinations. When the *beau idéal* of such as these shall have an existence in reality—when the individual shall ever reck of his work, as a sweep of his soot—and when, instead of his having to maintain the character of "an officer and a gentleman," the *gentleman* shall be lost altogether, and the *officer* require a new definition, —'twill be but like a foretaste of a still more future state; and, looking forward, we get a glance at a blessed era, when a "Glorious Commonwealth," with Mr. Beales as Protector, shall usurp the place of the Constitution of which we are so proud—dragging all men and all things down to its own low level, and tearing out root and branch whatever is not as base as itself.

Well! Of the tiffin it is sufficient to say that Signor Pasquale did his best for us, and that more attention was paid to the champagne-cup than to the band. At any rate, the two combined are always wonderfully effective in promoting sociability; and thus, conversation, at first a buzz, soon loudened almost into a roar.

It would be difficult to find a much more mixed assemblage. Military—French and English; naval— French, Austrian, Italian, American, and English; civilians of all nations—members of the different legations, and others.

The Aide, on the strength of his reputation as a linguist, sat between two French officers; and having once started them, he prudently retired from taking an active part in the debate, merely keeping them up to the mark by putting in an animated *oui* whenever the opportunity offered.

E E 2

What an amiable weakness is it, common to all Frenchmen,—what a welcome assistance to him who, only half-proficient or half-confident in his knowledge of their language, is called upon to make himself agreeable through its medium,—that they delight in nothing better than hearing their own tongues wag!

Right well was the Aide aware of this! and right well did he turn it to advantage for the entertainment of his guests, and for his own aggrandisement!

"*Oui*," he would drawl out meditatively, with head half averted, and hands slowly revolving round each other, as he showed himself carried away by the flowing eloquence he attempted not to interrupt.

"*Oui, oui*," more decidedly, as he gave an unreserved agreement in confirmation of a fact stated or an anecdote told—raising his eyes to the face of the speaker, and affecting the most intense interest in the subject in hand.

"*Certainement oui*," affirmatively, in answer to an appeal, more understood than expressed, as to the coincidence or difference of his opinion with that given by one of his guests; and here he would bow gracefully, and smile with the politeness of a D'Orsay.

"*Oui!!*" he would sing in a high treble of astonishment; elevating his eyebrows, and throwing his hands up like two notes of exclamation.

"*Oui? vraiment?*" interrogatively and half-doubtingly, when he thought some slight spur was needed to prevent his friends flagging; and this never failed to draw both of them out, volubly anxious to maintain their statements. Nay, such a torrent of words would it evoke, that for fear of its overwhelming him in its rush, he dared venture on this only as a last resource, and as an alternative for embarking in person on the treacherous waters of connected conversation.

But 'twould take pages to tell of half the changes he rang on that single word, aided by the power of expression conveyed by hands, arms, shoulders, and eyebrows, the flexibility of his musical voice, and the wondrous variations of time and aspiration.

"Oui" delightedly, "Oui" merrily, "Oui" sorrowfully, "Oui" sympathetically!

The "Oui" of approval; the "Oui" of argument; the "Oui" of apology.

All the feelings, all the emotions, even the passions of human nature, did he throw, as occasion required, into this one exclamation.

Thus—not only suffered, but encouraged, in their fondness for the sound of their own voices; urged on, as it were, to give full scope to a taste which, had the indulgence in it appeared to be received as in any degree irksome, their politeness would have instantly repressed —his two neighbours talked on delightedly; both vowing inwardly that they had never met a more agreeable companion, or more wonderfully astute member of society.

Had the Aide but clung to the prop that upheld him so long, and stifled all feelings of vain ambition, he might have continued without accident his hitherto successful career, and given a permanency to the feelings of respectful admiration which his less-favoured comrades were already beginning to entertain towards him —as they observed, almost awe-stricken, the fluent ease with which he appeared to converse with his Gallic friends.

But, as he dipped more frequently into the cup, as subject succeeded subject, and tale followed tale, he became inflamed with the desire of shining still further; and as the officer on his right finished a graphically-told little anecdote,—of which by some accident our friend had contrived to catch the point,—he rashly determined to cap the story, and proceeded to treat them to a reminiscence of his childhood.

For this purpose he cleared his throat, and began as follows: "Eh moi, monsieur, quand j'étais *fille*——"

Not even the natural *politesse* of the Frenchmen, not even the respect with which they had already learnt to regard his obvious talent, nor the knowledge of what was due from guest to host, could prevent the simultaneous burst of laughter that interrupted the Aide's narration; and it was some time before they could control themselves sufficiently to offer apology or explanation.

The cloak in which he had wrapped himself having once been torn open, and the nakedness within disclosed, the Aide was fain to throw it off altogether, and finished his story with the most extraordinary display of courage. Indeed, as the meal proceeded, he was not the only one who plunged with reckless intrepidity into the dangerous sea. Others were to be heard discoursing the most villainous French—or, ofttimes, a mixture of French, Japanese, and English—with a fluency that could only be Bacchanalian. A tolerably good specimen of this style of dialect was B.'s polite question, as they rose from the table. Seeing one of the Frenchmen seeking in vain for his cap among the heap on a table, he addressed him with—

"Ah, monsieur, doko (the Japanese for *where*) votre chapeau blanc?"

As before stated, the mess-room had been fitted up for a ball, and as the anteroom had also to undergo certain preparations for the same event, there was no place for dinner; and thus it fell out, that the hosts of the noon had nearly all to thank their guests for holding out the hand of hospitality to them in the evening.

"I say, B., what can we do all the afternoon? It's killing work sitting down, as we have done, in the middle of the day."

"I'm sure I don't know, unless we walk out to Treaty Point and have a swim. I shan't be fit for much this evening, if we don't work off the tiffin somehow. What do you suggest, Bones?"

"Well, you know, I don't go in much for dancing, but I'm game for anything. If the crops were not so high, we might take our nags out and have a shy across country."

"Good idea!" cried another; "never mind the crops! It won't hurt them for once. We've not had a lark for months. Let's go in for a spin this afternoon! Who'll come?"

"I will," from the Aide; "I will," from Podgy; "I will," from half-a-dozen others.

Such a proposal at *such* a time suited *such* fellows to a T; and away they went in a body to order their ponies and equip themselves for . . . . .

"Land on the port bow!"

* * * * * *

This was what caused us to break off so suddenly;

and can you wonder that such a sound—coming like a voice of welcome from the loving hearts that are once again so close—should act upon us so powerfully that we can scarce even sit down to bid you farewell?

As regards the chapter we have left unfinished, we need add but little.

The party did ride off their tiffin, and *did* also—we regret to say—some little damage to the crops; besides bringing misfortune, in two instances, on individuals.

Of these latter, the one sufferer was Belleville, who got into the water-jump on the steeple-chase course, and came out with his auburn tresses and new patrol jacket dyed to much the same hue. The other was a still more cruel case—though, true, in this latter the injury sustained was rather by the delicate feelings of the mind than the rougher susceptibility of the body.

A black-letter day was this to Mr. Pop.

The events of the morning still preyed heavily on him; silent and reserved had he been throughout the tiffin; and after the other party had set out for what they called "a lark," he bethought himself of ordering Bouncer—whose misconduct of the morning had gained for himself a fast while others were feasting—and rode slowly out to brood over his misfortunes.

As he jogged quietly along the broad road,—Bouncer and himself for the time on the best of terms,—a hideous yell, another, and again the same, re-echoed from a dozen throats, smote fearfully on his startled ear; and, not three fields off, he beheld what appeared to be a body of wild demons tearing across country to his destruction. With the instinct of self-preservation strong within him, he actually drove his spurs into Bouncer with a determination that so took the noble steed by surprise, that, forgetting to resent the liberty, he set off at once at the best speed he could muster.

It seems that the band of adventurers afore-mentioned had chanced in their rambles to sight the unhappy Mr. Pop afar off; when one heartless youth immediately suggested that they should "play at pig-sticking and make a race for first spear."

The idea was seized upon at once; and waiting till they were fairly in line, a view-holloa from Bones gave the signal to go, and, with the savage chorus that had reached their intended victim, they set off in mad pursuit.

Not knowing what object they might have in view, or what atrocity they might intend to commit, the bewildered imagination of Mr. Pop conjured up all sorts of horrors, and, with a desperate courage, he applied whip and heel unremittingly to the astonished Bouncer.

Nearer and nearer came his pursuers, like a pack of hungry wolves thirsting for his blood; till, as he felt his own strength failing, and the respiration of his gallant steed became thicker and louder than that of a walrus, despair began to take possession of his soul.

Succour often comes when least expected; and so it happened that, as Mr. Pop turned a corner of the road, —his dread tormentors now but a hundred yards behind,—it suddenly occurred to him that here a dense wood ran close beside his left hand.

The discovery reached him like the reprieve to the criminal awaiting his doom. With renewed hope, he turned Bouncer quickly into the cover; and, taking advantage of the thickest parts, plunged into the depths of the wood and escaped—though his nervous system suffered so severely from his trying adventure, that he rode not for many days after.

Meanwhile, his eager followers had overshot the mark; and, finding to their disgust, after casting in all directions, that they were unable to hit off the line of their quarry, betook themselves elsewhere in search of further mischief.

One item that they succeeded in perpetrating, consisted in B. and the Child jumping over the bamboo palings into Parson Duckworth's garden, and riding *through* the locked gate out of it.

This outrage we mention more as an opportunity for inserting the apology that the two graceless striplings themselves forgot to offer—though they had the effrontery on the following guest-night (when Parson D. was present), to gather a select circle round the injured divine, and commence a conversation by remarking "that they supposed some horses had been in his garden, as they had noticed the gate broken down and hoof-marks on the cabbage-beds, while riding by." Should, however, this 'meet the eye' of the reverend pastor, 'he may learn something to his advantage,' in the satisfaction of hearing that the Child smashed his head by coming into violent contact with the wooden arch over the gateway.

A description of the Ball would be out of place, even if we had time to give it. Our light nonsense about the rougher sex will fall as harmlessly as it is meant; but of those who are better and purer than ourselves, and to whose influence we owe the little that is good in our natures, the less we irreverently speak the better. We believe that on this particular occasion they enjoyed themselves—at all events, they did the next best thing, viz., to say that they did.

The floor was, perhaps, hardly as good as it might have been; but their little feet twinkled none the less merrily over it, nor the less brightly and joyously shone the sparkling eye or rang the silvery laugh—for when people congregate together in the East, they do it for the purpose of enjoyment, and think not of the little trifles that at home are so often suffered to mar pleasure.

At one moment, we remember,—and *this* we cannot help recalling,—considerable astonishment was caused by noticing a tall lady, somewhat inclined to *embonpoint* and quick dancing, apparently taking a turn by herself, as a member of the royal family might do. Round and round she went, evidently delighted with the brisk waltz that was holding its charm over others besides herself, while we stood watching the strange freak in wonder and amazement. At length she stopped, and the phenomenon was explained. From under her arm peeped the shock head and flushed face of the little Fenian, like an enormous peony pinned there to set off the black muslin dress, from among whose voluminous folds his body shortly followed.

* * * * * *

We should apologise for breaking off thus unceremoniously and abruptly, but for the conviction that you who have borne with us thus far, will also make allowance for the whirl of excitement, that the near prospect of realising the day-dreams of past years has thrown us into. Delight, fear, anticipation, and doubt are already turning our poor brains round, till it is no easy matter to pen even these few lines.

Our daily intercourse during the last three months seems to have attached and bound us to you, till we are loth, indeed, to break off the intimacy: and though we can hardly ask you to return the feeling, we shall be amply rewarded if we can know that what has so successfully lightened the monotony of a long sea-voyage, has also afforded you a few hours' amusement. We used to look upon the idea of authors regretfully taking leave of their unknown readers as but a strain of fancy, or as a kind of stereotyped winding-up to a book; but we can vouch to this—that had we been fated to three months' longer incarceration on board ship, we could have communed with you still, with a grateful feeling of companionship. Possibly you may say—"Thank goodness, you hadn't the opportunity!" but that matters not. We have had our own enjoyment in recalling these incidents in the life of the Holy Boys in a distant but pleasant country, and we offer them to you as they stand. It is quite probable that we may not again put pen to paper on these subjects, when once safely landed in the dear old country, where never a moment lacks its own special occupation for amusement or pleasurable employment. Thus, we shall lay our scribblings before you in their present unfinished, unrevised state; professing nothing, aiming at little; but cherishing still an inward assurance, that many among you will say to yourselves as you read these pages—"I, too, would throughly have been one of them had Fate thrown me there!"

www.ingramcontent.com/pod-product-compliance
Lightning Source LLC
Chambersburg PA
CBHW021427300426
44114CB00010B/691